Calvin for Today

Calvin for Today

edited by
Joel R. Beeke

Reformation Heritage books
Grand Rapids, Michigan

Calvin for Today
Copyright © 2009 Puritan Reformed Theological Seminary

Published by
Reformation Heritage Books
2965 Leonard St., NE
Grand Rapids, MI 49525
616-977-0599 / Fax 616-285-3246
e-mail: orders@heritagebooks.org
website: www.heritagebooks.org

Library of Congress Cataloging-in-Publication Data

Calvin for today / edited by Joel R. Beeke.
    p. cm.
  Includes bibliographical references.
  ISBN 978-1-60178-084-3 (hardcover : alk. paper) 1. Calvin, Jean, 1509-1564.
2. Calvinism. 3. Reformed Church--Doctrines. I. Beeke, Joel R., 1952-
  BX9418.C366 2010
  230′.42--dc22
                          2010004576

*For additional Reformed literature, both new and used, request a free book
list from Reformation Heritage Books at the above address.*

With heartfelt appreciation for

Richard A. Muller

mentor, encourager, and friend;
Reformation and Post-Reformation scholar, and
promoter of an educated Reformed ministry

Contents

Calvin the Ethicist

Calvin and His Contemporary Impact

Abbreviations

CO
Ioannis Calvini Opera quae supersunt omnia. Eds. Guilielmus Baum, Eduardus Cunitz, and Eduardus Reuss. 59 vols. Corpus Reformatorum, Volumes 29–87. Brunsvigae: C. A. Schwetschke et filium, 1863–1900.

Commentary
Commentaries of Calvin. Various editors and translators. 46 vols. Edinburgh: Calvin Translation Society, 1843–55; repr., in 22 vols., Grand Rapids: Baker, 1979. Also, *Calvin's New Testament Commentaries.* Ed. David W. Torrance and Thomas F. Torrance. Various translators. Grand Rapids: Eerdmans, 1972.

Institutes
Institutes of the Christian Religion. Ed. John T. McNeill. Trans. Ford Lewis Battles. 2 vols. Library of Christian Classics, no. 20–21. Philadelphia: Westminster Press, 1960.

OS
Joannis Calvini Opera Selecta. Ed. Peter Barth and Wilhelm Niesel. Munich: Chr. Kaiser Verlag, 1926–52.

Preface

A study of the Western world in the past five hundred years reveals the overwhelming influence of individuals, for good or ill. World War Two, with its appalling loss of human lives, the horrific Holocaust, and the wholesale destruction of cities was largely due to one man, Adolf Hitler. As historian John Lukacs recently argued, that war might well be called "Hitler's War."[1] On a different note, the course of Western history since the Reformation would have been quite different if a Frenchman named Jean Cauvin, better known today as John Calvin, had not been forced into exile in Geneva. The republic of the United States, for instance, would have a very different structure.[2] Calvin rightly has been named one of ten people who defined the second millennium A.D.[3]

Not surprisingly, the five hundredth anniversary of Calvin's birth in 2009 was celebrated in numerous conferences around the world. One of the more significant events was hosted by Puritan Reformed Theological Seminary in Grand Rapids, Michigan. This conference was significant in bringing together a number of academic scholars and ministers who propounded Calvin's theological ideas. The conference presenters are convinced it is important to remember Calvin because of his ongoing influence on the church and in the world, and

---

1. John Lukacs, *The Legacy of the Second World War* (New Haven: Yale University Press, 2010).

2. See Mark J. Larson, *Calvin's Doctrine of the State: A Reformed Doctrine and Its American Trajectory, The Revolutionary War, and the Founding of the Republic* (Eugene, Ore.: Wipf & Stock, 2009).

3. Alister McGrath, "Calvin and the Christian Calling," in *The Second One Thousand Years: Ten People Who Defined a Millennium*, ed. Richard John Neuhaus (Grand Rapids: Eerdmans, 2001), 66–75.

because Calvin was right in so many of his theological perspectives. Like Calvin, they believe remembering such theology is deeply beneficial to the church today. The fruit of their labor is what you hold in your hands.

The opening conference sermon, preached by David Murray, is the first chapter of this book, reminding us of Calvin's stress on the importance of preaching the Word. Then this book goes on to show how Calvin, who defined himself pre-eminently as a preacher of the gospel, can benefit aspiring preachers today (note especially chapters by Gerald Bilkes on Calvin as a Bible-centered man and David Murray on Calvin as an expositor of the Old Testament). Calvin was the finest theologian among a generation of Christian thinkers that included Martin Luther, Ulrich Zwingli, Heinrich Bullinger, Pierre Viret, Thomas Cranmer, John Knox, and Peter Martyr Vermigli. Of them, only Calvin was known as "the theologian," an epithet bestowed on him by Luther's co-worker Philipp Melanchthon. This volume explores the contemporary importance of Calvin as the "theologian of the Holy Spirit," which is what B. B. Warfield once called Calvin (Joey Pipa). It also explores three other vital areas of his teaching as a theologian: redemption (Derek Thomas), union with Christ (Cornelis Venema), and reprobation (Donald Sinnema).

Love for the church was another hallmark of Calvin's theology. He affirmed with the early church fathers that no one can have God for his Father who does not have the church for his mother. Four chapters explore his ecclesiology: an overview of his thinking about the church (Cornelis Pronk); a study of how best to reform her (Derek Thomas); her mission (Michael Haykin); and finally, Calvin's interest in the ancient church (Ligon Duncan).

Those deeply shaped by Calvin's thought have sought to apply his theology to all human life and thought. This volume contains two studies in this regard: a general summary of Calvin's ethics (Nelson Kloosterman) and an examination of his thinking about marriage (Michael Haykin). Finally, two studies explore the impact of Calvin today: one traces the growing influence of Calvinism in America (Ligon Duncan) and the other, which closes the volume with a parting word about Calvin, offers twelve reasons why Calvin is important today.

Much more could be said about Calvin, of course. But, hopefully, the chapters in this book will whet your appetite to learn more about walking with God as Calvin sought to walk.

In editing this volume, which is primarily designed for educated laypeople and ministers, I have let the speakers decide to what degree to retain the spoken style in their respective chapters, which explains why some of the chapters are a bit more formal than others. I hope you will enjoy the mixture.

I heartily thank all the speakers for their diligent work on their excellent addresses and their willingness to turn them into chapters. I thank Greg Bailey and Phyllis Ten Elshof for their invaluable assistance in editing this volume, Gary and Linda den Hollander for their able typesetting and proofreading, Amy Zevenbergen for another great cover design, Michael Haykin for his graciousness in assisting with this preface, and Pauline GeBuys for giving the book a final proofing. Thanks, too, to Chris Hanna and the staff at Puritan Reformed Seminary, who worked hard in planning a very successful first annual conference on behalf of our school. I am also deeply grateful for the kindness and understanding of my patient wife, Mary, and my dear children, Calvin, Esther, and Lydia. Without them, this work would not have been possible.

This book coincides with my completion of twenty-five years of seminary teaching and my first sabbatical, which is enabling me to complete a few projects like this book. For these years and decades, I owe wholehearted gratitude to our ever-faithful triune God who delights to be merciful to sinners (Micah 7:18). With all my heart, I confess with Samuel Rutherford that I don't know which divine person I love the most, but I do know that I love each of Them and need Them all. *Soli Deo gloria!*

—Joel R. Beeke

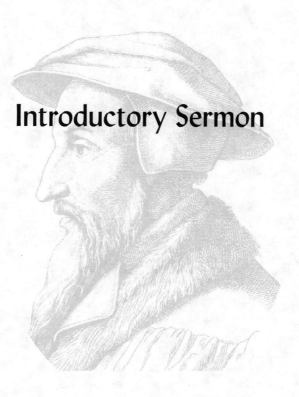

Introductory Sermon

CHAPTER 1

What Kind of Love is This?

David Murray

There remains a strange fascination with all things extraterrestrial, such as aliens and unidentified flying objects. There is a whole genre of literature, numerous Web sites, and repeated newspaper reports of sightings of this or that, usually couched in a context of hostility. If it is something from outside this world, something alien, something extraterrestrial, it must be hostile, it must be an enemy, and it must be something to be feared.

The apostle John brings before us something alien, something extraterrestrial, something from outside this world. But this is not something to be feared. It is not a force of hostility. Rather, it is a force full of adopting love. In 1 John 3:1, the apostle writes, "Behold, what manner of love the Father hath bestowed upon us, that we should be called the sons of God: therefore the world knoweth us not, because it knew him not." If you were to translate the first words of this verse literally, it would be something like this: "Behold what foreign love is this, what out-of-this-world love is this, what extraterrestrial love is this."

It is interesting that John Calvin's *Institutes of the Christian Religion* does not have one chapter on adoption. Did he miss it? Did he not see it? No, the reason he didn't have a chapter on it was due in part to the fact that Calvin saw the doctrine of adoption woven throughout the whole tapestry of God's marvelous work in the salvation of sinners. The doctrine of adoption was not peripheral but central to Calvin's whole theology. As we think about the love of God in His adoption of sinners, we are, in a sense, considering the controlling emphasis in all of Calvin's work.

John invites us to *behold*, which means "to study," "to investigate," "to dig deep," or "to research." That is what we want to do here. We will behold three things. First, we will behold the "we": "Behold, what manner of love the Father hath bestowed on *us*..." (emphasis added). Second, we will behold the "Father" that is mentioned here: "...that we should be called the sons of *God*" (emphasis added). What kind of Father is this? Third, we will behold the *love* that we are invited to dig into in this verse.

Behold the "*We*"

First of all, let us ponder the "we" or the "us" that is mentioned here: "Behold, what manner of love the Father hath bestowed upon *us*, that *we* should be called the sons of God." It is really stunning to John that God should have bestowed His love on people. It is beyond his comprehension.

The experts tell us that when people take steps to adopt a child, there are usually five factors in their decision as to which child to adopt: (1) the *genes* of the child; (2) the *environment* of the child — where he or she has been brought up; (3) the *education* of the child — what he or she has been taught; (4) the *record* of the child — especially if he or she is older — as to problematic or criminal behavior; and (5) the *prospects* of the child when all of this is put together. There are panels and experts who can tell us, when they look at these factors, what kind of future an individual child is likely to have. Of course, every adoptive parent is trying to get all these ducks in a row, as it were, hoping to get all these factors right so that the adoption will go well. So let's use these categories to look at the "we" and the "us" who the Father adopts.

First, think of our *genes*. When a couple adopts a child, they want to know who the natural parents are. Is there any genetic history they should be aware of? Are there any genetic factors that are going to prove problematic in the future? How about us? What kind of genes do we have? The Bible tells us. David says that we are conceived in sin and shaped in iniquity (Ps. 51:5). It doesn't get better. Another psalm says that we go astray from the womb, speaking lies (Ps. 58:3). Paul tells us of a spirit that right now works in the children of disobedience, and it is the spirit of the devil (Eph. 2:2). In fact, Jesus Himself summed it up when He spoke to the sinners of His own day and said, "Ye are of your father, the devil" (John 8:44). These are not good genes.

Second, maybe our *environment* will improve our prospects. Clearly, most adoptive parents are concerned about the kind of environment in which prospective adoptive children are brought up. What kind of health problems will they have? One of the adoption Web sites I looked at had this question listed under "FAQs": "Are the children healthy?" The answer was: "Yes, all our programs have healthy children available. However, it must be clarified that in international adoption, children are referred to as healthy if they are not known to have significant medical, emotional conditions. Healthy children often have effects of institutionalization, which can include malnutrition, delayed development, and other medical conditions, such as rickets, and scabies." What about us? Are we spiritually healthy? Like these children, we suffer the effects of our environment—the sin environment in which we are brought up. We are infected with the virus of sin. We are institutionalized in the ways of sin. Apparently certain foreign countries cannot get their children adopted by anyone from anywhere because they have terrible records of pollution, of poisoning the water or the air, and all the health problems associated with that. What kind of atmosphere have we been brought up in? What air have we breathed? It is polluted and poisoned with sin. We are spiritually poisoned, spiritually polluted.

Third, what about our *education*? Education can repair much damage. Adoptive parents often think that if children have received a good education, their prospects are better and brighter. Well, we are educated—in the ways of sin. We don't need our parents to teach us. Do you teach your children how to lie, how to fight, how to deceive, how to steal? You don't need to; they are self-taught, self-directed learners. They—and we—have learned every bad habit and evil way. We get straight A's in these subjects.

Fourth, what about our *record*? It is black, isn't it? In the United Kingdom, a couple sued an adoption agency for not revealing to them the nature of their adopted child's behavioral problems. They said, "This is unfair; if we had known the contents of this report, we would never have adopted this child." That was reasonable. I wonder what our records are like?

Fifth, what about *prospects*? The Bible tells us our prospect is eternal death. We have one horizon when we are born into this world, and it is hell. That is our prospect.

It staggers John that this kind of person should be adopted by God! It goes against everything this world knows about love. It goes against everything terrestrial, natural, and logical. God comes to you, believer, looks at you, and says: "Your genes couldn't be worse. Your environment is polluted and poisoned. When it comes to your education, you fail, fail, fail in everything good, but you pass with flying colors in everything evil. Your record has no white on the pages; it is all black. Your prospects are stark—you are going to hell. You have blasphemed Me, defied Me, attacked Me, and rejected Me. But…you shall be My child." This is what staggers John. Behold, where does this love come from, "that we should be called the sons of God"? It is little wonder that he uses the word *behold*. He is saying, "Dig deep into this; meditate on it; never leave it; soak in it; saturate yourself in this until it thrills you, excites you, and makes you soar in love, back to this loving heavenly Father."

Have you ever evaluated your own life according to these categories? Maybe you don't like the above description of yourself. Maybe you are willing to check off one or two factors, but not all. If so, God is not interested in adopting you. You have to check every box—*genes, environment, education, report, and prospects.* If you do, as we will see, He is on His way in adopting love. Behold the "we."

Behold the *"Father"*
If you were to ask a group of children who want to be adopted, "What kind of father would you like?" what kinds of things would they say? A number of them probably would say, "I'd like a forgiving father," probably because their experience has been quite the reverse. Or they might say, "I'd like a father who is full of grace."

Have you seen any of the adoption orphanages in Eastern Europe? I have visited one or two. When wealthy adopting parents come to these orphanages, the children are all lined up. When everyone walks in the room, the children are looking up, thinking: "Is this my father? Could this be my father?" Obviously they are really trying to make themselves look good and impressive, standing out from the crowd. The orphanage staff members already know, from experience, who is going to be picked. It is a pitiful sight to see the children who have been rejected before and who know they are going to be rejected again. Most adopters are looking for the archetypal perfect son or daughter.

If God is like that, we have no hope. But God is not looking for archetypal sons and daughters. God is not looking for those who have spruced themselves up and made themselves look better. The children God chooses to adopt cannot be predicted. He often picks the worst and passes by those who seem to be much more deserving. This is because He is a *gracious* Father!

He is also a *rich* Father. If you ask a child, "What kind of daddy would you like?" he will say, "I'd like a daddy with lots of money." What doesn't God have? He's got everything. Of course, many modern views of fatherhood have been perverted by money, so that good fatherhood is equated with giving children everything they want. Because great wealth is often not accompanied by great wisdom, the children are ruined. Even though the Father has everything and could give every single one of His children everything they ever wanted, He doesn't do that. He is wiser than the wisest human father. He knows what to give and He knows what not to give. He knows when to take back what He has given. He is a *wise* Father with His resources.

He is also a *tender* and *gentle* Father. He is depicted in Scripture as a Father who will wipe away every tear from our eyes. A story was told of an American Christian whose husband was killed in the Vietnam War. Friends were visiting with her when the news came to the home, and she quietly left the company and disappeared upstairs. After a while, her friends became concerned about her, and one of them went up to the door of her bedroom, which was closed, and listened. This is what she heard: "Oh Father, oh Father, oh my Father!" The man who told this story said this: "The now-widowed lady buried herself into the arms of her heavenly Father." This was not a sudden, desperate reaction to tragedy. Those comforting arms were well known to her from her experience of lesser troubles. This is your God, dear believer, a Father who feels for you and at the same time helps you, whose sympathy is matched by His ability and willingness to strengthen you. He is a gentle and tender Father with all the time in the world. He is a Father who never says, "I'm too busy." He is a Father who never has duties that keep Him from caring for His beloved children. He is always there as soon as we cry, like this widow, "Abba, Father!" As soon as He hears that in heaven, He races to the scene.

This Father has a _wonderful record of adoption_. In some countries, one in every five adoptions fails, and the children are returned. Has God ever failed in an adoption? Has He ever taken on a child, only to come to the point where He said: "No more; I can't take it. I never expected it to be so tough! Somebody else can do a better job." Never! He is patient, and He has never failed. He will not give up on you.

Think of His _willingness to adopt_. Apparently the number of people willing to adopt in the Western world is falling by fifteen percent every year. Has God's willingness to adopt ever declined by even one percent? Never! It is no less now than it was when John wrote these words, when he said not just, "Behold, what manner of love the Father hath bestowed…that we should be called the sons of God," but that we should be adopted by a Father who is so full of grace, so rich, so wise, so tender, so gentle, with so much time, with such a perfect record, and with such a heart full of willingness to receive the worst and the most hopeless of cases. John is looking at the whole universe here. He says: "I don't see that love anywhere else. This is alien, it is extra-terrestrial, it is unique. This is _the_ Holy Father, _the_ perfect Father."

There is no reason for any single person to be an orphan any longer. Can you find a fault in this Father? Can you find any reason to keep yourself away from this Father? Can you really live any longer without this Father? Will you not bury yourself in His arms and plead for His love and His mercy? You can "argue" with Him and say: "Look, if Thou dost love me, what will people say about Thy love? Lord, the most amazing thing is that if Thou dost love me and I become Thy child, people will say, 'I don't understand it; this is baffling, that this person should be saved and become a child of God.' Maybe my whole view of Christianity has been wrong and my whole view of God has been wrong." This is what grace is. Can you not plead that with Him? "Make me a trophy child, that the whole world will look at me and say, 'What kind of love is this?'"

Friend, if you ever come to understand the love of God, you have not really understood it. For John, it is beyond comprehension. He is saying, "Behold the _we_; then behold the _Father_." Is that possible? That brings us to our third point.

Behold the "*Love*"

Behold, what manner of love, that we and the Father can come together in this Father/son relationship. What kind of love is this?

Behold the *initiative* of this love. We love Him because He first loved us (1 John 4:19). Who took the initiative? If you are a child of God, the initiative of this love should fill you with thankful worship because you know that you never would have taken the initiative. Think of all the needy children in all the orphanages and the initiative they are taking. They plan and strategize how to get in the front row when visitors come, how to stand, how to attract attention, how to make themselves more desirable. Did you take that kind of initiative? You didn't, did you? He came seeking you, and you love Him because He first loved you. It was His strategy. It was His decision, not yours. He made the first move, not you. The world doesn't understand, but the Christian loves to think about this great God taking the initiative to come down and pick him out.

Behold the *ease* of this love. We think, "To enjoy that love there must be a long process to go through." John covers this in his Gospel. You say, "How can I become a child of God?" John answers: "He came unto his own, and his own received him not. But as many as received him, to them gave he power to become the sons of God, even to them that believe on his name" (John 1:11–12). Does that sound like a long process to you? How do you become a son of God?" You open your hand, the hand of your soul, to receive. You are not coming with something but with nothing. It is not coming to give but to receive. It is coming to Christ and believing on Him. Through faith in Christ, we become adopted children. Could He make it any easier?

Behold the *speed* of this love. If any of you have been involved in the adoption process, you know it is lengthy. In Western Europe, it takes about twelve months, but adopting from a foreign country can take up to three years. You have to go through many stages. You apply, then they interview you, they check your health, they check your friends, they do home visits, they do familiarization visits, they do court hearings, they observe your body language and do psychological and psychometric testing, and only once you have gone through all these hoops do you have any hope of adopting. How long does it take God to adopt a child? How fast is the process? It is as fast as the period at the end of this sentence. As soon as you believe in the Son of God, you, too, are a son or daughter of God. As soon as you receive Christ as your only hope and Savior, you are Christ's brother or sister, and His Father's child.

Think of the *size* of this love. In the United Kingdom, there are twenty-five-hundred adoptions a year But that leaves five thousand every year unadopted. In the United States, there are fifty thousand adoptions every year. But that leaves one hundred thousand unadopted every year. The system can cope only with fifty thousand. Loving parents can be found for only fifty thousand children. There is a limit to the number of adoptions that is possible in the human realm. Is there any limit on the number of adoptions God can make? Does He ever reach a quota? Does He ever come to a point in the year when He says, "Enough; I can't take any more"? Does His heart of love have a limit? It does not. You can never use that as an excuse. It is large enough for everyone, if everyone would seek it. It is large enough for you, if you will seek it. There is capacity; there is room. Think of the size of this love.

Think of the *effects* of this love. Researchers say that there are seven adverse effects in adoption: feelings of rejection, a sense of loss, guilt, shame, grief, intimacy avoidance, and cost. Some of these effects are felt by the natural parents, some by the adoptive parents, and some by the adopted child. There are many benefits in adoption, but these are some of the painful side effects. Not so in a spiritual adoption. Instead of rejection, there is acceptance. Instead of guilt, there is forgiveness. Instead of shame, there is confidence. Instead of grief, there is gladness. Instead of intimacy avoidance, intimacy is created and sought. There is a cost, and we shall come to that. And there is loss, but the only loser in the divine adoption is our natural father, the devil. The strange thing about this natural father—unlike other natural fathers, who are glad to put their children up for adoption—is that he fights it tooth and nail. He does not give up easily, gladly, or willingly. Why not make the devil a loser? Do you want to be a child of God? Here is a blessed side effect—you cause pain, grief, loss, and a sense of rejection to the evil one.

The apostle here speaks of a very specific effect. He says, "Therefore the world knoweth us not, because it knew him not" (1 John 3:1). What happened to the Son of God when He came here? He was rejected; He was crucified. Don't expect anything different. Don't expect to be recognized as a son of God. Even if you are recognized as such, don't expect that recognition to result in favor toward you. There are some who say, "We don't believe in this son of God business." They reject any possibility that human beings can become sons of God. But there are unconverted people in this world who *do* recognize the sons of God. They see something different in people who are sons of God. Maybe you remember, before your conversion, when you met certain Christians, and you knew there was something different about them. There was a different spirit in them compared to yourself and others.

I was recently on a plane in Brazil. I spoke briefly to the man sitting beside me, then I took out my notes to prepare for a sermon on Genesis 3:15, on the crushing of the serpent's head by the seed of the woman. Within thirty seconds of my taking out my notes, this man became agitated and restless. I didn't know what was going on. I felt uncomfortable, but I tried to ignore his behavior. He would get up, walk up and down the aisle of the plane, then sit down again. He was breathing hard. I looked at his face, and he seemed to be getting angrier and angrier. He would get up and talk to other people on the plane, and they would turn and look at me. I was thinking, "What is going on here?" The missionary with whom I was traveling was way in the back of the plane. Thankfully, the plane landed soon. When I got off, the missionary came up to me and said, "You have just shared a plane with a group of devil worshipers." They had just been at a conference, a meeting of an occult group in the interior of Brazil. He started pointing out to me some of the people from this cult, some wearing special clothes and headdresses. Suddenly, I understood what had happened on the plane. There was recognition. A son of the devil had recognized a son of God. He had some sense that I was hostile to him, and he felt anger and aggression. This verse came to me: "Therefore the world knoweth us not, because it knew him not" (1 John 3:1). This is what Christ experienced in a far greater degree. This is one of the effects of being a son of God. We can expect hostility.

But think of the *great end* of this love. As we read in verse 2, "Beloved, now are we the sons of God." This is what we are. But there is still a future, because he goes on: "And it doth not yet appear what we shall be: but we know that, when he shall appear, we shall be like him; for we shall see him as he is." Whatever the enmity we experience in this world, the day is coming when we will not be just *called* sons of God, we will be *like* the Son of God. This is what inspires and motivates the apostle to keep going, to keep persevering. In fact, this is what motivates holiness, too: "And every man that hath this hope in him purifieth himself, even as he is pure" (v. 3). Behold the love, the initiative of it, the size of it, the speed of it, the ease of it, the effects of it, and the end of it.

Above all, there is the *cost* of this love. The average international adoption today costs between \$25,000 and \$35,000. That is nothing compared to the cost involved in your adoption as a child of God. It cost the blood of God; it cost His life and His death. This, as John says, is out-of-this-world love. It is love that can be explained only by moving into another dimension.

Conclusion

Sinclair Ferguson remarked, "Students of Calvin's theology have too rarely recognized how important the concept of sonship was to his understanding of the Christian life." He goes on, "For Calvin, piety meant recognizing that our lives are nourished by God's fatherly care. It meant knowing oneself to be a child of God, that the purpose of the incarnation and the atonement was the adoption of Christians, and that the first title of the Holy Spirit is the *Spirit of adoption*."[1]

May God send that Spirit into every one of our hearts, and into every heart of every loved one we have, that He may bring us together into His great family, that we may, not just in time, but for all eternity, behold, research, dig into, and saturate ourselves in this foreign, extraterrestrial, and amazing adopting love.

---

1. Sinclair B. Ferguson, "The Reformed Doctrine of Sonship," in *Pulpit and People, Essays in Honor of William Still*, ed. Nigel M. Cameron and Sinclair B. Ferguson (Edinburgh: Rutherford House, 1986), 81–6.

Calvin and the Bible

CHAPTER 2

Calvin on the Word of God

Gerald M. Bilkes

The success of the Reformation was undoubtedly bound up with its high view of the Word of God, specifically its authority. John Calvin's *Institutes of the Christian Religion* codified this view in a glorious way, and his extensive commentaries prove that Calvin's view of Scripture was not simply a formal point.[1] In a word, for Calvin, Scripture was the master and he its servant. In the words of J. I. Packer:

> [T]he brilliant boy from Noyon [was] transformed by conversion into a God-centered, God-mastered, God-honoring man who bowed humbly to God's will and listened humbly to God's Word, and [his] tremendous powers of penetration and insight were put wholly at the service of the Scriptures. This was the man whom God could and did use to preserve Protestantism.[2]

The influence of the Protestant church is currently sadly on the decline, and it is only a return to a high view of Scripture that will

---

1. With considerable material in print on the theme of Calvin on the Word of God, I will not attempt either to summarize or interact with the scholarly debates; instead, I offer this as a reader's look at Calvin's view on the Word of God. For further reading, see, among others, Richard A. Muller, *Post-Reformation Reformed Dogmatics: The Rise and Development of Reformed Orthodoxy, ca. 1520 to ca. 1725: Vol. 2: Holy Scripture, The Cognitive Foundation of Theology,* 2nd ed. (Grand Rapids: Baker, 2003): 63–79; T. H. L. Parker, "Calvin the Biblical Expositor," in G. E. Duffield, *John Calvin* (Grand Rapids: Eerdmans, 1966), 176–86; and Wilhelm H. Neuser, "Calvins Verständnis der Heiligen Schrift," in *Calvinus sacrae scripturae professor: die Referate des Congrès International des Recherches Calviniennes vom 20. bis 23. August 1990 in Grand Rapids* (Grand Rapids: Eerdmans, 1994), 41–71. I am deeply grateful to John Mustafa for graciously aiding me in the background research for this chapter.

2. J. I. Packer, "John Calvin: A Servant of the Word," in *Puritan Papers: Vol. 3, 1963–1964,* ed. J. I. Packer (Phillipsburg, N.J.: P & R, 2002), 177.

enable the church to recover from this lapse. This five-hundredth anniversary of Calvin's birth, then, comes none too soon if it helps draw us back to the foundation, which is the Word of God, as Calvin showed so masterfully and compellingly.

THE WORD OF GOD IN CALVIN'S LIFE

Before I enter into the specifics of Calvin's view of the Word of God, I would like to recall three vignettes that illustrate the place the Word of God occupied in his life.

Calvin's Conversion

Though Calvin wrote little of his conversion, the little he did write is very suggestive of how the Word of God came to function authoritatively in his life. In the well-known passage that refers to his conversion in the commentary on the Psalms, written in July 1557, Calvin said:

> But as he (David), was taken from the sheepfold, and elevated to the rank of supreme authority; so God having taken me from my originally obscure and humble condition, has reckoned me worthy of being invested with the honorable office of a preacher and minister of the gospel.... And first, since I was too obstinately devoted to the superstitions of Popery to be easily extricated from so profound an abyss of mire, God by a sudden conversion subdued and brought my mind to a teachable frame, which was more hardened in such matters than might have been expected from one at my early period of life. Having thus received some taste and knowledge of true godliness, I was immediately inflamed with so intense a desire to make progress therein, that although I did not altogether leave off other studies, I yet pursued them with less ardor.
>
> I was quite surprised to find that before a year had elapsed, all who had any desire after purer doctrine were continually coming to me to learn, although I myself was as yet but a mere novice and tyro.[3]

Notice how Calvin wrote that he was extricated from the papacy by a "sudden conversion." He was suddenly enflamed by an intense desire to make progress. We surmise that this took place during

3. CO 31.21.

his years as a student. He lost his taste for his ordinary studies and began to preach. Soon people were flocking to him for counsel, even though he loved obscurity. He was propelled into publicity. He was soon in Geneva, with Guillaume Farel thundering to him to stay and preach there,[4] which he did for the rest of his life, apart from the three years when he was exiled from the city (1538–1541).

Writing in 1538 in his *Reply to Sadoleto*, Calvin used the analogy of light to describe the reality of his conversion:

> My mind being now prepared for serious attention, I at length perceived, as if light had broken in upon me, in what a sty of error I had wallowed, and how much pollution and impurity I had thereby contracted. Being exceedingly alarmed at the misery into which I had fallen, and much more at that which threatened me in the view of eternal death, I, as in duty bound, made it my first business to betake myself to thy way, condemning my past life, not without groans and tears. And now, O Lord, what remains to a wretch like me, but, instead of defense, earnestly to supplicate Thee not to judge according to its deserts that fearful abandonment of thy word, from which, in thy wondrous goodness, Thou hast at last delivered me.[5]

Calvin clearly took from his conversion two things regarding the Word of God: first, that God's Word is like light driving away darkness, and second, complete submission to God's Word is the necessary condition of the Godward life.

Calvin's Preaching

Calvin believed the pulpit to be "the throne of God, and from that throne he wants to govern our souls."[6] In the words of a recent biographer, Calvin's preaching aimed "to change God's enemies into his children," and "second, it taught God's children to honor their Father more and more."[7] For that to happen, the preacher had to listen to

---

4. "I was held back in Geneva not by deliberation or persuasion, but rather by a terrible imprecation from Guillaume Farel, as if God straight from heaven violently laid his hand on me" (CO 31.23).

5. John Calvin, Jacopo Sadoleto, and John C. Olin, *A Reformation Debate: Sadoleto's Letter to the Genevans and Calvin's Reply* (New York: Harper & Row, 1966), 89.

6. CO 53.520.

7. Herman Selderhuis, *John Calvin: A Pilgrim's Life* (Downers Grove, Ill: IVP Academic, 2009), 111. I am indebted to Selderhuis for Calvin's quotes in this section on preaching.

his Master and "speak as if the mouth of the Teacher."[8] Concerning a pastor who did not first become a student of the Word, Calvin wrote that "it would be better if he were to break his neck while climbing into the pulpit."[9]

What preaching there was in Geneva throughout Calvin's ministry! In the three churches in Geneva, there were three services on Sundays, at sunrise, at 9 o'clock, and at 3 o'clock. At noon, there was a children's service for catechism instruction. Additional services were held in each church on selected weekdays. In 1549, the city council determined to expand the preaching schedule to include sermons on every day of the workweek. From then on, Calvin preached an average of ten new sermons every fourteen days.[10]

When he was forced out of Geneva in 1538, he still bore the ministry of the Word in Geneva on his heart. Though he said, when he was asked to return, that he would rather die a hundred other deaths than return to that Geneva cross, where he was sure to meet his end a thousand times a day, yet he wrote to Farel: "If I were able to choose, I would do anything but obey you, but since I know that I am not my own master, I offer my heart to the Lord as a sacrifice."[11] Selderhuis remarks: "He preferred the cross of Geneva to the judgment of God."[12] His first sermon after his return picked up with the text where he had left off three years earlier. This poignantly illustrates Calvin's unyielding submission to the Word of God and a desire to speak nothing but what is true to it.

Calvin's Deathbed

A final vignette that fittingly sums up Calvin's attitude to the Word of God involves some of his final words on his deathbed. He attested to those standing by:

> As for my doctrine, I have taught faithfully, and God has given me grace to write, which I have done as faithfully as I could; and I have not corrupted one single passage of Scripture nor twisted it so far as I know: and when I studied subtlety, I have put all

---

8. *CO* 35.424.

9. *CO* 26.304.

10. Selderhuis, *John Calvin: A Pilgrim's Life*, 112.

11. *CO* 11.100.

12. Selderhuis, *John Calvin: A Pilgrim's Life*, 117

that under my feet, and have always aimed at being simple. I have written nothing out of hatred against anyone, but have always set before me what I thought was for the glory of God.[13]

This testimony is consistent with what we have seen from Calvin's conversion and preaching. Until the end of his life, Calvin's view of the Word of God remained indissolubly connected with concepts of authority and submission, faithfulness, and an eye for God's glory.

With this background, I now turn to how Calvin wrote about the Word of God in the *Institutes*, his commentaries, and his sermons.

HOW GOD'S WORD COMES TO US

Calvin believed that in His Word, God accommodates Himself to our understanding.[14] In line with this, Calvin also was content to use metaphors or word pictures to speak of the character and force of the Word of God. In fact, Selderhuis quotes Calvin as follows:

Let those who want to do well in carrying out the task of the ministry of the Word learn not only to converse and to speak publicly, but especially to penetrate through into the conscience so that people can see the crucified Christ and his very blood as it flows. If the church has that kind of artists, it will need neither wood nor stone, that is to say dead representations, and will in fact not need any images any more at all.[15]

Calvin used many word pictures as he unfolded his understanding of the Word of God. Because of space constraints, I will mention only some of the more prominent ones.

Speech from God

Scripture makes the "Word" the dominant metaphor for that means of God's self-revelation other than creation. In fact, it is so dominant that we rarely stop to think of it as a metaphor. However, Calvin savored the significance of the metaphor at many points, as the fol-

---

13. J. I. Packer, "Calvin's View of Scripture," in John Warwick Montgomery, *God's Inerrant Word: Conference on the Inspiration and Authority of Scripture* (Ligonier, Pa.: Bethany, 1974), 95–6.

14. "For because our weakness does not attain to his exalted state, the description of him that is given to us must be accommodated to our capacity so that we may understand it" (*Institutes* 1.17.13).

15. Selderhuis, *John Calvin: A Pilgrim's Life*, 115.

lowing quote illustrates: "Whoever wishes to profit in the Scriptures, let him first of all lay down as a settled point this.... That it was the mouth of the Lord that spake (*os Domini loquutum esse*)...we owe to the Scripture the same reverence which we owe to God, because it has proceeded from him alone, and has nothing of man mixed with it."[16]

In his *Institutes*, Calvin explained this concept at some length:

> The full authority which they [the Scriptures] obtain with the faithful proceeds from no other consideration than that they are persuaded that they proceeded from heaven, as if God had been heard giving utterance to them.... Clear signs that God is its speaker are seen in Scripture, from which it is plain that its teaching is heavenly.... Being enlightened by [the Spirit]...we are made absolutely certain...that [Scripture] has come to us by the ministry of men from God's very mouth.[17]

Calvin carried this view of Scripture over to the pulpit, where Scripture is to be faithfully expounded. This view of the Word of God has implications for how we hear:

> It is certain that if we come to church we shall not hear only a mortal man speaking but we shall feel (even by his secret power) that God is speaking to our souls, that he is the teacher. He so touches us that the human voice enters into us, and so profits us that we are refreshed and nourished by it. God calls us to him as if he had his mouth open and we saw him there in person.[18]

Clearly this view of Scripture as proceeding from God's very mouth gives a weight, a glory, and a divinity to the Scriptures, in line with how Scripture presents itself.

The School of God

A second prominent word picture that Calvin used for the Word of God was that of a school. In the third book of the *Institutes*, when Calvin was speaking of predestination, he wrote:

> For Scripture is the school of the Holy Spirit, in which, as nothing is omitted that is both necessary and useful to know, so

16. *Commentary* on 2 Timothy 3:16.
17. *Institutes* 1.7.5; elsewhere, Calvin writes: "The apostles were the certain and authentic amanuenses of the Holy Spirit and therefore their writings are to be received as oracles of God" (*Institutes* 4.8.9).
18. *CO* 54.11.

nothing is taught but what is expedient to know. Therefore we must guard against depriving believers of anything disclosed about predestination in Scripture, lest we seem either wickedly to defraud them of the blessing of their God or to accuse and scoff at the Holy Spirit for having published what it is in any way profitable to suppress.[19]

What Calvin was driving at by using the picture of Scripture as a school is that if it is important enough for God to have the doctrine of predestination in the curriculum of His school, as it were, who are we to neglect it or ignore it?

Connected with this emphasis on the Word of God as a school is Calvin's frequent refrain that we ought to be students, scholars, or disciples of the Word:

While it becomes man seriously to employ his eyes in considering the works of God, since a place has been assigned him in this most glorious theatre that he may be a spectator of them, his special duty is to give ear to the Word, that he may the better profit. Hence it is not strange that those who are born in darkness become more and more hardened in their stupidity; because the vast majority instead of confining themselves within due bounds by listening with docility to the Word, exult in their own vanity. If true religion is to beam upon us, our principle must be, that it is necessary to begin with heavenly teaching, and that it is impossible for any man to obtain even the minutest portion of right and sound doctrine without being a disciple of Scripture. Hence, the first step in true knowledge is taken, when we reverently embrace the testimony which God has been pleased therein to give of himself.[20]

We ought to have the posture of a diligent student, eager to learn from the Word of God. If we have such a lowly spirit, then we will truly learn; but without it, the Word will not profit us. Calvin wrote:

God hath so communicated his word unto us, and in such sort framed and wrought it for our understanding, as that there is not the most simple and ignorant which shall not find himself capable to be the scholar [student] of God, yea so that we come unto it in all lowliness and humbleness.... [I]f we come unto it in

---

19. *Institutes* 3.21.3.
20. *Institutes* 1.6.2.

the pride of our own minds, presuming of our own fine heads, as in this point a great number of proud and glorious men do, who will rather control God than submit themselves unto him and to his word: no doubt of it we shall be left in the dark.[21]

Someone put it this way to me once: "How amazing that God uses white and black on a page to bring a man to heaven." Indeed, God's Word is a school, and a teachable spirit will bring us great and eternal good.

The Sun

A third word picture Calvin used for the Word of God was the sun.[22] He wrote: "Indeed the Word of God is like the sun, shining upon all those to whom it is proclaimed, but with no effect among the blind. Now, all of us are blind by nature in this respect. Accordingly, it cannot penetrate into our minds unless the Spirit, as the inner teacher, through his illumination makes entry for it."[23] Notice how Calvin paralleled the images of sun and teacher in this quote. His point was that just as there is no seeing without the light of the sun, so there is no knowledge unless our minds are turned to God as our Sun.

Elsewhere, Calvin related this picture of the sun to the face of God:

The whole, then, comes to this: As soon as the minutest particle of faith is instilled into our minds, we begin to behold the face of God placid, serene, and propitious; far off, indeed, but still so distinctly as to assure us that there is no delusion in it. In proportion to the progress we afterwards make (and the progress ought to be uninterrupted), we obtain a nearer and surer view, the very continuance making it more familiar to us. Thus we see that a mind illumined with the knowledge of God is at first involved in much ignorance,—ignorance, however, which is gradually removed. Still this partial ignorance or obscure discernment does not prevent that clear knowledge of the divine favor which holds the first and principal part in faith. For as one

---

21. John Calvin, *Sermons on Psalm 119* (repr., Audubon, N.J.: Old Paths Publications, 1996), 334.

22. A related word picture is that of a "mirror," as we see in the following quote: "The word itself, however it may be conveyed to us, is like a *mirror* in which faith may behold God" (*Institutes* 3.2.6).

23. *Institutes* 3.2.24.

shut up in a prison, where from a narrow opening he receives the rays of the sun indirectly and in a manner divided, though deprived of a full view of the sun, has no doubt of the source from which the light comes, and is benefited by it; so believers, while bound with the fetters of an earthly body, though surrounded on all sides with much obscurity, are so far illumined by any slender light which beams upon them and displays the divine mercy as to feel secure.[24]

Ultimately, as Calvin made clear, this light from the sun is essentially Christ Himself. It is essentially the glory of Christ that is the sun of the Scriptures, as Calvin taught in his comments on 2 Corinthians 3: "We cannot magnify enough, or treat with too much reverence, the glory of Christ which shines in the gospel, as the brightness of the sun shines in its rays. It is in bad taste, and a foolish profanation of the gospel, when the power and majesty of the Spirit, which draw the minds and hearts of men to heaven, are withheld from the people."[25]

This word picture, then, strongly conveys to us the sense of illumination without which we are left to deadness and dullness.

Spectacles
A fourth and well-known word picture Calvin used was that of spectacles or glasses:

Not in vain, therefore, has he added the light of his Word in order that he might make himself known unto salvation, and bestowed the privilege on those whom he was pleased to bring into nearer and more familiar relation to himself. For, seeing how the minds of men were carried to and fro, and found no certain resting-place, he chose the Jews for a peculiar people, and then hedged them in that they might not, like others, go astray. And not in vain does he, by the same means, retain us in his knowledge, since but for this, even those who, in comparison of others, seem to stand strong, would quickly fall away. For as the aged, or those whose sight is defective, when any book however fair, is set before them, though they perceive that there is something written are scarcely able to make out two consecutive words, but, when aided by glasses, begin to read distinctly,

---

24. *Institutes* 3.2.19.
25. *Commentary* on 2 Corinthians 3:13.

so Scripture, gathering together the impressions of Deity, which, till then, lay confused in our minds, dissipates the darkness, and shows us the true God clearly.[26]

Of course, as we implied above, Scripture without the aid of the Holy Spirit is not sufficient to enlighten depraved and sinful man, who will not know God as he should. Calvin made clear, as Scripture also teaches, that man is blind and needs more than just an objective means, namely the spectacles of Scripture. He needs a subjective means as well. Commenting on Hebrews 11:3 in the *Institutes,* Calvin wrote: "The invisible divinity was represented indeed by such displays of his power, but that we have no eyes to perceive it unless they are illuminated through faith by the inner revelation of God."[27]

Scripture's glorious function, then, is like that of spectacles on the eyes of someone who otherwise can barely see. The Spirit, of course, needs to illumine our minds subjectively as well.

Strength and Sword

A fifth word picture Calvin was fond of was of a sword or another object indicating strength. Of course, the strength of the Word of God works in two ways. The first is against us. God's Word is a sword that is wielded to slay the sinner and bring him low. In his comments on Hebrews 4, Calvin said:

> If any one thinks that the air is beaten by an empty sound when the word of God is preached, he is greatly mistaken; for it is a living thing and full of hidden power, which leaves nothing in man untouched.... [H]e would have it effectually to constrain the consciences of men, so as to bring them under his authority; and that he has put power in his word for this purpose, that it may scrutinize all the parts of the soul, search the thoughts, discern the affections, and, in a word, shew itself to be the judge.... [T]here is nothing so hard or strong in man, nothing so hidden, that the powerful word cannot pervade it.[28]

But the Word of God, according to Calvin, is also a weapon in the hand of the believer. By it, God graciously supplies the believer

---

26. *Institutes* 1.6.1.

27. *Institutes* 1.5.14. See also Benjamin B. Warfield, *Calvin and Calvinism* (New York: Oxford University Press, 1931), 70, who elaborates on this point.

28. *Commentary* on Hebrews 4:12.

his armor, as it were. "We had need to be armed with the word of God, which is our sword, with the buckler of faith, and the helmet of hope."[29] On Acts 9:19–25, he wrote: "Whence had Paul this victory, save only because the Scripture was his sword? Therefore, so often as heretics stand up to resist the true faith, so often as wicked men endeavor to overthrow all godliness, so often as the ungodly do obstinately resist, let us remember that we must fet [seek] armor hence."[30]

Thus, Calvin pictured God's Word functioning as an instrument of strength, both against us and for us, aiding believers in the Christian warfare.

Shield, Safety, and Solace

The Word of God is not just a means of power and strength to attack, but also a means by which to be secure and safe. When discussing Christ's temptation by the Devil, Calvin noted how Christ quoted Scripture. He wrote: "Christ uses Scripture as his shield: for this is the true way of fighting, if we wish to make ourselves sure of the victory.... Those who voluntarily throw away that armor, and do not laboriously exercise themselves in the school of God, deserve to be strangled, at every instant, by Satan, into whose hands they give themselves up unarmed."[31]

Elsewhere, Calvin compared the Word of God to other means of safety and security for believers. Commenting on Isaiah 9:1, he wrote: "A man may happen to be drowned in a small stream, and yet, though he had fallen into the open sea, if he had got hold of a plank he might have been rescued and brought on shore. In like manner the slightest calamities will overwhelm us if we are deprived of God's favor; but if we relied on the word of God, we might come out of the heaviest calamity safe and uninjured."[32]

Another way God's Word comes to us, according to Calvin, is as a solace or shelter in trouble or adversity. He wrote:

[T]here is no other solace, and no other remedy for adversity, but our reposing upon the word of God, and our embracing the

---

29. Calvin, *Sermons on Psalm 119*, 140.
30. *Commentary* on Acts 9:19–25.
31. *Commentary* on Matthew 4:1–4.
32. *Commentary* on Isaiah 9:1.

grace and the assurance of our salvation which are offered in it.... The prophet declares that he was grievously oppressed by a weight of afflictions enough to overwhelm him; but that the consolation which he derived from the Divine law in such desperate circumstances, was as life to him.[33]

Here we see the experiential and pastoral significance that Calvin gave to the Word of God in the often perplexing and difficult reality of the life of Christians.

Sweetness

Closely related to this word picture of solace is Calvin's frequent and thoroughly biblical mention of the Word of God in terms of sweetness, like that of honey. I. John Hesselink has devoted a very helpful article to this subject in Calvin's corpus.[34] Typical of Calvin is a statement we find in his commentary on Micah: "God's word is good and sweet to all the godly. Let us then learn to become submissive to God, and then he will convey to us by his word nothing but sweetness, nothing but delights; we shall then find nothing more desirable than to be fed by this spiritual food; and it will ever be a real joy to us, whenever the Lord will open his mouth to teach us."[35]

According to Calvin, God uses the sweetness of His Word early in the Christian life. Calvin wrote, "The commencement of a good life consists in God's law attracting us to him by its sweetness."[36] By it, God allures us away from sin, Calvin said: "In our natural state, what is more agreeable to us than that which is sinful? This will be the constant tendency of our minds, unless the delight which we feel in the law carry us in the opposite direction."[37]

This has implications for preaching. Preachers should be concerned that the savor of the Word goes forth. Commenting on 2 Corinthians 2:14, Calvin wrote: "He [Paul] carries out, however, the metaphor of *odor*, by which he expresses both the delectable sweetness of the gospel, and its power and efficacy for inspiring life. In

---

33. *Commentary* on Psalm 119:89–96.

34. I. John Hesselink, "Calvin, Theologian of Sweetness," *Calvin Theological Journal* 37:2 (2002): 318–32. I thank Joel R. Beeke for bringing this article to my attention.

35. *Commentary* on Micah 2:7.

36. *Commentary* on Psalm 119:15.

37. Ibid.

the mean time, Paul instructs them, that his preaching is so far from being savorless, that it quickens souls by its very *odor*. Let us, however, learn from this, that those alone make right proficiency in the gospel, who, by the sweet fragrance of Christ, are stirred up to desire him, so as to bid farewell to the allurements of the world."[38]

Commenting on Psalm 119:103, Calvin wrote:

O how sweet have been thy words to my palate!... [David] was so powerfully attracted by the sweetness of the Divine Law, as to have no desire after any other delight. It is possible that a man may be affected with reverence towards the Law of God; but no one will cheerfully follow it, save he who has tasted this sweetness. God requires from us no slavish service: he will have us to come to him cheerfully, and this is the very reason why the prophet commends the sweetness of God's word so often in this psalm.[39]

Repeatedly in his *Sermons on Psalm 119*, Calvin returned to this theme of the sweetness of God's Word. In one of his prayers, he said:

According to this holy doctrine, let us prostrate ourselves before the majesty of our good God, in acknowledging our offences, beseeching him that it would please him to make us to see the sweetness of his word, as his servant David hath been thereon thoroughly settled: to the end we might have such a fervent affection to it, as that it might cause us to forget all the desires of this world, wherein we are too much plagued: and that we might cut off all the superfluities of our flesh: to the end we might be dedicated in all holiness unto our God, and to be confirmed more and more in his service.[40]

Later in this series, he wrote of the Word of God as the most superlative sweetness: "[T]he word of God ought to be more dear and precious unto us than all the riches of the world, and more sweet than all other sweetness in the earth."[41] A little later, again, Calvin wrote: "[T]he word of God ought to be more dear and sweet unto us, than all other things, and...we ought to take all our delight and pleasure therein, desiring nothing else, but to order and hold ourselves

---

38. *Commentary* on 2 Corinthians 2:14.
39. *Commentary* on Psalm 119:103.
40. Calvin, *Sermons on Psalm 119*, 309–310.
41. Ibid., 335.

to it: knowing that whatsoever God hath, is to this end, to communi-
cate the same unto us, that we might taste of his bounty and love."[42]

Clearly, the analogy of "sweetness" for the way in which the
Word of God comes to us was a dear one for Calvin.

Song

Connected to this last point of sweetness, Calvin used the word picture of a song book or song.

In his *Sermons on Psalm 119*, as he reflected on verse 54, Calvin
wrote:

> *Thy Statutes have been my song in the house of my pilgrimage*—Not
> estranged from God, nor yet from the knowledge of salvation
> but contrariwise, that he was the rather stirred up to sing praises
> unto God, and those Psalms which God did put in his mouth,
> yea, even such as were taken out of the law.... David...drew
> them from it as out of a Fountain.[43]

Calvin went on to apply David's profession. Christians "conform
themselves the best they can to the word of God, take all their delight
and pleasure therein, and make the law of God their song, which
maketh them to withdraw themselves from all the vanities and corruptions which they commit, so that they keep themselves within
this compass."[44]

Calvin has been especially responsible for bringing the Psalms
into the worship of families and churches everywhere. To use the
words of Selderhuis, "The Psalms became songs for a pilgrim church,
for believers who knew heaven to be their home country and were at
home nowhere on earth."[45]

This wide array of word pictures and others that we cannot pursue show us how Calvin unfolded the doctrine of the Word of God.
In all these ways, God's Word comes to us. It brings light, knowledge, comfort, defense, nourishment, joy, and so much more. How
multi-faceted, rich, and especially glorious is Calvin's view of the
Word of God.

---

42. Ibid., 419.
43. Ibid., 148.
44. Ibid., 149.
45. Selderhuis, *John Calvin: A Pilgrim's Life*, 133.

HOW WE SHOULD COME TO GOD'S WORD

I do not intend now to treat the precise method Calvin outlined and practiced for the way in which Scripture should be interpreted.[46] Instead, I wish to simply indicate with what disposition Calvin urged us to approach Scripture, especially in light of how it comes to us. I have found Calvin's *Sermons on Psalm 119* to be a repository of helpful insights on this matter.

Reverently

An attitude of reverence for the Word should be first. Calvin wrote: "There is a frank and free fear in those which are governed by the Spirit of God, which beareth a reverence unto his word, to make them tremble before it…they conceive his incomprehensible majesty in his word, and thereupon are humbled."[47] Of course, this does not negate a love and boldness with respect to God, as Calvin went on to state: "But yet they cease not for all that, to come boldly unto GOD, knowing that he will be their merciful Father and desireth nothing else but to receive them. This humble fear then, may well be conjoined with the love of God, agree with faith, and with a taste which we might take in the word of God, urging ourselves wholly thereto."[48]

Calvin complained that the Word of God, sadly, is not viewed this way by many:

> When God at this day speaketh unto us, what ear give we unto him? And how reverently? See here, he hath bestowed upon us a singular grace at this day, when as his word hath been once again published. Let us behold our unthankfulness. Let us lay all these things together, and we shall see that the majesty of God [in] his word is not more esteemed than the very peel of an onion, as we say.[49]

---

46. Thomas F. Torrance, *The Hermeneutics of John Calvin*, monograph supplements to the *Scottish Journal of Theology* (Edinburgh: Scottish Academic Press, 1988); Richard C. Gamble, *Calvin and Hermeneutics: Articles on Calvin and Calvinism*, Vol. 6 (New York: Garland, 1992); David Less Puckett, *John Calvin's Exegesis of the Old Testament* (Louisville: Westminster John Knox Press, 1995).

47. Calvin, *Sermons on Psalm 119*, 309.

48. Ibid.

49. Ibid., 325.

Dependently

In light of our innate blindness and even remaining darkness, we are wholly dependent on God when it comes to understanding and heeding His Word. With this prayer, Calvin gave us a good model of what it means to come dependently to the Word of God:

> Alas, dear Father, it is so far off that I am able to keep thy word, as that I should not be able to understand any whit thereof, if thou guidest me not thereto: For it is thou which must both begin the same, and also perform it wholly in me. Let us not think that through our own labor and industry, and by our own sharpness of wit, to come so far as to understand the secrets of God, but let us know that we had need to be enlightened with the grace of his holy Spirit, to open our eyes, for without it we are poor blind souls. Let us then learn, if we will be good Doctors and teachers, to proceed in all humbleness and fear, knowing that the least sentence in the Scripture surmounteth our understanding and that we are too dull and blockish to attain unto so high wisdom, except the Lord our God guideth and leadeth us thereto.[50]

Ardently

The final posture that I wish to mention from Calvin is that of longing or desire. We ought to approach Scripture with an ardency to receive all that God has to give us through His Word. Preaching on Psalm 119:125, Calvin said:

> [W]e should be always like beasts, until such time as God had opened unto us the spirit or understanding of humane things.... [W]hen we shall talk of the secrets of the heavenly life, and of the wisdom which God showeth unto us in his word: there must all men confess, that all their senses fail them, and that all their reason is dead and buried. What is then to be done? Let us come to the remedy which David here giveth us: to wit, that we desire of God to have understanding, that we might become very well learned. For without that, we must continue and remain still in our beastliness.[51]

A few pages further, Calvin expressed that ardency again vividly and memorably:

---

50. Ibid., 119, 75.
51. Ibid., 322.

[W]e should be enlightened...after we are known to be lowly and humbled, feeling our want and necessity, let us sigh and groan unto the majesty of our God, in beseeching him to instruct us. For we shall not need to be greatly learned for our right and perfect walking, if we truly and earnestly desire to be his scholars, and to prefer his word before all other things.... David... opened his mouth, as a forepined [languished] spirit, who was no longer able to abide it. And afterward he saith that he drew in his breath, that he was so zealous, as that it took away as it were his very speech from him.... Now then we have here to note, that even then we shall be enflamed with the word of God, when as we shall have yea even such a vehement desire, as hereof is mention made and as hath been before spoken of.[52]

Psalm 119 certainly furnishes great material for writing at length on ardency. Commenting on Psalm 119:20, "My heart breaketh out, for the desire, unto thy judgments always," Calvin said, "We need more than just cold prayer; instead, we need to come with such a true desire as 'carrieth us even out of ourselves' and to make no such accompt [account] of this present life, but to be well advised, to shoot at an higher matter."[53]

Conclusion

In our day, when the dominant approaches to the Word of God seem to regard it as a source either of inspirational stories to help us feel better about our circumstances or of maxims to help us get ahead in this world and life, Calvin's doctrine of the Word of God is both radically other and profoundly needed.

If I were allowed only three words to characterize Calvin's view of the Word of God, I would choose these three:

First, *exalted*. Above all, it is an exalted view. God's Word is an authority of the highest sort. It reveals a majestic God, and it does so in such a way that the Word itself is the extension of His domain—a scepter as it were, whereby He extends His rule. It is exalted because its authority is revealed to us by the attestation of the Holy Spirit, whereby God impresses on us the veracity and authority of the Word of God. And it is exalted because it deals with the redemption and

---

52. Ibid., 335.
53. Ibid., 54.

glory of God. It is all of God, it is Trinitarian, and for that reason it is greatly exalted.

Second, *experiential*. It reaches into the reality and vicissitudes of our lives, and it supplies every need that believers could ever have. When God needs to bring us low, He does it through the Word as a sword. When He needs to shield us in temptation and affliction or from undue sorrow, He does it through His Word. When He needs to comfort us so that we experience His solace and shelter, He does it through His Word. When He needs to draw us away from sin, He does it through the sweetness of His Word. In each of these cases, Calvin had a keen sense of how the Word of God fits our many needs and ministers to us.

Third, *expectant*. Throughout his commentaries and sermons, Calvin modeled an approach to the Word of God that is hungry for what God's mouth has to say. He projected such an earnest yet humble readiness to hear what God was saying—it was as if he stood before the text and would not be denied. Calvin said it best in this final quote, a prayer:

> Grant, Almighty God, as thou daily and familiarly deignest to grant us the light of heavenly doctrine, that we may come to thy school with true humility and modesty. May our docility be really apparent; may we receive with reverence whatever proceeds from thy lips, and may thy majesty be conspicuous among us. May we taste of that goodness which thou dost manifest to us in thy word, and be enabled to rejoice in thee as our Father; may we never dread thy presence, but may we enjoy the sweet testimony of thy paternal grace and favor. May thy word be more precious to us than gold and worldly treasures, and, meanwhile, may we feed upon its sweetness, until we arrive at that full satiety which is laid up for us in heaven through Christ our Lord.—Amen.[54]

---

54. *Commentary* on Daniel, vol. 2, prayer for Lecture 55.

CHAPTER 3

Calvin on Preaching Christ from the Old Testament

David Murray

There is a widespread crisis in preaching from the Old Testament today, and consequently in preaching Christ from the Old Testament. Fewer and fewer sermons are being preached from this part of the Bible, and those that are preached do not appear to command the same interest or respect as New Testament sermons.

Some surveys have found that only twenty percent of Christian sermons are from the Old Testament. The editor of *Preaching,* an evangelical journal for preachers, laments: "I annually receive hundreds of sermon manuscripts from ministers in a variety of Protestant denominations.... Less than one-tenth of the sermons submitted to *Preaching* are based on Old Testament texts."[1] Another complains that on the relatively rare occasion when an Old Testament text is announced, "it is often only the text for some topical treatise that soon departs from its context."[2]

This imbalance in the spiritual diet of most Christians explains many of the spiritual problems in the modern church and the modern Christian. How can we expect our congregations to be healthy when they are being largely deprived of thirty-nine of the sixty-six books (60 percent) of the Bible—the very books that provided the spiritual nourishment of Christ and His apostles?

There are many reasons for the reduced quantity and quality of Old Testament preaching today—liberalism, ignorance, dispensationalism (in both patent and latent forms), pastoral laziness, lack of good models, desire for academic credibility, etc. Even some

---

1. Michael Duduit, "The Church's Need for Old Testament Preaching," in *Reclaiming the Prophetic Mantle,* ed. George L. Klein (Nashville: Broadman, 1992), 10.

2. W. A. Criswell, "Preaching from the Old Testament," in *Tradition and Testament,* ed. J. S. Feinberg (Chicago: Moody, 1981), 298.

Reformed churches, churches that claim to be Calvinistic, have failed in these areas.

I have surveyed John Calvin's *Institutes of the Christian Religion* and his Old Testament commentaries and sermons, and I have identified and extracted a number of principles that undergirded his extensive Old Testament teaching and preaching. These principles are the pillars upon which we should restore, rebuild, and renew our Old Testament teaching and preaching, and specifically our preaching of Christ from the Old Testament. We will look first at theological pillars and then at some practical pillars.

THEOLOGICAL PILLARS

Pillar 1: By preaching the Old Testament, we are preaching Christ's words

When Calvin commented on the Old Testament, he repeatedly used phrases such as, "Here Christ comforts his church.... By these words, Christ convicts his people.... Christ therefore spoke to Israel."

Calvin, therefore, encourages us to hear the words of the Old Testament as the very words of Christ, and to preach them as such.

Pillar 2: Christ is the only teacher of His church

T. H. L. Parker identified this vital principle in Calvin's preaching and writing.[3] Whatever stage of biblical revelation we look at in the Old or New Testament, Christ was the one and only schoolmaster of His church.

For example, when commenting on Matthew 11:27, Calvin wrote, "I mean that God has never manifested himself to men in any other way than through the Son, that is his sole wisdom, light, and truth."[4] Patriarchs, prophets, and apostles all received their spiritual knowledge through the Son of God.

In *Calvin's Preaching,* Parker argues strongly against the tendency to conclude that because perfection and completeness have come in Christ, we need not concern ourselves with the Old Testament much beyond illustrations and proof-texts. Together with Calvin, he force-

---

3. T. H. L. Parker, *Calvin's Preaching* (Louisville: Westminster John Knox Press, 1992), 6.

4. *Institutes* 4.8.5.

fully concludes that "this overlooks the main point, that the Teacher of the Old Testament Church is the same Christ as the Teacher of the New Testament Church."[5]

Pillar 3: By preaching God, we preach Christ

Calvin did not feel the need to say the name of Christ, or to focus specifically on the second person of the Godhead, in order to preach Christ. Many of his Old Testament sermons did not specifically mention Christ. That is because, for Calvin, a God-centered sermon was implicitly Christ-centered. For example, he wrote in the *Institutes*, "Whenever the name of God is mentioned without particularization, there are designated no less the Son and the Spirit than the Father."[6]

We, too, when preaching from the Old Testament, must train our congregations to hear references to "God" and "LORD" with Trinitarian ears.

Pillar 4: The Old and New Testaments are united by the covenant of grace

This is one area where Calvin differed significantly from Martin Luther. Luther saw more of a contrast between the testaments, whereas Calvin emphasized their unity.

Calvin accepted that there were differences between the two testaments, as we shall see, but that did not in any way lessen the fundamental unity. He said, "The covenant made with all the patriarchs is so much like ours in substance and reality that the two are actually one and the same."[7] For Calvin, the covenants differ only in how they are managed or administered. In other words, the old covenant, the covenant God made with Israel, is fundamentally the same as the new covenant. Calvin put it like this:

> Now as to the *new* covenant, it is not so called, because it is contrary to the first covenant; for God is never inconsistent with himself, nor is he unlike himself.... God could never have made a new, that is, a contrary or a different covenant. For whence do we derive our hope of salvation, except from that blessed seed promised to Abraham?... These things no doubt suffi-

---

5. Parker, *Calvin's Preaching*, 7.
6. *Institutes* 1.13.20.
7. *Institutes* 2.10.2.

ciently shew that God has never made any other covenant than that which he made formerly with Abraham, and at length confirmed by the hand of Moses.... Let us now see why he promises to the people a *new* covenant. It being new, no doubt refers to what they call the form.... But the substance remains the same. By substance I understand the doctrine; for God in the Gospel brings forward nothing but what the Law contains.[8]

The relation between the testaments was absolutely central to Calvin's thought—so much so that Book II of the *Institutes*, which is all about redemption in Christ, is summarized in the title: *The Knowledge of God the Redeemer in Christ, first disclosed to the fathers under the Law, and then to us in the Gospel.*

Pillar 5: What was said to Israel was said also to us

The fundamental unity of the two testaments is also the basis for Calvin's view that what was said to Israel was, in some significant ways, also said to us: "True it is that the things which are contained here were spoken to the people of Israel, and might have profited them in their time; but yet do they also belong unto us at this day, and they be as a common treasure whereof God will have us to be partakers."[9]

One example of this can be found in his introductory sermon on Micah. He spoke of God's anger against Jerusalem and Samaria, then identified "us" with "them." Parker summarizes a part of this sermon thus: "We too [like Jerusalem and Samaria] do not like to hear of God's wrath, but only of his kindness. But if we are to know God's love, we must first feel his wrath and be wounded to the bottom of our hearts."[10]

Having surveyed Calvin's teaching on this, David Puckett concludes: "The people of God are one and God's revelation to his people as recorded in scripture is one. The differences between the revelation under the old and new covenants pale when compared with that which remains the same."[11]

---

8. *Commentary* on Jeremiah 31:31–32.
9. John Calvin, *Sermons on Deuteronomy* (Edinburgh: Banner of Truth Trust, 1987, facsimile reprint of 1583 publication), 5.
10. T. H. L. Parker, *Calvin's Old Testament Commentaries* (Edinburgh: T & T Clark, 1986), 40; *Supplementa Calviniana*, 5, 4–7.
11. David L. Puckett, *John Calvin's Exegesis of the Old Testament* (Louisville: Westminster John Knox Press, 1995), 37.

Parker points out that although in Calvin the New Testament believer has more clarity and assurance of Christ than the Old Testament believer, insofar as they both live by hope rather than by possession they are in the same experimental position.[12]

Pillar 6: Every Old Testament believer was saved through faith in Christ

On this, Calvin was crystal clear. He had to be. He faced the opposition of Anabaptists who insisted that the Old Testament was fundamentally different from the New. They said that the Old Testament was legalistic and that people's relation to God was by their good works, not the grace of Christ. Let us hear Calvin's emphatic response:

> Indeed the ancient fathers were saved by no other means than by that which we have.... They had their salvation grounded in Christ Jesus, as we have: but that was after an obscure manner, so as they beheld the thing afar off which was presented unto them.[13]

> Accordingly, apart from the Mediator, God never showed favor toward the ancient people, nor ever gave hope of grace to them.[14]

> From this it is now clear enough that, since God cannot without the Mediator be propitious toward the human race, under the law Christ was always set before the holy fathers as the end to which they should direct their faith.... Here I am gathering a few passages of many because I merely want to remind my readers that the hope of all the godly has ever reposed in Christ alone.[15]

> The Gospel was not given in order to add anything to the Law and the Prophets. Let us read, let us run through everything contained in the New Testament; we shall not find one syllable added to the Law and the Prophets. It is only a declaration of what had already been taught there. It is true that God has shown greater favour to us than to the Fathers who lived before

---

12. Parker, *Calvin's Old Testament Commentaries*, 46.
13. Ralph A. Smith, "Calvin's Covenantal Pronomianism"; http://www.berith. org/essays/cal/cal04.html, see note 9.
14. *Institutes* 2.6.2.
15. Ibid.

the coming of our Lord Jesus Christ, so that things are much clearer to us now. But yet nothing has been added.[16]

As to whether the Old Testament believers understood that their salvation was in Christ alone, again Calvin gave an emphatic "yes!" He underlined how the Old Testament prophets often addressed the needs of God's overwhelmed and despairing people with prophecies of Christ. Puckett comments:

> This is how Calvin explains a stylistic peculiarity of the prophets. They abruptly break into whatever they were writing in order to speak of Christ, "for in him are ratified all the promises which would otherwise have been doubtful and uncertain." Thus, the major issue of life for the people of the Old Testament was no different than in the New Testament—faith in Christ.[17]

Pillar 7: The Old Testament believers had the Holy Spirit

Calvin compared the promise-fulfillment relationship of the Old and New Testaments using the figures of shadow to light, shadow to body, child to adult, and sketch to painting. These analogies applied not just to Christ in the Old Testament but also to the Holy Spirit. Though not to the same degree or power as in the New Testament, the "power and grace of the Spirit was vigorous and reigned in the very truth of the shadows."[18]

Pillar 8: The hope of Old Testament believers was spiritual and heavenly

Anabaptists said not only that Old Testament salvation was legalistic, but also that those saved in this way were materialistic. Their hope was for the blessing of earthly prosperity, not heavenly immortality.

Calvin acknowledged that Old Testament promises seemed to be focused on the earthly and the temporal. However, he insisted that they actually were promises of eternal life. He highlighted New Testament verses that equated the Old Testament hope with that of the New Testament (Rom. 1:2; 3:21; Heb. 11:9ff) and concluded: "If the doctrine of the gospel is spiritual, and gives us access to the possession of incorruptible life, let us not think that those to whom it had

---

16. CO 54.294. 24-35

17. Puckett, *John Calvin's Exegesis of the Old Testament*, 40.

18. *Commentary* on Exodus 30:22ff.

been promised and announced omitted and neglected the care of the soul, and sought after fleshly pleasures like stupid beasts."[19]

But did the old covenant believers themselves consciously look for eternal life and immortality? In his *Institutes,* Calvin appealed to the consciousness of numerous Old Testament characters to prove that they had set their minds on a better life, a heavenly one.[20]

Calvin taught that God used the earthly promises to direct the minds of His people upward to the heavenly reality, and the Old Testament saints knew this and followed this course. For example, when commenting on Isaac's seemingly earthly blessing upon Jacob, Calvin said that God appointed the land of Canaan "as a mirror and pledge to them of the celestial inheritance.... Therefore, although Isaac makes the temporal favors of God prominent, nothing is further from his mind than to confine the hope of his son to this world."[21]

Pillar 9: The law was a schoolmaster that led Old Testament believers to Christ

Calvin's understanding of the law as a schoolmaster (Gal. 3:24) was heavily influenced by his own education, especially the way he learned Latin. He spent years learning the trivium: grammar, rhetoric, and dialectic. This was for the purpose of eventually being freed from the schoolmaster so that he could go on to the joys of higher education. Calvin saw the law as a schoolmaster that performed a number of exercises to lead worshipers to Christ. This view was not just descriptive of the redemptive-historical change from the old covenant to the new covenant, but was true personally in the lives of Old Testament believers. In summary, "The whole law, in short, was nothing but a manifold variety of exercises in which the worshippers were led by the hand to Christ."[22]

Pillar 10: There were differences between the Old and New Testaments

For all that we have said about the fundamental unity of the two testaments—and that is an important foundation to lay—Calvin

---

19. *Institutes* 2.10.3.
20. *Institutes* 2.10.10–23.
21. *Commentary* on Genesis 27:27.
22. *CO* 50.221.

identified several differences between them. However, these differences in no way detract from or balance the similarities.

First, God used more earthly means and instruments to train His people in the Old Testament than in the New. In the New Testament, the gospel is declared plainly and directly, but in the Old Testament, God set the same gospel before people using the language of earthly blessings. Puckett remarks: "The people of the old covenant were not blind to the fact that the Lord accommodated his message to their weakness in using earthly means to train them. They were attracted all the more to the goodness of God who would stoop to speak to them through such means."[23]

Second, the New Testament is much clearer than the Old due to the Old Testament's use of symbols and signs of truth in place of the reality. But it is only when compared with the outstanding clarity of the New Testament that the obscurity of the Old is so noticeable. Although Calvin allowed the term *gospel* to be used of the promises of salvation found in the law, he admitted that the term pre-eminently belonged to the New Testament proclamation of grace manifested so much more clearly and fully in Christ.

Third, the old covenant was more letter and less Spirit, whereas the New Covenant has more Spirit to accompany the letter. Parker summarizes this difference thus: "In comparison with the Gospel, the Law is an outward teaching, not penetrating to the heart. In comparison with the Law, the Gospel teaches spiritually, as the effectual instrument of God's grace."[24]

Fourth, the old covenant often produced fear and bondage, whereas the new covenant gives freedom and assurance. Calvin did not deny that old covenant believers knew freedom and forgiveness, but "they received this, not from the Law in itself as Law, but from the Gospel promises in the Law."[25]

While holding to a gracious salvation through faith in Christ for all Old Testament believers, Calvin accepted that even spiritually mature believers sometimes knew the fear and bondage of the law. He explained: "For, however much they enjoyed the privilege that they had received through the grace of the gospel, they were still

23. Puckett, *John Calvin's Exegesis of the Old Testament*, 40.
24. Parker, *Calvin's Old Testament Commentaries*, 54.
25. Ibid., 55.

subject to the same bonds and burdens of ceremonial observances as the common people."[26]

Fifth, since Christ, salvation is extended beyond the Jews to the nations.

PRACTICAL PILLARS

Having proposed ten theological pillars upon which to rebuild our Old Testament preaching, let me now outline eight practical pillars, eight principles that should guide the practical implementation of the theological principles.

Pillar 1: The aim of all Old Testament study is to find and preach Christ

Calvin, of course, recognized the need for academic training if one was to be an able Bible teacher. However, as Puckett highlights, he also recognized that "the possession of such skills does not guarantee proper understanding of the Old Testament. It is far more important that he read scripture with the proper goal—that of finding Christ."[27] Calvin put it even more succinctly and pungently: "Whoever turns aside from this object, even though he wears himself out with all his learning, will never reach the knowledge of the truth."[28]

It is this principle that led Calvin to be so critical of Jewish exegesis. He said that their Christless exegesis was the result not so much of misunderstanding the text but of a spiritual rebellion manifested in their refusal to recognize their need of a mediator.

For example, when he attacked the efforts of a certain rabbi to prove that Daniel 7:27 contains no reference to Christ, he said:

> We must not be surprised at the shameful ignorance of these rabbis, and at their blundering at the very rudiments, since they do not acknowledge the necessity of a Mediator, through whom alone the Church can obtain any favor before God.... [T]heir separating the Church from the Mediator is like leaving a mutilated body apart from its disjoined head.[29]

---

26. *Institutes* 2.11.9.
27. Puckett, *John Calvin's Exegesis of the Old Testament*, 82.
28. *Commentary* on John 5:39.
29. *Commentary* on Daniel 7:27.

I wonder how many "Christian" sermons on the Old Testament could be similarly described?

Pillar 2: The New Testament is our exegetical guide to the Old Testament

Calvin did not believe only in contextual interpretation, but also in canonical interpretation. The context of any passage or book of Scripture was the rest of Scripture. He would never interpret any book as if it stood outside of the Bible. Puckett comments: "For all his emphasis on historical interpretation, Calvin does not depart from the belief that scripture interprets scripture. The Prophets interpret the Law, and more importantly, the New Testament interprets the Old Testament."[30]

For Calvin, the New Testament was the most reliable guide in interpreting the Old Testament. For example, he based his belief that the law is a perfect rule for holy living on the New Testament interpretation of the Old, specifically the way Christ and His apostles refer believers to the law. "When we say that this is the meaning of the law, we are not thrusting forward a new interpretation of our own, but we are following Christ, its best interpreter," Calvin said.[31]

Pillar 3: If you cannot be Christ-centered in exegesis, be so in application

Calvin did not impute full New Testament understanding to Old Testament authors. He saw their understanding as determined by their place on the timeline of redemptive history. One result of this is that in some of his sermons, many paragraphs and pages can pass with little or no mention of Christ. I will critique Calvin for this a bit later. However, we have to acknowledge that this can be the justifiable and appropriate result of some of our Old Testament sermons. Calvin's solution was to have Christ-centered application for his New Testament hearers. Parker comments, "Calvin pursues the same course in all his Old Testament sermons of interpreting according to the historical context but applying within the context of the Christian Faith."[32] He goes on to say: "For page after page he can

30. Puckett, *John Calvin's Exegesis of the Old Testament*, 88.
31. *Institutes* 2.8.7.
32. Parker, *Calvin's Preaching*, 92.

look like Calvinus Judaeus and then suddenly show that, in his voluntary exile among the men of the Old Covenant, living with them in shades and shadows, he has not forgotten the Sun of righteousness who, as he himself already knows, will in their future rise with healing in his wings."[33]

Pillar 4: Preach the original message to the original audience

Prior to the sixteenth century, most people used the Old Testament as a source for proof texts or extended allegories. Very few were concerned with interpreting the text historically—considering the original author, circumstances, meaning, and context.

Calvin admitted that the allegorical method was appealing and plausible. He accepted that Paul used allegory in Galatians 4. However, he said this fact did not exclude the literal historical meaning and could not be used to justify finding allegory in other passages. He turned his back on allegorizing in favor of a more sober treatment of Scripture that explained the grammatical and historical meaning. In fact, Calvin insisted on this so much that some accused him of Judaizing. Calvin's retort was that allegorical interpretation was diabolical—that the devil had used this method to undermine the Bible.

Take as an example a weekday lecture on Micah. Calvin began with an explanation of the author and his circumstances, saying, "[Micah's] sermons would be useless to us today, or at any rate, frigid, unless we reckon with his times, so that we can compare and contrast our own circumstances with those of men of his age."[34]

A sermon on the same passage had similar introductory information. However, in the sermon, Calvin emphasized that the prophet's message was not only for his own times and people but for all times and people. To those who said the church did not need the prophets but had enough in the gospel, he retorted, "C'est un blaspheme execrable."[35]

As Calvin believed that the application of much of the Old Testament was through analogy, he insisted that unless the original setting was given full weight, there was a real danger of drawing the wrong

33. Parker, *Calvin's Old Testament Commentaries*, 7.
34. *CO* 43.281–2.
35. *SC* (*Supplementa Calviniana*) 5,1–4.

analogy. True application had to be based on the similarity of the past and present circumstances.

Pillar 5: Highlight partial fulfillments before highlighting the final fulfillment

This principle flows out of the previous one. Calvin saw that Christian exegetes were often impatient to proceed from Old Testament prophecy to New Testament fulfillment. However, he insisted on doing full justice to the original historical fulfillments before proceeding to the New Testament fulfillments. So, for example, the prophets' magnificent promises to exiled Israel of a restoration to and renewal of their land had to be seen first of all as fulfilled in the post-538 B.C. restorations before being interpreted as promises of a restoration and renewal of the kingdom of God in the gospel age.

Pillar 6: Preach Christ from all genres of Old Testament literature

Most preachers preach Christ from the Old Testament to a very limited degree—perhaps from the promises of Christ found in the prophets or the precepts of Christ found in the law. But there are two areas on which Calvin majored but on which we tend to minor. The first is preaching on Christ's pictures—typology. Here are a few samples from Calvin's work:

> For what is more vain or absurd than for men to offer a loathsome stench from the fat of cattle in order to reconcile themselves to God? Or to have recourse to the sprinkling of water and blood to cleanse away their filth? In short, the whole cultus of the law, taken literally and not as shadows and figures corresponding to the truth, will be utterly ridiculous…if the forms of the law be separated from its end, one must condemn it as vanity.[36]

> Our Heavenly Father willed that we perceive in David and his descendants the living image of Christ.[37]

The second is preaching on Christ's presence—the christophanies. Again, here are a few samples:

> But the orthodox doctors of the church have rightly and prudently interpreted that chief angel to be God's Word, who

---

36. *Institutes* 2.7.1.
37. *Institutes* 2.6.2.

already at that time, as a sort of foretaste, began to fulfill the office of Mediator. For even though he was not yet clothed with flesh, he came down, so to speak, as an intermediary, in order to approach believers more intimately.[38]

In the books of Moses, the name of Jehovah is often attributed to the presiding Angel, who was undoubtedly the only-begotten Son of God.[39]

Let us learn from Calvin to preach Christ from all genres of Scripture: His promises, His precepts, His pictures, His presence, etc.

Pillar 7: The Old Testament should be preached frequently

The natural and obvious outworking of Calvin's Christ-centered view of the Old Testament was a multitude of Old Testament sermons. In fifteen years of Genevan pulpit ministry, from 1549 onward, he preached more than two thousand Old Testament sermons—most of them connected expositions of Old Testament books. Job took a year, Deuteronomy sixteen months, and Isaiah three years. If we look at his lectures, we find that he gave sixty-six lectures on Daniel, 193 on Jeremiah, and sixty-five on Ezekiel. Parker calculates that when we take into account the written commentaries, lectures, and sermons, "Calvin expounded in one way or another, sometimes with duplication, about three quarters of the books of the Old Testament."[40]

Calvin explained this Old Testament emphasis somewhat in his sermon on 2 Timothy 3:16–17: "To sum it up, St Paul here pronounces that men must not take out parts and bits that they approve of and what meets their fancy in Holy Scripture. Without exception they should conclude that, since God has spoken in his Law and in his Prophets, they must keep to the whole."[41]

Pillar 8: Build Christ-centered Old Testament preaching slowly and safely

Calvin was quite a severe critic of certain types of Christian exegesis that mistakenly saw Christ in every verse of the Old Testament. In

---

38. *Institutes* 1.13.10.
39. *Commentary* on Joshua 5:14.
40. Parker, *Calvin's Old Testament Commentaries*, 33.
41. CO 54.283.[39-45]

his view, this damaged the credibility of true Christ-centered Old Testament preaching.

For example, he rejected a christological exegesis of Psalm 72 because it gave Jewish interpreters reason to criticize by applying to Christ what, Calvin said, did not apply to Him.

Although Calvin was a great exponent of typology, he argued that we do not seek for meaning in every detail of every type. He cautioned:

> It was by no means the intention of God to include mysteries in every hook and loop; and even although no part were without a mystical meaning, which no one in his senses will admit, it is better to confess our ignorance than to indulge ourselves in frivolous conjectures. Of this sobriety, too, the author of the Epistle to the Hebrews is a fit master for us, who, although he professedly shows the analogy between the shadows of the Law and the truth manifested in Christ, yet only sparingly touches upon some main points, and by this moderation restrains us from too curious disquisitions and deep speculations.[42]

We can learn from Calvin here. We have to recognize that due to the problems we highlighted earlier, preaching Christ from the Old Testament is going to meet some skeptical resistance. So let us wisely preach the obvious, the clear, and the unambiguous in order to build trust and confidence, rather than inviting just or unjustified ridicule by preaching Christ from more obscure and difficult passages and texts.

DON'T FOLLOW CALVIN IN EVERYTHING

As many have noted, Calvin probably would have been appalled at the focus on him on the five hundredth anniversary of his birth. He was never one to seek a personal following and would have emphatically rejected any address or essay that said Calvin should be one's model. So let me conclude by urging you to follow Calvin only insofar as he follows Christ.

I am happy to follow Calvin for about nine steps out of every ten he takes. But I do believe he makes the odd misstep, and I wish

---

42. *Commentary* on Exodus 26:1.

to highlight three of these in order to caution against making Calvin alone our guide.

First, I believe he was too critical of the New Testament writers' use of the Old Testament. Some of the language he used to describe how the apostles used the Old Testament inadvertently undermines the inspiration of Scripture to some degree.[43] Calvin would have benefitted from the more recent research and writing in this important area.

Second, in his desire not to unnecessarily alienate some Jewish scholars of his day, Calvin rejected the traditional Christological interpretations of some important Old Testament passages (e.g. Isa. 4:2; Zech. 6:12; 13:6; Isa. 42:19; Jer. 16:16, Pss. 50; 72). I believe he was sometimes too concessive to their Christless interpretations of some Old Testament texts. He seemed at times to be a bit over-anxious not to incur their ridicule.[44]

Third, for all his excellent theory of preaching Christ from the Old Testament, I believe that Calvin sometimes became too fixated on the historical meaning and failed to proceed to Christological interpretation. His application was almost always Christological, but in his desire to limit his interpretation to the historico-grammatical meaning, his exegesis was sometimes not sufficiently Christ-centered. Some scholars have argued that Calvin's regular hearers were so well trained that he assumed they would make their own Christological exegesis of his theocentric words. However, our hearers are not so well trained, and need every help and prod they can get.

CONCLUSION

In my own experience, nothing has so expanded my heart and warmed my soul as preaching Christ from the Old Testament. When I look back over my seventeen years of preaching the gospel, I can say that I have never known so much of the Spirit's power, never known so much pulpit unction, as when preaching Christ from the Old Testament. Also, I have found that the godliest people I have preached to found the most edification and expressed the most appreciation for Christ-centered Old Testament sermons. Now, experience is not

43. See Puckett, *John Calvin's Exegesis of the Old Testament*, 91–100.
44. Ibid., 53ff.

our final arbiter and judge. However, I believe that the Holy Spirit especially blesses preaching that honors portions of God's Word that are widely neglected or even abused. Let us follow not just Calvin but Christ, and preach Christ from the Old Testament.

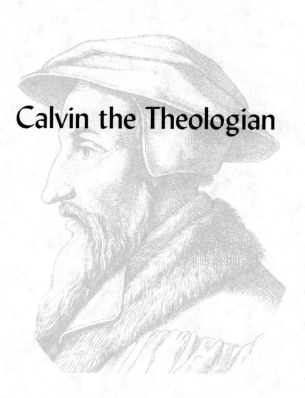

Calvin the Theologian

CHAPTER 4

Calvin on the Holy Spirit

Joseph A. Pipa Jr.

O ne of the continuing areas of confusion in the modern church concerns the role of the Holy Spirit in the life of the Christian and the church. In many respects, those who ought to be teaching others need to be taught (although many consider themselves teachers, "understanding neither what they say, nor whereof they affirm"; 1 Tim. 1:7). Confusion abounds regarding not just the gifts of the Spirit but His role in the Christian life and the church. Moreover, those of us in the Reformation tradition too often live and conduct our ministries as if there were no unique role for the Holy Spirit today. John Calvin is a sane and biblical voice in the midst of the cacophony as he teaches us of the role and the importance of the Spirit.

Among his many contributions to theology, Calvin's development of the doctrine of the Holy Spirit towers as one of his most significant. Benjamin B. Warfield called Calvin the "theologian of the Holy Spirit" and went on to say that Calvin's development of the doctrine of the Holy Spirit was his greatest contribution to the church: "It is probable...that Calvin's greatest contribution to theological science lies in the rich development...which he was the first to give...to the doctrine of the work of the Holy Spirit.... The *Institutes* is...just a treatise on the work of God the Holy Spirit in making God savingly known to sinful man, and bringing sinful man into holy communion with God."[1]

Therefore, let us learn from Calvin about the person and work of the Holy Spirit. I will deal with the person of the Spirit and His relation in the Godhead, the Spirit and Scripture, the Spirit and the

---

1. Benjamin B. Warfield, "John Calvin the Theologian," in *Calvin and Augustine,* ed. Samuel G. Craig (Philadelphia: Presbyterian and Reformed, 1956), 484–5.

Christian life, the Spirit and the means of grace, and the Spirit and His gifts. I will further demonstrate Calvin's relevance by comparing his teaching with our confessional standards.

The Person of the Spirit

Each generation of believers needs to be grounded in the great truths of the faith. Many Christians today have little or no practical grasp of the doctrine of the Trinity. Calvin offers us sound, practical instruction.

Although he was attacked by Pierre Caroli as being anti-Trinitarian,[2] Calvin was clearly an orthodox Trinitarian; in fact, he considered the knowledge of the triune personhood of God, along with His immensity and spirituality, as necessary elements of the knowledge of God.[3] Warfield asserted, "The tripersonality of God is conceived by Calvin, therefore, not as something added to the complete idea of God, or as something into which God develops in the process of His existing, but as something which enters into the very idea of God, without which He cannot be conceived in the truth of His being."[4]

Calvin asserted with the ancient church that God is one being who exists in three persons. He wrote:

> And that passage in Gregory of Nazianzus vastly delights me: "I cannot think on the one without quickly being encircled by the splendor of the three; nor can I discern the three without being straightway carried back to the one." Let us not, then, be led to imagine a trinity of persons that keeps our thoughts distracted and does not at once lead them back to that unity. Indeed, the words "Father," "Son," and "Spirit" imply a real distinction—let no one think that these titles, whereby God is variously designated from his works, are empty—but a distinction, not a division.[5]

---

2. See Benjamin B. Warfield, "The Doctrine of the Trinity," in *Calvin and Calvinism* (Grand Rapids: Baker, 1981), 189–284, for a thorough discussion of the attacks and Calvin's response. For a contemporary discussion, see Douglas F. Kelly, "The True and Triune God: Calvin's Doctrine of the Holy Trinity," in *Theological Guide to Calvin's Institutes,* ed. David W. Hall and Peter Lillback (Phillipsburg, N.J.: P&R, 2008), 65–89.

3. *Institutes* 1.13.1.

4. Benjamin B. Warfield, *The Person and Work of the Holy Spirit* (Amityville, NY: Calvary Press, 1997), 190–1.

5. *Institutes* 1.13.17.

In accord with orthodoxy, Calvin taught that the Holy Spirit is the third person of the Godhead and is completely and equally God. Calvin offered the classical arguments for the deity of the Spirit in the *Institutes*, 1.13.14. Warfield summarizes his arguments:

> The deity of the Spirit is similarly argued on the ground of certain Old Testament passages (Genesis i.2; Is. Xlviii.16) where the Spirit of God seems to be hypostatized; of the divine works attributed to Him, such as ubiquitous activity, regeneration, and the searching of the deep things of God on the one hand and bestowing of wisdom, speech and all other blessings on men on the other; and finally of the application of the name God to Him in the New Testament writings (e.g., I Cor. iii.16, vi.19; II Cor. vi. 16; Acts v.3; xxviii.25; Mat. xii.31).[6]

Douglas F. Kelly writes, "Calvin, again in common with many church fathers, demonstrates from the Old and New testaments the full deity of the Holy Spirit especially in light of the divine works wrought by the Spirit that Calvin shows him to be fully God."[7]

Calvin demonstrated the eternal deity of the Spirit from His work as Creator, Revealer, Giver of life, Sanctifier, and Author of spiritual gifts. Calvin wrote:

> In short, upon him, as upon the Son, are conferred functions that especially belong to divinity. "For the Spirit searches...even the depths of God" [I Cor. 2:10], who has no counselor among the creatures [Rom. 11:34]; he bestows wisdom and the faculty of speaking [I Cor. 12:10], although the Lord declares to Moses that it is his work alone [Ex. 4:11].... For if the Spirit were not an entity subsisting in God, choice and will [referring to 1 Cor. 12:11] would by no means be conceded to him. Paul, therefore, very clearly attributes to the Spirit divine power, and shows that he resides hypostatically in God.[8]

The Holy Spirit, therefore, must be confessed as the third person of the Trinity, equal in substance, power, and glory with the Father and the Son.

Calvin taught that the Spirit exists as the third person of the God-

---

6. Warfield, *Calvin and Calvinism,* 227. See Kelly, "Calvin's Doctrine of the Holy Trinity," 80.

7. Ibid.

8. *Institutes* 1.13.14.

head who proceeds from the Father and the Son. Although some have objected to terms such as *person* to describe the subsistence of the Spirit distinct from the Father and the Son, because they are not found in Scripture, Calvin defended the use of terms such as *person* or *hypostasis*. He wrote:

> "Person," therefore, I call a "subsistence" in God's essence, which, while related to the others, is distinguished by an incommunicable quality. By that term "subsistence" we would understand something different from "essence." For if the Word were simply God, and yet possessed no other characteristic mark, John would wrongly have said that the Word was always with God [John 1:1]. When immediately after he adds that the Word was also God himself, he recalls us to the essence as a unity. But because he could not be with God without residing in the Father, hence emerges the idea of a subsistence, which, even though it has been joined with the essence by a common bond and cannot be separated from it, yet has a special mark whereby it is distinguished from it. Now, of the three subsistences I say that each one, while related to the others, is distinguished by a special quality. This "relation" is here distinctly expressed: because where simple and indefinite mention is made of God, this name pertains no less to the Son and the Spirit than to the Father. But as soon as the Father is compared with the Son, the character of each distinguishes the one from the other. Thirdly, whatever is proper to each individually, I maintain to be incommunicable, because whatever is attributed to the Father as a distinguishing mark cannot agree with, or be transferred to, the Son. Nor am I displeased with Tertullian's definition...that there is a kind of distribution or economy in God which has no effect on the unity of essence.[9]

Calvin based his defense of the terms *person* and *hypostasis* on his understanding of Hebrews 1:3, that Christ is the "image of his *hypostasis*." However, although Calvin's assertion is true, Warfield points out that his exegesis was faulty, since the writer to the Hebrews is asserting the full deity of the Son and not His distinct personality.[10]

---

9. *Institutes* 1.13.6.

10. Warfield, *Calvin and Calvinism*, 214. See Westminster Larger Catechism, Q&A 9; Shorter Catechism, Q&A 6; Heidelberg Catechism, Q&A 24.

The Belgic Confession reflects Calvin and all orthodoxy when it states:

> According to this truth and this Word of God, we believe in one only God, who is one single essence, in which are three persons, really, truly, and eternally distinct according to their incommunicable properties; namely, the Father, and the Son, and the Holy Ghost. The Father is the cause, origin, and beginning of all things, visible and invisible; the Son is the word, wisdom, and image of the Father; the Holy Ghost is the eternal power and might, proceeding from the Father and the Son. Nevertheless God is not by this distinction divided into three, since the Holy Scriptures teach us that the Father, and the Son, and the Holy Ghost have each His personality, distinguished by their properties; but in such wise that these three persons are but one only God. Hence then, it is evident that the Father is not the Son, nor the Son the Father, and likewise the Holy Ghost is neither the Father nor the Son. Nevertheless these persons thus distinguished are not divided nor intermixed; for the Father hath not assumed the flesh, nor hath the Holy Ghost, but the Son only. (Art. 8)

With respect to the development of the doctrine of the Trinity, Calvin's significance for today is two-fold. First, he advanced the doctrine of the Trinity in carefully defining that each member of the Godhead is *autotheos*; namely, each is essentially God *a se ipso* (of Himself). In other words, the procession of the Spirit from the Father and Son has to do only with His person and not His being. The question is whether the Son and the Spirit eternally derive their divinity from the Father or eternally derive their persons from the Father. Calvin insisted that with respect to being, God is eternally one, but with respect to personal distinctions, the Son is eternally begotten and the Spirit proceeds from the Father and the Son. Kelly concludes,

> Here we find the contribution of Calvin to trinitarian theology in the luminous way he clarifies the full deity of the Son and the Spirit (who are distinct persons from the Father), while at the same time affirming the absolute oneness and simplicity of the essence the three persons share in common from all eternity. Calvin shows that the personal distinctions of the three always refer to their personal relationships within the one essence, in which there is a certain "economic order," according to which the Father has priority. This order of personal relationship "takes

nothing away from the deity of the Son and the Spirit." Calvin holds that the Scriptures teach that "God is one in essence, and hence that the essence both of the Son and of the Spirit is unbegotten...." Thus God without particularization is unbegotten; and the Father also in respect to his person is unbegotten.[11]

This concept is stated in the Belgic Confession: "The Father hath never been without His Son, or without His Holy Ghost. For they are all three coeternal and coessential. There is neither first nor last; for they are all three one, in truth, in power, in goodness, and in mercy" (Art. 8).

Second, Calvin's significance for the development of the doctrine of the Trinity is found in his approach to the doctrine. He eschewed all speculation about the Trinity and the Spirit, approaching the matter practically for the sake of God's people. Warfield pointed out:

> The main thing was, he insisted, that men should heartily believe that there is but one God, whom only they should serve; but also that Jesus Christ our Redeemer and the Holy Spirit our Sanctifier is each no less this one God than God the Father to whom we owe our being; while yet these three are distinct personal objects of our love and adoration. He was wholly agreed with his colleagues at Geneva in holding that "in the beginning of the preaching of the Gospel," it conduced more to edification and readiness of comprehension to refrain from the explanation of the mysteries of the Trinity, and even from the constant employment of those technical terms in which these mysteries are best expressed, and to be content with declaring clearly the divinity of Christ in all its fullness, and with giving some simple exposition of the true distinction between the Father, Son, and Holy Spirit.[12]

Joel R. Beeke's insight is very helpful:

> The great danger of discussing the ontological Trinity, Calvin knows, is that well-meaning theologians may produce all kinds of unnecessary words on the subject. "In the one essence of God there is a trinity of persons; you will say in one word what Scripture states, and cut short empty talkativeness" [*Institutes*, 1.3.5]. Calvin's great interest is in the practical work of

---

11. Kelly, "Calvin's Doctrine of the Holy Trinity," 86–7.
12. Warfield, *Calvin and Calvinism*, 198–9.

the relational Trinity rather than the theological abstractions of the ontological Trinity. His major goal is to promote practical, experiential Christian living. Thus, in his first catechism (1538), Calvin writes, "When we name Father, Son, and Holy Spirit, we are not fashioning three Gods, but in the simplest unity of God, Scripture and the very experience of godliness disclose to us the Father, his Son, and the Spirit" [*Catechism*, sec. 20].[13]

The Spirit and Scripture

One of the most contested doctrines in the church today is that of the inerrancy and infallibility of Scripture. Calvin instructs us in the Bible's self-testimony and the role of the Holy Spirit in producing Scripture. He believed that the sixty-six books of the Bible are God's inspired and infallible Word. Calvin's teaching on Holy Scripture is found in 1.7–9 of the *Institutes*. He wrote, "Scripture is from God... it has flowed to us from the very mouth of God by the ministry of men."[14] Elsewhere, he said, "The Sacred Scriptures, which so far surpass all gifts and graces of human endeavor, breathe something divine."[15]

Time and again he emphasized that the Spirit was the divine author of Scripture. He pointed out that the presence of distinct styles among the writers was not contrary to the full divinity of Scripture: "I admit that some of the prophets had an elegant and clear, even brilliant, manner of speaking, so that their eloquence yields nothing to secular writers...while [the Holy Spirit] elsewhere used a rude and unrefined style. But whether you read David, Isaiah, and the like, whose speech flows sweet and pleasing, or Amos the herdsman, Jeremiah, and Zechariah, whose harsher style savors of rusticity, that majesty of the Spirit...will be evident everywhere."[16] With respect to Paul's epistles, he said: "You see then that the first lesson which we have to gather from this passage is that our faith must not waver one way or another, but have a sure and immovable foundation to rest on, namely, God's truth, even as it is contained in the gospel. And seeing that St. Paul is sufficiently acknowledged by us, let us not

---

13. Joel R. Beeke, "Calvin on the Holy Spirit" (unpublished manuscript), 4.
14. *Institutes* 1.7.5.
15. *Institutes* 1.8.1.
16. *Institutes* 1.8.2.

doubt that God's Spirit speaks to us as this day by his mouth, neither let us hear the doctrine as if it were subject to our judgment."[17] In quoting Scripture, he regularly used the formula, "The Holy Spirit says."

Of course, the Reformed standards uniformly assert this high view of Scripture. The Westminster Larger Catechism gives a succinct summary: "The Holy Scriptures of the Old and New Testament are the Word of God, the only rule of faith and obedience" (Q&A 3; cf. Belgic Confession, Art. 3).

Because the Spirit is the author, Calvin insisted that the Scriptures are self-authenticating. He refuted the idea that the authority of Scripture is dependent on the church. He wrote:

> Thus, while the church receives and gives its seal of approval to the Scriptures, it does not thereby render authentic what is otherwise doubtful or controversial…. As to their question—How can we be assured that this has sprung from God unless we have recourse to the decree of the church?—it is as if someone asked: Whence will we learn to distinguish light from darkness, white from black, sweet from bitter? Indeed, Scripture exhibits fully as clear evidence of its own truth as white and black things do of their color, or sweet and bitter things do of their taste.[18]

With respect to Scripture's internal testimony, he anticipated the Westminster Confession of Faith:

> We may be moved and induced by the testimony of the Church to an high and reverend esteem of the holy scripture, and the heavenliness of the matter, the efficacy of the doctrine, the majesty of the style, the consent of all the parts, the scope of the whole, (which is to give all glory to God,) the full discovery it makes of the only way of man's salvation, the many other incomparable excellencies, and the entire perfection thereof, are arguments whereby it doth abundantly evidence itself to be the word of God. (1.5)[19]

But he also anticipated the confession's conclusion, "yet notwithstanding, our full persuasion and assurance of the infallible truth,

17. John Calvin, *Sermons on Ephesians*, trans. Arthur Golding (1577; repr., Edinburgh: Banner of Truth Trust, 1973), 10.

18. *Institutes* 1.7.2.

19. See also *Institutes* 1.8 for Calvin's development of these things and Robert L. Reymond, "Calvin's Doctrine of Holy Scripture," in *Theological Guide to Calvin's Institutes*, 51–4; Belgic Confession, Art. 5.

and divine authority thereof, is from the inward work of the Holy Spirit, bearing witness by and with the word in our hearts" (1.5).

As Robert L. Reymond writes: "The Holy Spirit speaking in Holy Scripture is the believer's final and ultimate authority in all matters of belief and behavior. But the inner witness of the Holy Spirit, working by and with the Word in his heart, Calvin argued, confirms to the believer that the Bible is God's Word. That is to say, the Christian's confidence in Holy Scripture as the Word of God is produced by the Holy Spirit who graciously bears witness in the believer's heart at regeneration to the truthfulness of God's Word being proclaimed to him."[20]

Calvin said that to seek authority elsewhere was to mock the Holy Spirit.[21] He wrote:

> If we desire to provide in the best way for our consciences—that they may not be perpetually beset by the instability of doubt or vacillation, and that they may not also boggle at the smallest quibbles—we ought to seek our conviction in a higher place than human reasons, judgments, or conjectures, that is, in the secret testimony of the Spirit. True, if we wished to proceed by arguments, we might advance many things that would easily prove...that the law, the prophets, and the gospel come from him [God]. Indeed, ever so learned men, endowed with the highest judgment, rise up in opposition and bring to bear and display all their mental powers in this debate. Yet, unless they become hardened to the point of hopeless impudence, this confession will be wrested from them: that they see manifest signs of God speaking in scripture. From this it is clear that the teaching of Scripture is from heaven.... The testimony of the Spirit is more excellent than all reason. For as God alone is a fit witness of himself in his Word, so also the Word will not find acceptance in men's hearts before it is sealed by the inward testimony of the Spirit. The same Spirit, therefore, who has spoken through the mouths of the prophets must penetrate into our hearts to persuade us that they faithfully proclaimed what had been divinely commanded.[22]

He added in the next section: "For even if it wins reverence for

---

20. Reymond, "Calvin's Doctrine of Holy Scripture," 49.
21. *Institutes* 1.7.1.
22. *Institutes* 1.7.4.

itself by its own majesty, it seriously affects us only when it is sealed upon our hearts through the Spirit. Therefore, illumined by his power, we believe neither by our own nor by anyone else's judgment that Scripture is from God; but above human judgment we affirm with utter certainty (just as if we were gazing upon the majesty of God himself) that it has flowed to us from the very mouth of God by the ministry of men."[23]

Convinced of this reality, we need not be hesitant in using the Bible. We do not need to prove it is the Word of God before we use it; we must simply use it. God through His Spirit will do the convincing.

The Spirit and the Christian Life

In expounding the doctrines of the Trinity and Scripture, Calvin taught what the orthodox church has always confessed. In his doctrine of conversion and the Christian life, however, Calvin, building on the foundation of Augustine, expounded Paul more clearly and profoundly than those who had come before him. Of course, when one thinks about soteriology, one thinks about the five points of Calvinism, but Calvin's other contribution was with respect to the doctrine of union with Christ.

Union with Christ

For Calvin, the entire application of the work of salvation is bound up in union with Christ. As union with Christ is a central element in the theology of the apostle Paul, so it is in the theology of Calvin. Calvin taught that union with Christ is essential to every aspect of the Christian life, and that the Spirit is essential to this union. The Spirit is the agent of union as He produces faith by which we come into union with Christ, and, as the Spirit of Christ, He indwells us.

In answering the question of how we participate in the benefits purchased by Christ, Calvin wrote:

> First, we must understand that as long as Christ remains outside of us, and we are separated from him, all that he has suffered and done for the salvation of the human race remains useless and of no value for us. Therefore, to share with us what he has received from the Father, he had to become ours and to dwell within us. For this reason, he is called "our Head" [Eph. 4:15],

---

23. *Institutes* 1.7.5.

and "the first-born among many brethren" [Rom. 8:29]. We also, in turn, are said to be "engrafted into him" [Rom. 11:17], and to "put on Christ" [Gal. 3:27]; for, as I have said, all that he possesses is nothing to us until we grow into one body with him. It is true that we obtain this by faith. Yet since we see that not all indiscriminately embrace that communion with Christ which is offered through the gospel, reason itself teaches us to climb higher and to examine into the secret energy of the Spirit, by which we come to enjoy Christ and all his benefits.... To sum up, the Holy Spirit is the bond by which Christ effectually unites us to himself.[24]

Commenting on the title of the Spirit in John 14:16, "another Comforter," he wrote: "He calls Him *another* because of the difference in the blessings we obtain from each. Christ's proper work was to appease the wrath of God by atoning for the sins of the world, to redeem men from death and to procure righteousness and life. That of the Spirit is to make us partakers not only of Christ Himself, but of all His blessings."[25]

This theme of union is often reiterated in our standards. For example, the Westminster Confession: "All saints that are united to Jesus Christ their head by his Spirit, and by faith, have fellowship with him in his graces, sufferings, death, resurrection, and glory" (26:1; see also Heidelberg Catechism, Q&A 32).

Conversion

The Spirit's work begins in securing our union with Christ; He is the author of the new birth. Reformed theology traditionally has referred to this work of the Spirit as regeneration. Calvin often used the term *regeneration* more broadly to refer to sanctification; as William Edgar wrote: "The general term that encompasses the Christian life for Calvin is 'regeneration.' Unlike our modern tendency to reduce regeneration to the moment of the new birth, Calvin sees it as a process which moves the believer forward from sin and vice to eternal life."[26] But even though Calvin often used the term *regenera-*

---

24. *Institutes* 3.1.1.
25. *Commentary* on John 14:16.
26. William Edgar, "Ethics: The Christian Life and Good Works according to Calvin," in *Theological Guide to Calvin's Institutes*, ed. David W. Hall and Peter Lillback (Phillipsburg, N.J.: P&R, 2008), 322.

tion to include sanctification, he also used the term in its later, more traditional meaning. For example, commenting on Psalm 100:3, he wrote, "It is clear from the context that he is speaking of regeneration, which is the beginning of the spiritual life...."[27] He referred to the Spirit as the Spirit of regeneration in light of His initial work in conversion.[28]

The Spirit begins by removing spiritual blindness. Commenting on John 6:44, Calvin said:

> But nothing is accomplished by preaching him if the Spirit, as our inner teacher, does not show our minds the way. Only those men, therefore, who have heard and have been taught by the Father come to him. What kind of learning and hearing is this? Surely, where the Spirit by a wonderful and singular power forms our ears to hear and our minds to understand.... It therefore remains for us to understand that the way to the Kingdom of God is open only to him whose mind has been made new by the illumination of the Holy Spirit.... Because these mysteries are deeply hidden from human insight, they are disclosed solely by the revelation of the Spirit. Hence, where the Spirit of God does not illumine them, they are considered folly.[29]

Calvin taught that this work is necessary because the sinner is dead in his sins and unable to come to Christ or do any spiritual good on his own: "If anyone wants a clearer answer, here it is: God works in his elect in two ways: within, through his Spirit; without, through his Word. By his Spirit, illuminating their minds and forming their hearts to the love and cultivation of righteousness, he makes them a new creation. By his Word, he arouses them to desire, to seek after, and to attain that same renewal."[30]

This doctrine is summarized in the Westminster Larger Catechism. The catechism teaches that union with Christ is a product of effectual calling: "The union which the elect have with Christ is the work of God's grace, whereby they are spiritually and mystically, yet really and inseparably, joined to Christ as their head and husband; which is done in their effectual calling" (Q&A 66). Furthermore, the

---

27. *Institutes* 2.3.6. See also 2.7.11.
28. *Institutes* 3.3.21; 3.21.7.
29. *Institutes* 2.2.20.
30. *Institutes* 2.5.5.

catechism highlights the Spirit's role, namely, that in effectual calling the Father draws sinners to Christ by His Word and Spirit: "Effectual calling is the work of God's almighty power and grace, whereby (out of his free and special love to his elect, and from nothing in them moving him thereunto) he doth, in his accepted time, invite and draw them to Jesus Christ, by his word and Spirit; savingly enlightening their minds, renewing and powerfully determining their wills, so as they (although in themselves dead in sin) are hereby made willing and able freely to answer his call, and to accept and embrace the grace offered and conveyed therein" (Q&A 67).

No doctrine is more encouraging to the gospel enterprise than that of the sovereign work of the Holy Spirit in conversion. When we recognize that conversion is completely the work of God, we are liberated to evangelize; we become bold. Moreover, we learn to plead with God for the lost. Regardless of one's theology of conversion, when one prays for conversion, he follows the teaching of Calvin.

Consequences of Union

According to Calvin, union with Christ leads to both justification and sanctification: "Let us sum these up. Christ was given to us by God's generosity, to be grasped and possessed by us in faith. By partaking of him, we principally receive a double grace: namely, that being reconciled to God through Christ's blamelessness, we may have in heaven instead of a Judge a gracious Father; and secondly, that sanctified by Christ's spirit we may cultivate blamelessness and purity of life."[31] Although in the *Institutes*, Calvin dealt with sanctification first, he recognized the priority of justification, writing that it "is the main hinge on which religion turns."[32]

He defined justification thus: "He is said to be justified in God's sight who is both reckoned righteous in God's judgment and has been accepted on account of his righteousness.... Therefore, we explain justification simply as the acceptance with which God receives us into his favor as righteous men. And we say that it consists in the remission of sins and the imputation of Christ's righteousness."[33]

---

31. *Institutes* 3.11.1.
32. *Institutes* 3.11.1.
33. *Institutes* 3.11.2.

Justification is received by Spirit-generated faith and imputed on the basis of union with Christ through His Spirit.

Calvin emphasized that justification is always accompanied by sanctification: "Why, then, are we justified by faith? Because by faith we grasp Christ's righteousness, by which alone we are reconciled to God. Yet you could not grasp this without at the same time grasping sanctification also. For he 'is given unto us for righteousness, wisdom, sanctification, and redemption' [I Cor. 1:30]. Therefore Christ justifies no one whom he does not at the same time sanctify. These benefits are joined together by an everlasting and indissoluble bond, so that those whom he illumines by his wisdom, he redeems; those whom he redeems, he justifies; those whom he justifies, he sanctifies."[34]

The Belgic Confession clearly relates justification to sanctification: "We believe that this true faith, being wrought in man by the hearing of the Word of God and the operation of the Holy Ghost, doth regenerate and make him a new man, causing him to live a new life, and freeing him from the bondage of sin. Therefore it is so far from being true, that this justifying faith makes men remiss in a pious and holy life, that on the contrary without it they would never do anything out of love to God, but only out of self-love or fear of damnation" (Art. 24; cf. Westminster Confession of Faith, 13.1; Larger Catechism, Q&A 75). But note well, these two works of God are not two aspects of union but are two distinct things: the act of justification and the work of sanctification.

Calvin defined sanctification as that act by which "God renews us by His Spirit, and confirms in us the grace of renewal and continues it to the end."[35] It is the process by which the believer is renewed in the image of God in the whole man, being enabled more and more to die to sin and to live unto righteousness—two aspects that Calvin referred as mortification and vivification.[36]

The Holy Spirit is the powerful, divine agent of sanctification. Sanctification grows out of regeneration and is the fruit of the Spirit's work in the life of the one whom He indwells. With respect to Christ's endowment with the Spirit, Calvin wrote: "We must bear in mind that Christ came endowed with the Holy Spirit in a special

---

34. *Institutes* 3.16.1.
35. *Commentary* on John 17:17.
36. *Institutes* 3.3.8

way: that is, to separate us from the world and to gather us unto the hope of the eternal inheritance. Hence he is called the 'Spirit of sanctification' [cf. II Thess. 2:13; I Peter 1:2; Rom. 1:4] because he not only quickens and nourishes us by a general power that is visible both in the human race and in the rest of the living creatures, but he is also the root and seed of heavenly life in us."[37]

Calvin taught that the Spirit was the compelling source of sanctification, working in the believer to motivate him to seek sanctification. In discussing titles of the Spirit, Calvin said He is called "water" (Isa. 55:1; 44:3), for "by his secret watering the Spirit makes us fruitful to bring forth the buds of righteousness."[38] He related this motivating work to the believer's union with Christ: "By the grace and power of the same Spirit we are made his members, to keep us under himself and in turn to possess him."[39]

The product of the new life is called the fruit of the Spirit, because it all proceeds from Him. Calvin wrote on Galatians 5:22, "Just as earlier he had condemned the whole nature of man as producing nothing but evil and worthless fruits, so he now tells us that all virtues, all good and well-regulated affections, proceed from the Spirit, that is, from the grace of God and the renewed nature which we have from Christ."[40] He concluded by commenting on how one lives by the Spirit: "Now in his usual way, Paul draws an exhortation out of the doctrine. The death of the flesh is the life of the Spirit. If God's Spirit lives in us, let him govern all our actions. There will always be many who impudently boast of living in the Spirit, but Paul challenges them to prove their claim. As the soul does not live idly in the body, but gives motion and vigour to every member and part, so the Spirit of God cannot dwell in us without manifesting himself by the outward effects. By 'life' is here meant the inward power and by 'walk,' the outward actions."[41]

Beeke summarizes Calvin's doctrine in this way: "In sanctification, the believer offers himself to God as a sacrifice. To be sure, this never comes without a great struggle, for it requires cleansing from

37. *Institutes* 3.1.2.
38. *Institutes* 3.1.3.
39. *Institutes* 3.1.3.
40. *Commentary* on Galatians 5:22.
41. *Commentary* on Galatians 5:25.

the pollution of the flesh and the world.[42] Further, it entails prayer, repentance, mortification, self-denial, cross-bearing, obedience, daily conversion, and separation from pollution."[43]

Therefore, we ought to pray often to be filled with the Spirit. Again Beeke writes:

> Calvin stressed that the Spirit is fulsome. His gifts are full, Pentecost was full; the wind filled the house where the followers of Jesus were sitting, and it filled their hearts. This is what we need today—the fullness of the Spirit.
>
> Our forefathers often compared the fullness of the Spirit to a sailboat in full gale. This is the church's need today. How we should be praying, "Give us the fullness of the Spirit, Lord. Come, north and south winds, and blow on Christ's garden. Come, Savior, walk in the garden of the church and smell her sweet spices. Work mightily by the Holy Spirit in us, our children, our church, our community, and our nation" (cf. Song of Sol. 4:16–5:2).[44]

Closely related to justification and sanctification is adoption. Adoption is a central element in Calvin's theology, although, like the doctrine of the Holy Spirit, he did not devote a section to it in the *Institutes*. Beeke writes, "Calvin's repeated references to adoption embrace 'the whole ethos of the Christian life,' despite his lack of giving adoption its own specific section in the *Institutes*."[45] For Calvin, adoption is the apex of salvation, as well as the halfway point between justification and sanctification.[46]

Calvin wrote of the role of the Spirit in adoption, "The Spirit of God gives us such a testimony, that when he is our guide and teacher our spirit is made sure of the adoption of God; for our mind of itself, without the preceding testimony of the Spirit, could not convey to us

---

42. *Commentary* on John 17:17–19.

43. *Commentary* on 1 Corinthians 1:2.

44. Beeke, "Calvin on the Holy Spirit," 23.

45. Joel R. Beeke, *Heirs with Christ* (Grand Rapids: Reformation Heritage Books, 2008), 5–6. For a thorough study of Calvin on adoption, see Tim J. R. Trumper, "An Historical Study of the Doctrine of Adoption in the Calvinistic Tradition" (Ph.D. dissertation, University of Edinburgh, 2001), 38–214. See also Howard Griffith, "The First Title of the Spirit: Adoption in Calvin's Soteriology," *Evangelical Quarterly* 73, 2 (2001): 135–53.

46. Beeke, "Calvin on the Holy Spirit," 21.

this assurance."[47] The Westminster Confession calls the Spirit, "the Spirit of Adoption," and notes that all those who are justified "have access to the throne of grace with boldness; are enabled to cry, Abba Father; are pitied, protected, provided for, and chastened by him as by a father; yet never cast off, but sealed to the day of redemption, and inherit the promises, as heirs of everlasting salvation" (12; cf. Larger Catechism, Q&A 74).

As the Spirit of adoption, the Spirit enables the believer to call out boldly, "Abba, Father" (Larger Catechism, Q&A 95). He testifies to us that our sins are forgiven and we are the sons of God, heirs, even joint heirs with Christ, our Elder Brother.[48] As Beeke points out, "He does all of this without detracting from the role of Christ. As the Spirit *of Christ*, He assures the believer by leading him to Christ and His benefits, and by bringing those benefits to fruition in the believer."[49]

Closely related to adoption is the work of the Spirit as the seal of God's work in us. Commenting on 2 Thessalonians 2:13, Calvin wrote:

> The Gospel is not only a testimony to us of our adoption, but the Spirit also seals it, and those who are led by the Spirit are the *sons of God* (Rom. 8.14), and he that possesses Christ has eternal life (I John 5:12). We must note this carefully, so that we may not disregard the revelation of God, with which He bids us rest satisfied, and plunge into an endless labyrinth with the desire of seeking revelation from His secret counsel, the investigation of which he compels us to abandon. We are, therefore to be satisfied with the faith of the Gospel and the grace of the Spirit by which we have been regenerated. By this means we refute the depravity of those who make the election of God a pretext for every kind of wrong-doing, for Paul connects it with faith and

---

47. *Commentary* on Romans 8:16. Cf. *Institutes* 3:2, 11, 34, 41; *Commentary* on John 7:37–39; Acts 2:4; 3:8; 5:32; 13:48; 16:14; 23:11; Romans 8:15–17; 1 Corinthians 2:10–13; Galatians 3:2, 4:6; Ephesians 1:13–14, 4:30; *Tracts and Treatises*, trans. Henry Beveridge (Grand Rapids: Eerdmans, 1958), 3:253ff.; J. K. Parratt, "The Witness of the Holy Spirit: Calvin, the Puritans and St. Paul," *Evangelical Quarterly* 41 (1969): 161–8.

48. *Commentary* on Romans 5:5; *Institutes* 3.1.3; 3.2.11; *Commentary* on 1 Corinthians 2:12; Romans 8:33.

49. Beeke, "Calvin on the Holy Spirit," 17; *Institutes* 3.2.34.

regeneration in such a way that he would not have us measure it by any other standard.[50]

The Spirit also enables the believer to continue, which we call perseverance. As Calvin said, the Holy Spirit permanently resides in the believer, guaranteeing perseverance: "There is no danger of those who are renewed by spiritual grace becoming dry. And therefore, although we thirst throughout our life it is nevertheless certain that we have not drunk of the Spirit just for one day, or for any short time, but as of a perennial fountain that will never fail."[51]

The Larger Catechism teaches that believers, because of the electing love of God and the union of believers with Christ, "can neither totally nor finally fall away from the state of grace, but are kept by the power of God through faith unto salvation" (Q&A 79).

We should praise God for this reality. Our boldness as Christians grows out of our awareness that the Spirit who indwells us will complete His work in us and bring us into glory.

The Spirit and the Means of Grace

One of the neglected topics in the church today is the means of grace. The Westminster Shorter Catechism defines the means of grace as "The outward and ordinary means whereby Christ communicateth to us the benefits of redemption…especially the word, sacraments, and prayer; all which are made effectual to the elect for salvation" (Q&A 88). In the development of his theology, Calvin emphasized the role of the Spirit in all three areas.

The Word of God

With respect to the Word, he taught that the work of the Spirit is necessary for the illumination of the meaning of Scripture and for effectiveness in preaching. In response to the fanatics who exalted the work of the Holy Spirit above Scripture, Calvin said, "I should like to know from them what this spirit is by whose inspiration they are borne up so high that they dare despise the Scriptural doctrine as childish and mean.… By a heinous sacrilege these rascals tear apart those things which the prophet [Isa. 59:21] joined together with an

---

50. *Commentary* on 2 Thessalonians 2:13.
51. *Commentary* on John 4:13.

inviolable bond."[52] He continued in the next section, "We ought zealously to apply ourselves both to read and to hearken to Scripture if indeed we want to receive any gain and benefit from the Spirit of God."[53] He concluded: "The Holy Spirit so inheres in His truth, which He expresses in Scripture, that only when its proper reverence and dignity are given to the Word does the Holy Spirit show forth His power.... By a kind of mutual bond the Lord has joined together the certainty of his Word and of his Spirit so that the perfect religion of the Word may abide in our minds when the Spirit, who causes us to contemplate God's face, shines."[54] Reymond's summary is apt: "The Spirit without the word is a delusion and the word without the Spirit is dead. Word and Spirit ever belong together and must never be separated."[55]

Because of this relationship, the Spirit must be the ultimate teacher. In describing the Spirit's work as the Spirit of truth, Calvin wrote: "Christ gives the Spirit another title—that He is the Teacher of truth (*magister veritatis*). From this it follows that until we have been inwardly taught by Him all our minds are held by vanity and falsehood."[56] The Westminster Larger Catechism teaches, "The holy scriptures are to be read with an high and reverent esteem of them; with a firm persuasion that they are the very word of God, and that he only can enable us to understand them" (Q&A 157).

We have a concise summary of Calvin's doctrine of Spirit and Word in the Larger Catechism: "The Spirit of God maketh the reading, but especially the preaching of the word, an effectual means of enlightening, convincing, and humbling sinners; of driving them out of themselves, and drawing them unto Christ; of conforming them to his image, and subduing them to his will; of strengthening them against temptations and corruptions; of building them up in grace, and establishing their hearts in holiness and comfort through faith unto salvation" (Q&A 155; cf. Shorter Catechism, Q&A 89).

With respect to preaching, he developed the work of the Spirit under the concept of unction. One of the reasons Calvin preached

---

52. *Institutes* 1.9.1.
53. *Institutes* 1.9.2.
54. *Institutes* 1.9.3.
55. Reymond, "Calvin's Doctrine of Holy Scripture," 55.
56. *Commentary* on John 14:17.

extemporaneously was his desire to depend consciously on the Holy Spirit in preaching. In his famous letter to Lord Somerset, Calvin insisted on extemporaneous preaching so that Christ and the Spirit will be free to exercise their ministry:

> What I have thus suggested as to the manner of instruction, is only that the people be so taught as to be touched to the quick, and that they may feel that what the Apostle says is true, (Heb. iv.) that "the word of God is a two-edged sword, piercing even through the thoughts and affections to the very marrow of the bones." I speak thus, Monseigneur, because it appears to me that there is very little preaching of a lively kind in the kingdom [England], but that the greater part deliver it by way of reading from a written discourse.... But all these considerations ought not to hinder the ordinance of Jesus Christ from having free course in the preaching of the Gospel. Now, this preaching ought not to be lifeless but lively, to teach, to exhort, to reprove, as Saint Paul says in speaking thereof to Timothy, (2 Tim. iii.). So indeed, that if an unbeliever enter, he may be so effectually arrested and convinced, as to give glory to God, as Paul says in another passage, (1 Cor. xiv.). You are also aware, Monseigneur, how he speaks of the lively power and energy with which they ought to speak, who would approve themselves as good and faithful ministers of God, who must not make a parade of rhetoric, only to gain esteem for themselves; but that the Spirit of God ought to sound forth by their voice, so as to work with mighty energy.[57]

With respect to the role of the Spirit in Calvin's theology of preaching, Steven J. Lawson writes:

> The Holy Spirit, Calvin said, is actively at work in the preaching of the Word, and this powerful ministry of the Spirit was the *sine qua non* of Calvin's expository ministry. He stated that during public proclamation, "when the minister executes his commission faithfully, by speaking only what God puts into his mouth, the inward power of the Holy Spirit is joined with his outward voice." In fact, in all preaching, he affirmed, there must be an "inward efficacy of the Holy Spirit when He sheds forth

---

57. John Calvin, *Calvin's Selected Works*, ed. Jules Bonnet, trans. David Constable (Grand Rapids: Baker, 1983), 5:190.

His power upon hearers, that they may embrace a discourse by faith."[58]

This truth is also emphasized in the Larger Catechism: "They that are called to labour in the ministry of the word, are to preach sound doctrine, diligently, in season and out of season; plainly, not in the enticing words of man's wisdom, but in demonstration of the Spirit, and of power" (Q&A 159).

Calvin insisted on the importance of recognizing the sovereignty of the Spirit: "This does not mean that the grace of the Holy Spirit and his influence are tied to preaching, so that the preacher can, whenever he pleases, breathe forth the Spirit along with the utterance of the voice. We are, then, Ministers of the Spirit, not as if we held him enclosed within us, or as it were captive—not as if we could at our pleasure confer his grace upon all, or upon whom we pleased—but because Christ, through our instrumentality, illuminates the minds of men, renews their hearts, and, in short, regenerates them wholly."[59]

Surely we need to recover today in the Reformed churches the matter of the Spirit's role in preaching. Too often our preaching is dry and lifeless, and we depend on our preparation rather than the Spirit.

Prayer
Furthermore, Calvin greatly emphasized the Spirit's role in prayer. Because of weakness and imperfection, we will make no progress in this discipline on our own. He wrote,

> Therefore, in order to minister to this weakness, God gives us the Spirit as our teacher in prayer, to tell us what is right and temper our emotions. For, "because we do not know how to pray as we ought, the Spirit comes to our help," and "intercedes for us with unspeakable groans" [Rom. 8:26]; not that he actually prays or groans but arouses in us assurance, desires, and sighs, to conceive which our natural powers would scarcely suffice. And Paul, with good reason, calls "unspeakable" these groans which believers give forth under the guidance of the Spirit; for they who are truly trained in prayers are not unmindful that, perplexed by blind anxieties, they are so constrained as scarcely

58. Steven J. Lawson, *The Expository Genius of John Calvin* (Lake Mary, Fla.: Reformation Trust, 2007), 28–9.
59. *Commentary* on 2 Corinthians 3:6.

to find out what it is expedient for them to utter. Indeed, when they try to stammer, they are confused and hesitate.[60]

Calvin emphasized, however, that praying in dependence on the Holy Spirit must not lead us to sloth or passivity: "But rather our intention is that, loathing our inertia and dullness, we should seek such aid of the Spirit. And indeed, Paul, when he enjoins us to pray in the Spirit [I Cor. 14:15], does not stop urging us to watchfulness. He means that the prompting of the Spirit empowers us so to compose prayers as by no means to hinder or hold back our own effort, since in this matter God's will is to test how effectually faith moves our hearts."[61]

The Larger Catechism gives a useful commentary on praying in the Spirit: "We not knowing what to pray for as we ought, the Spirit helpeth our infirmities, by enabling us to understand both for whom, and what, and how prayer is to be made; and by working and quickening in our hearts (although not in all persons, nor at all times, in the same measure) those apprehensions, affections, and graces which are requisite for the right performance of that duty" (Q&A 182).

The Sacraments
Many today downplay the role of the sacraments in sanctification, but Calvin argued that God appointed them for the confirmation and increase of faith.[62] However, he was well aware that apart from the supernatural agency of the Spirit, they would be completely ineffective:

But the sacraments properly fulfill their office only when the Spirit, that inward teacher, comes to them, by whose power alone hearts are penetrated and affections moved and our souls opened for the sacraments to enter in. If the Spirit be lacking, the sacraments can accomplish nothing more in our minds than the splendor of the sun shining upon blind eyes, or a voice sounding in deaf ears. Therefore, I make such a division between Spirit and sacraments that the power to act rests with the former, and the ministry alone is left to the latter—a ministry empty and tri-

60. *Institutes* 3.20.5.
61. *Institutes* 3.20.5.
62. *Institutes* 4.14.9.

fling, apart from the action of the Spirit, but charged with great effect when the Spirit works within and manifests his power.[63]

He illustrated the role of the Spirit in the sacraments by the necessity of good vision to see and good ears to hear. Sight and hearing, he said, "are analogous to the work of the Holy Spirit in our hearts, which is to conceive, sustain, nourish, and establish faith. The both of these things follow: the sacraments profit not a whit without the power of the Holy Spirit, and nothing prevents them from strengthening and enlarging faith in hearts already taught by that Schoolmaster. There is only this difference: that our ears and eyes have naturally received the faculty of hearing and seeing; but Christ does the same thing in our hearts by special grace beyond the measure of nature."[64] He added that the Spirit prepares "our minds by his inward illumination to receive the confirmation extended by the sacraments."[65]

The Belgic Confession gives a good summary of the role of the Spirit in the sacraments: "For they are visible signs and seals of an inward and invisible thing, by means whereof God worketh in us by the power of the Holy Ghost. Therefore the signs are not in vain or insignificant" (Art. 33).

The Spirit and His Gifts

The last area to consider is the Spirit and His gifts. So many today, when they think about the work of the Holy Spirit, limit their thoughts to the extraordinary gifts of the Spirit. Calvin's teaching was broader and thus much more profitable. Calvin began his discussion of gifts by pointing out that whatever abilities the natural man has are of the Spirit. In dealing with the consequences of the fall, he pointed out that the natural man retains understanding of earthly things: government, household management, science, logic, rhetoric, mechanical skills, and liberal arts.[66] The Spirit bestows gifts in these areas:

> Meanwhile, we ought not to forget those most excellent benefits of the divine Spirit, which he distributes to whomever he

---

63. *Institutes* 4.14.9.
64. Ibid.
65. *Institutes* 4.14.10.
66. *Institutes* 2.2.13–15.

wills, for the common good of mankind. The understanding
and knowledge of Bezalel and Oholiab, needed to construct
the Tabernacle, had to be instilled in them by the Spirit of God
[Ex. 31:2–11; 35:30–35]. It is no wonder, then, that the knowledge of all that is most excellent in human life is said to be
communicated to us through the Spirit of God. Nor is there reason for anyone to ask, What have the impious, who are utterly
estranged from God, to do with his Spirit? We ought to understand the statement that the Spirit of God dwells only in believers
[Rom. 8:9] as referring to the Spirit of sanctification through
whom we are consecrated as temples to God [I Cor. 3:16]. Nonetheless he fills, moves, and quickens all things by the power of
the same Spirit, and does so according to the character that he
bestowed upon each kind by the law of creation.[67]

Calvin reminded us that we ought not to despise the accomplishments of the unconverted, but thank God for them and use them
with thankfulness: "But shall we count anything praiseworthy or
noble without recognizing at the same time that it comes from God?
Let us be ashamed of such ingratitude into which not even the pagan
poets fell, for they confessed that the gods had invented philosophy,
laws, and all useful arts."[68] He added: "But if the Lord has willed
that we be helped in physics, dialectic, mathematics, and other like
disciplines, by the work and ministry of the ungodly, let us use this
assistance. For if we neglect God's gift freely offered in these arts, we
ought to suffer just punishment for our sloths."[69] Give thanks to God
for the remarkable gifts we enjoy each day. They all flow from God
the Spirit to us and are primarily for the benefit of the elect.

As he discussed what we denominate as spiritual gifts, Calvin
insisted that we need to recognize that God gave them for the good of
the church.[70] He distinguished between those gifts that were extraordinary, given for the apostolic age, and those which continue.

He expounded the extraordinary gifts from Paul's list in 1 Corinthians 12:8–10: "But that gift of healing, like the rest of the miracles,
which the Lord willed to be brought forth for a time, has vanished
away in order to make the new preaching of the gospel marvelous

---

67. *Institutes* 2.2.16.
68. *Institutes* 2.2.15.
69. *Institutes* 2.2.16.
70. Beeke, "Calvin on the Holy Spirit," 19.

forever."[71] Along with healing he listed knowledge, faith (to perform miracles), speaking in tongues, and interpretation.[72]

He taught how we should look on these extraordinary gifts. First, they attested to the divinity of the gospel. In answering the Roman Catholic accusation that the Protestants had no new miracles, Calvin wrote:

> Perhaps this false hue could have been more dazzling if Scripture had not warned us concerning the legitimate purpose and use of miracles. For Mark teaches that those signs which attended the apostles' preaching were set forth to confirm it [Mark 16:20]. In like manner, Luke relates that our "Lord...bore witness to the word of his grace," when these signs and wonders were done by the apostles' hands [Acts 14:3]. Very much like this is that word of the apostle: that the salvation proclaimed by the gospel has been confirmed in the fact that "the Lord has attested it by signs and wonders and various mighty works" [Heb. 2:4; cf. Rom. 15:18–19].[73]

Second, in his typical experimental fashion, he directed our attention to how we should think about the extraordinary gifts practically:

> For although we do not receive [the Spirit], that we may speak in tongues, that we may be prophets, that we may cure the sick, that we may work miracles; yet it is given us for a better use, that we may believe with the heart unto righteousness, that our tongues may be framed unto true confession, (Rom. 10:10,) that we may pass from death to life, (John 5:24,) that we, which are poor and empty, may be made rich, that we may withstand Satan and the world stoutly.[74]

The church desperately needs to recover these emphases, if she is truly to profit from the gifts.

The ordinary gifts are for the well-being of the church: "God has bestowed superlative gifts upon us for the purpose of perfecting what He has begun." Instead of filling us with pride, this should greatly

---

71. *Commentary* on Acts 10:44; *Institutes* 4.19.18.
72. *Commentary* on 1 Corinthians 12:8–10.
73. *Institutes*, "Prefatory Address," 16.
74. *Commentary* on Acts 10:46.

humble us.[75] Among these, he listed knowledge ("acquaintance with sacred things" or "ordinary information"), prophecy (preaching),[76] teaching, exhortation, ministering, diaconal distribution of gifts, the care of the sick, and ruling.[77]

Conclusion

Calvin, therefore, continues to teach us today about the comprehensive work of the Holy Spirit in the world and in the lives of God's people. He brings sanity in the midst of confusion and above all teaches us to live in constant dependence on the Spirit.

Calvin teaches us to praise this ineffable being for His powerful work in giving Scripture; engrafting us into Christ for our justification; sanctifying, keeping, and assuring us; making effective the means of grace to us; and giving gifts in the world and particularly to His church.

We also should become all the more committed to prayer. It is through prayer we most intensely manifest our dependence on the Spirit and daily seek His work on our behalf.

---

75. *Commentary* on 1 Thessalonians 1:2.

76. *Commentary* on 1 Corinthians 12:8–10. See also Romans 12:6 for Calvin's interpretation of prophecy.

77. *Commentary* on Romans 12:6–8; 1 Corinthians 12:28–31.

CHAPTER 5

Redemption: Speaking Peace in the 21st Century

Derek W. H. Thomas

I have to admit that in seminary I found John Calvin's works a little inaccessible. That was entirely my fault and probably prejudicial on my part. The problem was, in part, unfamiliarity with the language and theological structures of the Reformation period—Calvin didn't read like John Owen or Richard Sibbes. It took me twenty years to really get Calvin under my skin and appreciate the lines of continuity from the sixteenth to the seventeenth century—the Puritans built on the foundation of Calvin.[1]

Since then, Calvin has been and is with me almost every day. Through the legacy of his writings, I commune with him on a daily basis; I cannot imagine preparing a sermon, engaging in pastoral ministry, or exercising the discipline of spiritual warfare without God's gift to us of John Calvin. However, as Robert Godfrey has reminded us: "The real Calvin was not in the first place a man who lived to influence future generations. Rather he was a spiritual pilgrim finding anew the apostolic Christianity expressed in the Bible and serving as a faithful minister of that Word in the church of his day."[2] Calvin, I think, would be bemused by the attention given to him in 2009, the five-hundredth anniversary of his birth.

Highlighting Biblical Teaching
Despite caricatures, the Genevan Reformer was a modest and humble man seeking to make the Scriptures the point of focus rather than

---

1. I have never subscribed to the so-called "Calvin vs. the Calvinists" school of thought, based as it is in part on poor scholarship and in part on a failure to appreciate what are in effect anachronistic expectations.

2. W. Robert Godfrey, *John Calvin: Pilgrim and Pastor* (Wheaton, Ill.: Crossway, 2009), 8.

himself. That Calvin continues to speak to us in meaningful ways in our time is a testimony to the fact that what he said and wrote reflected Scripture. As a theologian, pastor, preacher, communicator, correspondent, and pilgrim-Christian, Calvin sought to highlight the Bible's teaching in all of its variegated nature. As a child of the Renaissance, he championed redemptive-historical, grammatico-historical exegesis based on careful analysis of Hebrew and Greek, a carefully nuanced hermeneutic, and a belief (unlike in our postmodern times) in the abiding and knowable nature of objective truth.

I am painfully aware that talking and writing about Calvin can sometimes lead to confusion rather than light. Not every book about Calvin reveals the Reformer's mind and heart; too often, it reveals the prejudices of its author. Speaking over half a century ago, J. I. Packer commented, "The student will find that Calvin makes richer and more straightforward reading than all his expositors."[3] My aim in this chapter, therefore, is not to add to the confusion but to attempt to allow Calvin to speak for himself.

The cross (the theme of this chapter) was central in Calvin's theological reflections. In his commentary on the Synoptic Gospels, he wrote, "We must remember that upon the teaching of the cross… our salvation depends."[4] That puts matters rather bluntly and urgently. For Calvin, to err here was to fail foundationally. There is more at stake than mere opinion; salvation—*our* salvation—hangs in the balance.

Focus on Romans 8:31–32

In addressing the topic of "Redemption: Speaking Peace in the 21st Century," I want to narrow our focus to a particular text and follow Calvin's interpretation of it. The text in question is Romans 8:31–32: "What shall we then say to these things? If God be for us, who can be against us? He that spared not his own Son, but delivered him up for us all, how shall he not with him also freely give us all things?"

Two scholarly works in particular have received just praise for their illuminating insights into the Reformer's doctrine of the atonement. The first, by Paul van Buren, is *Christ in our Place: The*

---

3. J. I. Packer, quoted in Jean Cadier, *The Man God Mastered*, trans. O. R. Johnston (London: InterVarsity Press, 1960), 187.

4. *Commentary* on Matthew 27:11.

Substitutionary Character of Calvin's Doctrine of Reconciliation[5]; the second, by Robert A. Peterson, is *Calvin's Doctrine of the Atonement*.[6] The latter, as Peterson himself has since admitted, showed "a failure to give pride of place to penal substitution."[7] In addition, there are, among others, important studies by Mark Thompson, Henri Blocher, and Timothy George.[8] These studies provide valuable insights into the kaleidoscopic nature of Calvin's understanding of the biblical material on the atonement. Our task in this chapter is merely to extrapolate a few of the Reformer's lines of thought as he reflects upon the atoning work of Christ on behalf of sinners.

In order to evaluate Calvin's understanding of Romans 8, we will follow his exposition in his Romans commentary in both an English translation and a critical Latin edition.[9] The Romans commentary was Calvin's first commentary, written during his exile in Strasbourg and published in 1540. We might infer that the commentary represents a "young" rather than a more "mature" Calvin, but it is doubtful that such a consideration (essential in most biographical studies) is relevant in Calvin's case.[10] Even though the commentary was writ-

---

5. Paul van Buren, *Christ in our Place: The Substitutionary Character of Calvin's Doctrine of Reconciliation* (Edinburgh: Oliver and Boyd, 1957). Van Buren treats the atonement from the perspective of the incarnation, the satisfaction of Christ, and union with Christ.

6. Robert Peterson, *Calvin's Doctrine of the Atonement* (Phillipsburg, N.J.: Presbyterian and Reformed, 1983). In a foreword, J. I. Packer comments that no treatment of Calvin's doctrine of the atonement has (in 1983) "been tackled in print before in so adequate a manner," adding, "this essay is something of a milestone."

7. Robert Peterson, "Calvin on Christ's Saving Work," in David W. Hall and Peter A. Lillback, eds., *Theological Guide to Calvin's Institutes: Essays and Analysis* (Phillipsburg, N.J.: P&R, 2008), 245.

8. Mark D. Thompson, "Calvin on the Cross of Christ," in *John Calvin and Evangelical Theology: Legacy and Prospect*, ed. Sung Wook Chung (Louisville: Westminster John Knox, 2009), 107–127; Henri Blocher, "The Atonement in John Calvin's Theology," in *The Glory of the Atonement*, ed. C. E. Hill and F. A. James (Downers Grove, Ill.: InterVarsity, 2004), 279–303; Timothy George, *Theology of the Reformers* (Leicester, England: Apollos, 1988).

9. *The Epistle of Paul to the Romans and Thessalonians*, ed. and trans. R. Mackenzie, David W. Torrance, and Thomas F. Torrance (1973; repr., Grand Rapids: Eerdmans, 1991), hereafter *Romans*; *Iohannis Calvini Commentarius in Epistolam Pauli ad Romanos*, ed. T. H. L. Parker (Leiden: Brill, 1981), hereafter *Romans LC*.

10. Richard A. Muller comments that the preface to the 1540 edition of Calvin's Romans commentary offers "insight into the exegetical and theological agenda that Calvin undertook at quite an early age and prosecuted with remarkable consistency until his death in 1564." Richard A. Muller, *The Unaccommodated Calvin: Studies in*

ten before he reached his thirtieth birthday, Calvin's theological map was already well established. According to Richard A. Muller, it was Calvin's study of Romans (among other factors) that influenced the Reformer's decision to alter the *Institutes* from the more catechetical and instructional form of the first (1536) edition to the more foundational and academic shape of the second (1539) edition.[11]

THE INWARD TESTIMONY OF THE HOLY SPIRIT

The text in question, Romans 8:31–32, begins with two searching questions: "What shall we then say to these things? If God be for us, who can be against us?" (Rom. 8:31). Calvin, the pastoral theologian, waxed eloquent: "If God is not propitious to us, no sure confidence can be conceived, even though everything should smile upon us. On the other hand, however, His favour alone is a sufficiently great consolation for every sorrow, and a sufficiently strong protection against all storms of misfortune." Having cited several Scripture passages in support of God's consolation in times of trial, Calvin continued with this comment:

> There is no power under heaven or above it which can resist the arm of God.... That man alone displays true confidence in God who is content with His protection, and had no fear sufficient to make him despair. Believers are certainly often shaken, but are never utterly cast down. In short, the apostle's object was to show that the godly soul ought to stand on the inward testimony of the Holy Spirit, and not to depend on external things.[12]

For one who had been a pastor for only three or four years when he wrote these words, the sense of pastoral urgency and consolation in these sentences is remarkable.

Central to Calvin's convictions was the "inward testimony of the Holy Spirit" (*interior Spiritus sancti testimonio*[13]). Benjamin B. Warfield famously dubbed Calvin "pre-eminently the theologian of the

---

the Foundation of a Theological Tradition (Oxford: Oxford University Press, 2000), 22.

11. Ibid., 123–4. It would be interesting to know what Calvin would have changed had he re-written his Romans commentary, but the fact that he saw no need suggests that it represented, more or less, his "mature" thought on Paul's epistle despite the fact that he was not even thirty years old when he wrote it.

12. *Commentary* on Romans 8:31.

13. *Romans LC*, 185.

Holy Spirit."[14] But despite Warfield's attribution, Calvin's deeply thoughtful understanding of the Spirit's role in "closing the gap" between the ascended and glorified Christ and ourselves has often been overlooked. The descent of the Spirit (at Pentecost) was in order to raise us up into fellowship with Christ (cf. Col. 3:1–4). There is no Christ other than the *enfleshed* Christ in heaven, and, for Calvin, one of the marvels of the Christian life is the sheer possibility of our communion with this enfleshed Christ (*Logos ensarkos*) in heaven. This reaches sublime levels in Calvin's discussion of the Lord's Supper:

> Even though it seems unbelievable that Christ's flesh, separated from us by such great distance, penetrates to us, so that it becomes our food, let us remember how far the secret power of the Holy Spirit towers above all our senses, and how foolish it is to wish to measure his immeasurableness by our measure. What, then, our mind does not comprehend, let faith conceive: that the Spirit truly unites things separated in space.[15]

As rich as these sentences are in the context of the Reformer's discussion of the Supper, they encapsulate a lifelong emphasis on the believer's dependence on the inward work of the Holy Spirit in order to feed on Christ and be nourished through our union with Him.

To return to our text, Paul is asking, "How can I know that I am in a right relationship with God, one that will sustain me through the fiery trials that come my way?" In other words, we must address a twofold concern:

How can I know that God is *for* me?
How can I know that God is for *me*?

Is God *for* Me?
As to the first question, the issue relates to the reconciliation of the righteous and holy character of God with sinners. How is it possible for a sinner to find himself in a right relationship with such a God?

---

14. B. B. Warfield, "Calvin as a Theologian," in *Calvin and Augustine*, ed. Samuel Craig (Phillipsburg, N.J.: Presbyterian and Reformed, 1971), 484. Cf. a similar remark by Warfield: "And it is to John Calvin that we owe the first formulation of the doctrine of the work of the Holy Ghost; he himself gave it a very rich statement, developing it especially in the broad departments of 'Common Grace,' 'Regeneration,' and 'the Witness of the Spirit'," in an Introduction to Abraham Kuyper, *The Work of the Holy Spirit* (Grand Rapids: Eerdmans, 1975 [1900]), xxxiv.

15. *Institutes* 4.17.10.

The answer lies in *justification*, something that Paul alludes to in verse 30: "whom he did predestinate, them he also called: and whom he called, them he also justified: and whom he justified, them he also glorified." Justification, Calvin wrote, is the "unmerited imputation of righteousness."[16] Earlier in Romans, Calvin commented on the words, "Being justified freely by his grace" (Rom. 3:24): "...since there is nothing left for men in themselves but to perish, having been smitten by the just judgment of God, they are therefore freely justified by His mercy, for Christ comes to the aid of their wretchedness, and communicates Himself to believers, so that they find in Him alone all those things of which they are in want."[17]

Also in this location, Calvin is at his most Aristotelian, pointing out a fourfold distinction: "There is perhaps no passage in the whole of Scripture which more strikingly illustrates the efficacy of this righteousness, for it shows that the mercy of God is the efficient cause, Christ with His blood is the material cause, faith conceived by the Word the formal or instrumental cause, and the glory of both the divine justice and goodness the final cause."[18]

We may know, therefore, that God is *for* us through believing the promise of the gospel and embracing the Lord Jesus Christ. In this way, the righteousness of Christ is imputed to us and we are reckoned to be in a right standing with God. In terms that are clearly agreeable to later Reformed expressions of justification, Calvin set forth the logic of the gospel. How can I know that God is *for* me? The answer must be sought in the matrix of the gospel, beginning with the objectivity of what God promises to those who trust in Jesus Christ: "*There is* therefore now no condemnation to them which are in Christ Jesus" (Rom. 8:1, emphasis added). If we are "in Jesus Christ," there is no condemnation; the condemnation due to our sin and the guilt of our sin has been eradicated and taken away. It has been removed. Justification has brought us, as Paul elaborates in earlier chapters in Romans, into a judicial relationship with God in which we are right. We come into this right standing with God through faith alone in Jesus Christ alone. In the gospel, the righteousness of God has been revealed from faith to faith; "the just shall live by faith" (Rom. 1:17).

---

16. *Commentary* on Romans 8:30. "*Gratuita iustitiae imputation*," *Romans LC*, 184.

17. *Commentary* on Romans 3:24.

18. Ibid.

Is God for *Me*?

In answering the second question—"How can I know that God is for *me*?"—a more difficult issue rises to the surface. The first question (on justification) was objective. This question is more subjective. How can I know that God has justified *me*? This was a question that later Reformed and Puritan theology addressed in some detail, and it is fascinating to observe how Calvin dealt with the question in 1540. Even when dealing with the issue of justification (Rom. 8:30), Calvin saw its very objectivity as addressing the unwarranted conclusion: these present trials are evidence that God is angry with me and therefore I am not in a right relationship with him. Calvin wrote: "What is more desirable than to be reconciled to God, so that our miseries should no longer be signs of His curse, or lead to our destruction?"[19]

Calvin reflected on what is a modern preoccupation among Christians. If "fortune smiles," we all too easily conclude that God is smiling on us. If "fortune frowns," it can only be that God is angry with us. Such instant reward/retribution theology is a mark of the health-and-wealth movements of our time, but Calvin drew the opposite conclusion: "If God is not propitious to us, no sure confidence can be conceived, even though everything should smile upon us. On the other hand, however, His favour alone is a sufficiently great consolation for every sorrow, and a sufficiently strong protection against all the storms of misfortune."[20]

It was inconceivable to the Reformer to imagine the Christian life as free from trials and difficulties. The atonement, though it guarantees final victory over sin and Satan, disease and death, does not ensure a trouble-free existence in the present world-order. Nowhere did Calvin put it more eloquently than in his commentary on 1 Peter 1:11: "the government of the Church of Christ has been so divinely constituted from the beginning that the Cross has been the way to victory, and death the way to life."[21] Commenting on Romans 8:28, where the apostle assures us of God's comprehensive providence ensuring that "all things…work together for good," Calvin wrote,

---

19. *Commentary* on Romans 8:30.
20. Ibid.
21. *Commentary* on 1 Peter 1:11.

"The troubles of this life are so far from hindering our salvation that they rather assist it."[22]

Therefore, Christians may expect trouble, and for that reason the question, "How can I know that God is for *me*?" is even more poignant. The presence or absence of trials cannot be a sure indicator of a right standing with God. However, the *function* of trials differs greatly in believers and unbelievers: "Although the elect and the reprobate are exposed without distinction to similar evils, yet there is a great difference between them, for God instructs believers by afflictions, and procures their salvation."[23]

Through the inward testimony of the Spirit, we are reminded that earthly trials are God's way of disciplining us and weaning us from the temptations and allurements of this world. To the godly, trials are evidences of "the Fatherly love of God."[24]

THE FATHER'S ACTION: HE DID NOT SPARE HIS SON

In accord with Calvin's belief that commentaries should be both brief and simple,[25] the Reformer draws out in a single sentence what lies at the heart of the atonement: "It is a notable and shining proof of His inestimable love that the Father did not hesitate to bestow His Son for our salvation."[26] At the heart of Calvin's understanding of the atonement was a deep-seated Trinitarianism: the atonement was not and *could not* have been the work of Christ apart from the Father or the Spirit. In its design, accomplishment, and application, all three persons of the Godhead were intimately involved in furnishing the parameters of man's redemption from bondage to sin and Satan. In particular, Calvin placed a distinctive emphasis on the love of the Father in procuring for us our redemption. Far from viewing the atonement as the Son wrenching love from a reluctant Father, Calvin saw the very initiative of redemption within the con-

---

22. *Commentary* on Romans 8:28.

23. Ibid.

24. *Commentary* on Romans 8:32.

25. See, Richard C. Gamble "*Brevitas et simplicitas*: Toward an Understanding of Calvin's Hermeneutic," *Westminster Theological Journal* 47 (1985): 1–17; idem., "Calvin as Theologian and Exegete: Is There Anything New?" *Calvin Theological Journal* 23 (1988): 178–94.

26. *Commentary* on Romans 8:32.

tours of the Father's prior love for sinners. Commenting on John 3:16, "For God so loved the world, that he gave his only begotten Son...," Calvin wrote: "As the whole matter of our salvation must not be sought anywhere else than in Christ, so we must see whence Christ came to us, and why he was offered to be our Savior. Both points are distinctly stated to us: namely, that faith in Christ brings life to all, and that Christ brought life, because the Heavenly Father loves the human race, and wishes that they should not perish."[27]

The Father did not spare His Son. It is a remarkable thing, as John Lidgett points out, that Calvin frequently refers to the Fatherhood of God: "To those who only have a superficial acquaintance with the teachings of Calvin, it may be a surprise to find that no other writer of the Reformation makes such use of the Fatherhood of God as does Calvin. Throughout the *Institutes* the relationship of God to believers and their relationship to Him is set forth, above all, in terms of Fatherhood and sonship."[28]

It is important for us to grasp this point in Calvin, particularly since one recent biographer has suggested that Calvin betrays theological tensions in his understanding of God as Father due to underlying psychological unease resulting from a bad relationship with his earthly father.[29] The result for Calvin is a somewhat schizophrenic doctrine of God—one that is complex and anxiety-ridden, driven to contradictions, and torn between the labyrinth of one view and the abyss of another.

However, whatever Calvin's relationship to his earthly father might have been, he frequently reveals a tenderness in speaking about his heavenly Father. In commenting on Romans 8:31–32, Calvin exhorts us "to be thoroughly persuaded of the fatherly love of God."[30] This is reminiscent of something he writes in the *Institutes*. Citing Augustine, he said:

---

27. *Commentary* on John 3:16.

28. John Scott Lidgett, *The Fatherhood of God in Christian Truth and Life* (Edinburgh: T. & T. Clark, 1902), 253.

29. This, more or less, is the underlying psychological (and Freudian) interpretation provided by the influential biographer, William J. Bouwsma, in *John Calvin: A Sixteenth-Century Portrait* (Oxford: Oxford University Press, 1988). As a result, Calvin was "chiefly driven by a terror that took shape for him in the metaphor of the abyss" (230).

30. *Commentary* on Romans 8:31.

Therefore, he loved us even when we practiced enmity toward him and committed wickedness. Thus in a marvelous and divine way he loved us even when he hated us. For he hated us for what we were that he had not made; yet because our wickedness had not entirely consumed his handiwork, he knew how, at the same time, to hate in each one of us what we had made, and to love what he had made.[31]

THE SON: EXPOSED TO DEATH

If the Father did not spare His own Son, the Son Himself was "delivered up" (Rom. 8:32). In the briefest of comments, Calvin explained that "to *deliver us* here means to expose to death."[32] The word employed by the apostle in Romans 8:32 is the same word employed at several points in the Synoptic Gospels: Jesus was "delivered over" to Pilate (Matt. 27:2; Mark 15:1), the chief priests "delivered out of envy" (Mark 15:10; Luke 24:7), and they "delivered him to be crucified" (Matt. 27:26). Commenting on these passages in his *Harmony of the Gospels*, Calvin wrote against those who attempted to soften the doctrine of God's predestinating purpose that lies behind this term:

> By way of softening the doctrine, which appears to them to be somewhat harsh, they substitute the *foreknowledge* of God in place of the *decree*, as if God merely beheld from a distance future events, and did not arrange them according to his pleasure. But very differently does the Spirit settle this question; for not only does he assign as the reason why Christ was delivered up, that *it was so written*, but also that it was so *determined*.
>
> For where Matthew and Mark quote Scripture, Luke leads us directly to the heavenly decree, saying, *according to what was determined*; as also in the Acts of the Apostles, he shows that Christ *was delivered* not only *by the foreknowledge*, but likewise *by the fixed purpose of God*, (Acts 2:25), and a little afterwards, that *Herod and Pilate*, with other wicked men, did those things which had been fore-ordained by the hand and purpose of God (Acts 4:27, 28). Hence it is evident that it is but an ignorant subterfuge

---

31. *Institutes* 2.16.4. Calvin is citing (loosely) from Augustine, *John's Gospel* cx. 6 (MPL 35. 1923 f.; tr. NPNF VII. 411).

32. *Commentary* on Romans 8:32.

which is employed by those who betake themselves to bare fore-knowledge.[33]

The crucifixion was not an accident or a happenstance. It took place in accord with the predetermined divine purpose of almighty God — a plan to which the Son was already privy.

Understanding Jesus' reluctance

We ought to consider the reluctance of Jesus in the Garden of Gethsemane in light of this predetermination to which He Himself was privy. In the garden, Jesus cried, "O my Father, if it be possible, let this cup pass from me: nevertheless not as I will, but as thou *wilt*" (Matt. 26:39, emphasis added). Calvin was reflective as he approached this passage. Citing from Ambrose, he agreed that we would think less of Jesus had He *not* uttered these words:

> I not only do not think that there is any need of excuse, but there is no instance in which I admire more his kindness and his majesty; for he would not have done so much for me, if he had not taken upon him my feelings. He grieved for me, who had no cause of grief for himself; and, laying aside the delights of the eternal Godhead, he experiences the affliction of my weakness. I boldly call it *sorrow*, because I preach the cross. For he took upon him not the appearance, but the reality, of incarnation. It was therefore necessary that he should experience grief, that he might overcome sorrow, and not shut it out; for the praise of fortitude is not bestowed on those who are rather stupefied than pained by wounds.[34]

Calvin understood these words as reflective of the human nature of Christ, made to suffer in every respect like ourselves. It is a mark of the absolute nature of the incarnation that Jesus trembled in the face of a *bloody* death. We value and treasure Him all the more that in the face of such a death He resigned himself fully and unreservedly to do the will of His Father in heaven. His death was predetermined by divine counsel and covenant, but it was equally voluntary on Christ's part. His obedience was freely given, and given in full.

---

33. *Commentary on a Harmony of the Evangelists: Matthew, Mark, and Luke*, trans. Rev. William Pringle (1843; repr., Grand Rapids: Baker, 1981), 3:201 (comment on Matthew 26:24).

34. *Harmony* (comment on Matthew 26:39), 3:229–30.

Calvin then faces the dilemma head-on:

But it may be asked, How did he pray that the eternal decree of the Father, of which he was not ignorant, should be revoked? or though he states a condition, *if it be possible*, yet it wears an aspect of absurdity to make the purpose of God changeable. We must hold it to be utterly impossible for God to revoke his decree. According to Mark, too, Christ would seem to contrast the power of God with his decree. *All things, says* he, *are possible to thee.* But it would be improper to extend the power of God so far as to lessen his truth, by making him liable to variety and change. I answer, There would be no absurdity in supposing that Christ, agreeably to the custom of the godly, leaving out of view the divine purpose, committed to the bosom of the Father his desire which troubled him. For believers, in pouring out their prayers, do not always ascend to the contemplation of the secrets of God, or deliberately inquire what is possible to be done, but are sometimes carried away hastily by the earnestness of their wishes.[35]

It is all the more admirable that Christ, as our sin-bearer and substitute, without the benefit of divine knowledge that for a moment is blotted out, gave unyielding obedience even in the face of the horrors that lay before Him—not only the physical brutality of crucifixion but the spiritual torment of being regarded as one worthy of condemnation. Before Him lay the act of substitution: He would be made sin for us (2 Cor. 5:21), a statement that Calvin understood in this way:

For he assumed in a manner our place, that he might be a criminal in our room, and might be dealt with as a sinner, not for his own offenses, but for those of others, inasmuch as he was pure and exempt from every fault, and might endure the punishment that was due to us—not to himself. It is in the same manner, assuredly, that we are now *righteous in him*—not in respect of our rendering satisfaction to the justice of God by our own works, but because we are judged of in connection with Christ's righteousness, which we have put on by faith, that it might become ours.[36]

---

35. Ibid., 3:229.
36. *Commentary* on 2 Corinthians 5:21.

No wonder Jesus trembled at the prospect of enduring the Father's anger!

> Having undertaken to be our Surety He resolved actually to undergo in our room the judgment of God. No one that considers that Christ undertook the office of a Mediator on the condition of suffering our condemnation, both in His body and in His soul, will think it strange that He maintained a struggle with the sorrows of death, as if an offended God had thrown Him into a whirlpool of afflictions.[37]

INEXORABLE GOSPEL LOGIC:
WHAT IS CHRIST'S IS OURS

If Christ took our sin and bore its just condemnation, we through faith receive His righteousness reckoned to our account. It is the pastoral conclusion of the apostle: "how shall he not with him also freely give us all things?" (Rom. 8:32). Calvin wrote, "He has not been sent us void of blessings, or empty-handed, but filled with all heavenly treasures, so that those who possess Him may not want anything that is necessary for their complete happiness."[38] Every joy, every satisfaction, is found in union with Christ.

Nowhere did Calvin write more eloquently than in expounding upon this theme in the *Institutes*:

> We see that our whole salvation and all its parts are comprehended in Christ [Acts 4:12]. We should therefore take care not to derive the least portion of it from anywhere else. If we seek salvation, we are taught by the very name of Jesus that it is "of him" [I Cor. 1:30]. If we seek any other gifts of the Spirit, they will be found in his anointing. If we seek strength, it lies in his dominion; if purity, in his conception; if gentleness, it appears in his birth. For by his birth he was made like us in all respects [Heb. 2:17] that he might learn to feel our pain [compare to Heb. 5:2]. If we seek redemption, it lies in his passion; if acquittal, in his condemnation; if remission of the curse, in his cross [Gal. 3:13]; if satisfaction, in his sacrifice; if purification, in his blood; if reconciliation, in his descent into hell; if mortification of the flesh,

---

37. *Harmony*, 3:319 (comment on Matthew 27:46).
38. *Commentary* on Romans 8:32.

in his tomb; if newness of life, in his resurrection; if immortality, in the same; if inheritance of the Heavenly Kingdom, in his
entrance into heaven; if protection, if security, if abundant supply of all blessings, in his Kingdom; if untroubled expectation
of judgment, in the power given to him to judge. In short, since
rich store of every kind of good abounds in him, let us drink our
fill from the fountain, and from no other.[39]

As Sinclair B. Ferguson writes: "Salvation and all its benefits not
only come to us through Christ but are to be found exclusively in
Christ. Union with Christ brings the believer into fellowship with
Christ, crucified, resurrected, ascended, reigning, and returning."[40]

---

39. *Institutes* 2.16.19.
40. Sinclair B. Ferguson, "Calvin's Heart for God," in *John Calvin: A Heart for
Devotion, Doctrine, & Doxology*, ed. Burk Parsons (Orlando, Fla.: Reformation Trust,
2008), 35.

CHAPTER 6

Union with Christ, the "Twofold Grace of God," and the "Order of Salvation" in Calvin's Theology

Cornelis P. Venema

One of John Calvin's most significant contributions to the Reformed churches is his clear and compelling view of the believer's union with Christ and participation in the two benefits of His saving work, the grace of "free justification" and evangelical "repentance," or sanctification.[1] In his treatment of this "twofold grace of God" (*duplex gratia Dei*), Calvin resolutely opposed the Roman Catholic confusion of justification and sanctification. With Martin Luther, Calvin insisted that the gospel of Jesus Christ principally teaches us that our acceptance with God is based entirely on the gracious work of Jesus Christ on our behalf. Calvin, like Luther before him, was an uncompromising champion of the doctrine of justification by grace alone through faith alone. However, Calvin insisted with equal fervor that those who are justified through faith alone are never justified by a faith that is alone. The same Christ who justifies His people also sanctifies them by His indwelling Spirit. In this way, Calvin steered a careful course between the errors of nomism and antinomianism, which have often troubled the Christian church in general and the Reformed churches in particular since the sixteenth-century Reformation.

Interpreters of Calvin's doctrine of grace are generally familiar with his emphasis on the twofold grace of God. However, despite

---

1. In Reformed theology, the usual language of the "order of salvation" is "justification" and "sanctification." Calvin ordinarily used the terminology of "justification" and "regeneration" or "repentance." Only infrequently did he speak of "sanctification," though it was clearly for him a synonym for either regeneration or repentance. In what follows, I will often use the term "sanctification" rather than "regeneration" or "repentance" for the sake of clarity. I will also use the phrase "twofold grace of God" to refer to what Calvin, in theological shorthand, denominates the *duplex gratia Dei*.

a broad consensus regarding Calvin's understanding of the two benefits of the gospel, considerable debate continues regarding his view of the relation between the grace of free justification, the first of these benefits, and the grace of what Calvin terms "regeneration" or "repentance." This debate is due in part to Calvin's surprising decision in his *Institutes of the Christian Religion* to treat the second grace, regeneration or repentance, before the first, justification. Though Calvin designated justification the "main hinge" of the Christian religion, he adopted an "order of teaching" (*ordo docendi*) in the *Institutes* that seems to reverse the sequence of justification and sanctification. This odd ordering has been the occasion for considerable discussion among interpreters of Calvin's theology, not only in the past but more recently as well. Some even appeal to this sequence as evidence that Calvin's view of the "order of salvation," or *ordo salutis*, differed from that of later Calvinism.

To address Calvin's understanding of the twofold grace of God, especially the debate regarding the relation of its two aspects, I will begin with a summary of his understanding of justification and sanctification. In the course of my summary, I will note how Calvin distinguished but refused to separate these two graces. With this summary as background, I will then assess a recent illustrative debate regarding Calvin's view of the relation between justification and sanctification. Finally, I will conclude with several observations regarding the theological and pastoral significance of Calvin's position.

CALVIN'S DOCTRINE OF THE TWOFOLD GRACE OF GOD

Calvin treated the topic of the twofold grace of God in Book III of the *Institutes*, which offers a comprehensive exposition of the believer's participation in the saving work of Christ as Mediator. As the title of Book III indicates, Calvin aimed to describe the two benefits of salvation in Christ that believers enjoy through faith-union with Him. In order for believers to enjoy the fruits of Christ's saving work, which Calvin described at length in Book II, they must be joined to Christ by the work of the Spirit and through faith. Accordingly, Calvin introduced the subject of the twofold grace of God by noting that any discussion of faith would be "barren and mutilated and well-nigh useless" unless it included an explanation of its twofold benefit[2]:

> Let us sum these up: Christ was given to us by God's generosity, to be grasped and possessed by us in faith. By partaking of him, we principally receive a double grace (*duplicem gratiam*): namely, that being reconciled to God through Christ's blamelessness, we may have in heaven instead of a Judge a gracious Father, and secondly, that sanctified by Christ's Spirit we may cultivate blamelessness and purity of life.[3]

Throughout his writings, Calvin consistently spoke of these two benefits as the distinct, yet inseparable, fruits of the believer's union with Christ through faith.

Justification: the First Benefit of Union with Christ

According to Calvin, justification through faith is the first benefit that believers receive through union with Christ. Whereas sanctification or repentance is the second benefit, justification or reconciliation is "the main hinge on which religion turns."[4] When Calvin treated the benefits of our reception of God's grace in Christ, he clearly granted a kind of priority to justification as the first aspect of the twofold grace of God. The pre-eminence of this benefit is affirmed in various ways throughout his writings. For example, Calvin argued that, since the knowledge of our salvation chiefly depends on a proper conception of this benefit, it may be termed the "leading tenet of the gospel."[5]

---

2. *Institutes* 3.3.1 (*OS* 4.55). When referring in what follows to Calvin's works in the *Opera Selecta*, ed. P. Barth and G. Niesel, 5 vols. (München: Kaiser, 1926–52), I will use the abbreviation *OS*. When referring to the *Calvini Opera* (*Ioannis Calvini opera quae supersunt omnia*), ed. G. Baum, E. Cunitz, E. Reuss et al., 59 vols. (vols. 29–87, *Corpus Reformatorum*) (Brunsvigae, Schwetschke, 1863–1900), I will use the abbreviation *CO*.

3. *Institutes* 3.11.1 (*OS* 4.182). Cf. French ed., 1560: "double grace"; *Institutes* 3.11.14 (*OS* 4.198); 3.2.8 (*OS* 4.18); *Commentary* on Deuteronomy 30:19 (*CO* 25.56): "duplicem Christi gratiam."

4. *Institutes* 3.11.1 (*OS* 4.182): "...praecipuus esse sustinendae religionis cardo"; French ed., 1560: "...c'est le principal article de la religion Chrestienne." Cf. *Institutes* 3.15.1 (*OS* 4.239): "Praecipuum autem hunc esse causae cardinem"; Sermon on 2 Samuel 12:13 (*SC* 1.332): "...c'est le principal poinct de nostre salut"; *Sermon sur la prophetie de Jesus Christ* (*CO* 35.626): "...c'est le principal article de nostre salut"; *Sermon sur la Justification* (*CO* 23.688): "...voici le fondement de la vraye Religion"; *Sermon sur la Justification* (*CO* 23.694): "...la principale clef de tout Evangile."

5. *Commentary* on Luke 1:77 (*CO* 45.51): "...praecipuum evangelii caput." Cf.

Reconciliation, or the forgiveness of sins, constitutes the chief end in the preaching of the gospel of Christ,[6] since it concerns His chief office.[7] The gospel primarily differs from secular philosophy by placing our salvation in free forgiveness and in conceiving it to be the source of all God's blessings to us, including that of sanctification, the second aspect of the twofold grace of God.[8] Because justification expresses the "true logic of piety" itself, it may be termed the first benefit of our reception of God's grace in Christ.[9]

According to Calvin, justification is the first benefit of the gospel because it concerns the believer's acceptance in the presence of God on the basis of the righteousness of Christ[10]:

> He is said to be justified in God's sight who is reckoned righteous in God's judgment and has been accepted on account of his righteousness.... On the contrary, justified by faith is he who, excluded from the righteousness of works, grasps the righteousness of Christ through faith, and clothed in it, appears in God's sight not as a sinner but as a righteous man. Therefore, we explain justification simply as the acceptance with which God receives us into his favor as righteous men. And we say that it consists in the remission of sins and the imputation of Christ's righteousness.[11]

Justification, as Calvin's formal definition indicates, is a *juridical* or forensic act, a gracious judgment of God whereby the believer is accepted into His favor. As a gracious judgment of God, it constitutes a complex transaction, including the forgiveness of sins and the imputation of Christ's righteousness.[12]

Commentary on Matthew 1:14 (*CO* 45.139); *Commentary* on Luke 1:6 (*CO* 45.10): "foedus...cuius primum caput est gratuita reconciliato...."

6. *Commentary* on John 20:23 (*CO* 47.440): "Hic ergo praecipuus est evangelii praedicandi finis, ut Deo reconcilientur homines, quod fit gratuita peccatorum venia."

7. *Commentary* on John 1:29 (*CO* 47.25): "...praecipuum Christi officium."

8. *Commentary* on John 20:23 (*CO* 47.440).

9. *Commentary* on Micah 7:19 (*CO* 43.431–2): "...dialectica pietatis."

10. Cf. *Institutes* 3.11 (*OS* 4.181), which bears the title: "De iustificatione fidei, ac primo de ipsa nominis et rei definitione."

11. *Institutes* 3.11.2 (*OS* 4.182–3). Cf. *Institutes* 3.17.8 (*OS* 4.261); 3.11.4 (*OS* 4. 184–5).

12. For a consideration of Calvin's understanding of the "righteousness" of Christ that is imputed to believers for their justification, particularly whether it

Because justification involves the believer's acquittal and acceptance as righteous before God's judgment seat, Calvin repeatedly took issue with the more common medieval and Scholastic tendency to identify being justified (*iustificari*) with "to make just" (*iustum facere*).[13] Our justification does not depend on the possession of righteousness as an inherent "quality" of our person, since the righteousness that justifies us is a "relative righteousness."[14] Neither does it depend on "an infused habit or quality,"[15] such that God's judgment and acceptance of us rest on what "men are in themselves."[16] Because only Christ's obedience suffices for perfect righteousness before God, and since only in Him do we find righteousness inhering as a quality of His person,[17] the believer's justification rests on Christ's work alone, and may not be understood to depend causally on his character (*habitus*) or upon an "infused righteousness."[18]

Sanctification: The Second Benefit of Union with Christ

Calvin usually termed the second benefit of our reception of God's grace in Christ "regeneration" or "repentance."[19] Though inseparably joined with justification and faith, this benefit must not be confused with it: "As faith is not without hope, yet faith and hope are different things, so repentance and faith, although they are held together by a permanent bond, require to be joined rather than con-

---

includes what later Reformed theologians termed the "active" obedience of Christ, see my recent article, "Calvin's Doctrine of the Imputation of Christ's Righteousness: Another Example of 'Calvin Against the Calvinists'?" *Mid-America Journal of Theology* 20 (2009): 15–47.

13. E.g., *Sermon sur la Justification* (*CO* 23.706). Cf. *Acta Synodi Tridentinae Cum Antidoto*, 1547 (*CO* 7.447): "Quaestio est verbi, quid sit iustificatio. Negant [i.e., the Catholic authors of Trent's declaration concerning justification] solam esse remissionem peccatorum: sed renovationem et santificationem simul contineri volunt."

14. *Commentary* on Habakkuk 2:4 (*CO* 43.534–5). Cf. *Institutes* 3.11.3 (*OS* 4.183): "...nempe relative, non autem ut qualitatem aliquam denotet."

15. *Commentary* on Galatians 3:6 (*CO* 50.205). Cf. *Sermon sur la Justification* (*CO* 23.692).

16. *Commentary* on Romans 4:3 (*CO* 49.70).

17. *Commentary* on Romans 5:19 (*CO* 49.101).

18. *Commentary* on Acts 13:39 (*CO* 48.306): "...iustitia infusa." Cf. *Commentary* on Luke 18:14 (*CO* 45.421); *Commentary* on 2 Corinthians 5:21 (*CO* 50.74).

19. *Institutes* 3.3 (*OS* 4.55) bears the title: "Fide nos regenerari; ubi de poenitentia." Calvin used a variety of terms to describe this aspect of God's grace in Christ and made no effort to distinguish between them. Among the more important of these are "sanctification," "renewal" or "reformation of life," "rebirth," and "conversion."

fused."[20] Between this aspect of God's grace and the first there exists an "unbreakable connection,"[21] yet it is distinct from it in conception and nature. Whereas justification refers to our *status* as forgiven sinners, sanctification refers to the *process* by which our sinfully corrupted natures are transformed through the work of the Spirit of Christ. Therefore, though justification is by faith alone, exclusive of the righteousness of works, Calvin contended that it is always accompanied by good works and the reformation of life. Sanctification or repentance, as the second benefit of the believer's union with Christ, constitutes Calvin's comprehensive category for understanding the redirection and alteration of the lives of those who are indwelt by Christ through the Spirit.

Calvin's use of the terms "repentance," "regeneration," and "sanctification" as synonyms reflected his understanding that the reformation of human life, which comes about through faith, is not so much something we accomplish of ourselves as it is a gift of God, effected by the Holy Spirit. In other words, our sanctification is no less the fruit of the creative power of the Spirit of Christ than our justification:

> For Christ imparts the Spirit of regeneration to us in order that he may renew us within, and that a new life may then follow the renewal of mind and heart. For if the function of giving repentance belongs to Christ, it follows that it is not something that has been put in the power of man. And since it is truly something of a wonderful reformation, which makes us new creatures, restores the image of God in us, transfers us from the slavery of sin to the obedience of righteousness, men will no more be able to convert themselves than to create themselves.[22]

Consequently, Calvin repudiated any suggestion that sanctification or the reformation of life is something we can effect of ourselves to complement the free grace of God in Christ. Christ Himself, through the operation of His Spirit, is the sole source of our purity, righteousness, and regeneration.[23] Since sanctification is effected in

---

20. *Institutes* 3.3.5 (*OS* 4.59).

21. *Commentary* on Acts 20:21 (*CO* 48.463): "…individuo nexu inter se cohaereant poenitentia et fides."

22. *Commentary* on Acts 5:31 (*CO* 48.111).

23. E.g., *Commentary* on Acts 11:16 (*CO* 48.257); *Commentary* on Acts 13:39 (*CO*

us through the Spirit, it is as much the peculiar gift of God's grace to us as our justification.[24] For this reason, both repentance and regeneration are *by faith*, and both are the free gift of Christ, who imparts them to us in the power of His Spirit. [25]

The Relation of Justification and Sanctification: "Distinction Without Separation"

In his formulation of the relation between justification and sanctification, Calvin employed the language of the Chalcedonian Christological settlement, which speaks of the two natures of Christ being "without confusion" and "without separation." The relation between justification and sanctification is analogous to the relation and union between the divine and human natures in the one person of Christ. Justification and sanctification are *distinct in conception*, yet they are *inseparable in reality*, since they are simultaneously bestowed and necessarily conjoined benefits of our union with Christ through the operation of His Spirit.

For Calvin, justification and sanctification must be conceptually distinguished lest they be confused and our relation to God adversely affected. For example, in his *Institutes*, Calvin, while acknowledging their inseparability, insisted that justification and sanctification must be distinguished in order that the proper object of faith, God's goodness, might be fully appreciated:

> Repentance is preached in the name of Christ when, through the teaching of the gospel, men hear that all their thoughts, all their inclinations, all their efforts are corrupt and vicious. Accordingly, they must be reborn if they would enter the kingdom of heaven. Forgiveness of sins is preached when men are taught that for them Christ became redemption, righteousness, salvation, and life, by whose name they are freely accounted righteous and innocent in God's sight. Since both kinds of grace are received

---

48.307); *Commentary* on 1 John 2:17 (*CO* 55.320); *Commentary* on 1 John 3:5 (*CO* 55.333); *Commentary* on Malachi 4:2 (*CO* 44.491).

24. *Commentary* on Ezekiel 11:19, 20 (*CO* 40.246); *Commentary* on Ezekiel 18:32 (*CO* 40.456).

25. Calvin offered a general definition of sanctification in *Institutes* 3.3.5 (*OS* 4.60): "Repentance can thus be well defined: it is the true turning of our life to God, a turning that arises from a pure and earnest fear of him; and it consists in the mortification of our flesh and of the old man, and in the vivification of the Spirit."

by faith, as I have elsewhere proved, still because the proper object of faith is God's goodness, by which sins are forgiven, it was expedient that it should be carefully distinguished from repentance.[26]

Unless the difference between justification and sanctification is carefully maintained, the goodness and mercy of God will be seriously impugned and the assurance of faith will be threatened.

Though Calvin emphasized the conceptual distinction between justification and sanctification for these reasons, he was equally concerned to emphasize the second part of the Christological formula, "without separation." Though justification and sanctification are conceptually distinct, they are inseparable in reality. Speaking of repentance and faith, Calvin argued that they "are indeed things wholly distinct, and yet not contrary, and ought never to be separated, as some inconsiderately do."[27] In his development of this inseparable relation between justification and sanctification, Calvin did not hesitate to take issue with those who improperly interpreted the phrase "faith without works justifies" and who inadequately treated the relation between justification and sanctification. Commenting on the proper interpretation of the former phrase, Calvin noted:

> [I]t still remains true, that faith without works justifies, although this needs prudence and a sound interpretation; for this proposition, that faith without works justifies, is true and yet false, according to the different senses which it bears. The proposition, that faith without works justifies by itself, is false, because faith without works is void.... Thus faith can be no more separated from works than the sun from its heat; yet faith justifies without works, because works form no reason for our justification.[28]

It would not be prudent interpretation of this proposition to allow that a dead faith could justify even though it does not work through love.[29] Such an interpretation reflects an inadequate concep-

---

26. *Institutes* 3.3.19 (*OS* 4.77).

27. *Commentary* on Jeremiah 26:17–19 (*CO* 38.532): "Sunt quidem res distinctae, sed tamen non diversae, nec separari debent, ut quidem parum considerate faciunt." Calvin then added, "Nam poenitentia est conversio totius vitae et quasi renovatio: fides autem reos confugere docet ad Dei misericordiam."

28. *Commentary* on Ezekiel 18:14–17 (*CO* 40.439). Cf. *Sermon sur la Justification* (*CO* 23.733).

29. Calvin expressed his position briefly when he noted that "it is faith alone

tion of the relation between justification and sanctification, since it allows a separation between them. Only a living faith may be said to justify us. Only those indwelt by the Spirit of Christ and consecrated to the Lord, having hearts framed to obedience to the law, may be said to have been forgiven and accounted righteous by God.[30]

UNION WITH CHRIST AND THE
"ORDER OF SALVATION" IN CALVIN'S THEOLOGY

In my introductory comments, I noted that there has been considerable debate regarding Calvin's view of the relation between justification and sanctification.[31] Though it is generally acknowledged that Calvin viewed these two benefits as distinct in conception yet inseparable in reality, Calvin's decision to treat the second of these benefits before the first in his *Institutes* has prompted some to argue that Calvin "coordinated" them under the more basic rubric of "union with Christ." In so doing, Calvin is said to have taken a different approach than that of later Calvinists, who articulated an "order of salvation" in which sanctification *follows* or is a "fruit" of justification. This debate regarding the twofold grace of God in Calvin's theology is illustrated by a recent exchange between two interpreters of Calvin in the *Journal of the Evangelical Theological Society*. In the June 2007 issue of the *Journal*, Thomas L. Wenger identified and criticized what he characterized as a "new perspective" on Calvin's understanding of the twofold grace of God.[32] In response to Wenger's essay, Marcus

---

which justifies, and yet the faith which justifies is not alone." Cf. *Acta Synodi Tridentinae Cum Antidoto*, 1547 (*CO* 7.477): "Fides ergo sola est quae iustificet: fides tamen quae iustificat, non est sola. Quemadmodum solis calor solus est qui terram calefaciat: non tamen idem in sole est solus, quia perpetuo coniunctus est cum splendore." *Sermon sur la Justification* (*CO* 23.733). Calvin often used the metaphor of the relation between the sun and its heat or light to emphasize the invariable and necessary relation between justification and sanctification.

30. *Institutes* 3.14.9 (*OS* 4.228).

31. For an extended summary of this debate, see my *Accepted and Renewed in Christ: The "Twofold Grace of God" and the Interpretation of Calvin's Theology* (Göttingen: Vandenhoeck & Ruprecht, 2007), 13–30.

32. Thomas L. Wenger, "The New Perspective on Calvin: Responding to Recent Calvin Interpretations," *Journal of the Evangelical Theological Society* 50, 2 (June 2007): 311–28.

Johnson offered an extensive rebuttal in the September 2008 issue, which also included a response from Wenger.[33]

Wenger: The Priority of Justification to Sanctification

In his essay, Wenger observes that several recent interpreters of Calvin's teaching have claimed the traditional interpretation treats the gospel benefits of justification and sanctification too "disparately." In what Wenger terms the "new perspective on Calvin," the older claim that Calvin insisted on a distinct priority of justification to sanctification, as in the later Reformed scholastic doctrine of the *ordo salutis* [order of salvation], fails to appreciate the dominant theme of "union with Christ" in Calvin's soteriology. According to Wenger, the "new perspective on Calvin" exaggerates the theme of union with Christ in Calvin's theology and coordinates the two benefits of justification and sanctification in a way that differs from the later Calvinist doctrine of the relative priority of justification in the application of salvation.[34] Wenger cites the following passage from Richard Gaffin as representative of this new perspective:

> Calvin destroys Rome's charge [of antinomianism] by showing that faith, in its Protestant understanding, entails a disposition to holiness without particular reference to justification, a concern for Godliness that is not to be understood only as a consequence

33. Marcus Johnson, "New or Nuanced Perspective on Calvin? A Reply to Thomas Wenger," *Journal of the Evangelical Theological Society* 51, 3 (September 2008): 543–58; and Thomas L. Wenger, "Theological Spectacles and a Paradigm of Centrality: A Reply to Marcus Johnson," *Journal of the Evangelical Theological Society* 51, 3 (September 2008): 559–72.

34. Wenger cites the following sources to illustrate this alleged "new perspective on Calvin": Craig B. Carpenter, "A Question of Union with Christ? Calvin and Trent on Justification," *Westminster Theological Journal* 64 (2002): 363–86; Tim J. R. Trumper, "Covenant Theology and Constructive Calvinism," *Westminster Theological Journal* 64 (2002): 387–404; Jae Sung Kim, "*Unio cum Christo*: The Work of the Holy Spirit in Calvin's Theology" (Ph.D. diss., Westminster Theological Seminary, 1998); Ronald N. Gleason, "The Centrality of the *Unio Mystica* in the Theology of Herman Bavinck" (Ph.D. diss., Westminster Theological Seminary, 2001); David B. Garner, "Adoption in Christ" (Ph.D. diss., Westminster Theological Seminary, 2002); Kevin Woongsan Kang, "Justified by Faith in Christ: Jonathan Edwards's Doctrine of Justification in Light of Union with Christ" (Ph.D. diss., Westminster Theological Seminary, 2003); William Borden Evans, "Imputation and Impartation: The Problem of Union with Christ in Nineteenth Century American Reformed Theology" (Ph.D. diss., Vanderbilt University, 1996).

of justification. Calvin proceeds as he does, and is *free* to do so, because for him the relative "ordo" or priority of justification and sanctification is indifferent theologically. Rather, what has controlling soteriological importance is the priority to both of (spiritual, "existential," faith-) union with Christ.[35]

According to the new view of Calvin's doctrine of grace, Calvin offers a better account of the coordination of justification and sanctification than is found in the older sequential view of an order of salvation.

In his evaluation of the "new perspective on Calvin," Wenger offers two kinds of criticisms of this emphasis on the centrality of union with Christ, the first "historiographical" and the second "exegetical." In his assessment of the "new perspective on Calvin" from a historiographical point of view, Wenger identifies three problems with its approach. First, he observes that the "new perspective" amounts to another version of the "Calvin against the Calvinists" school of interpretation. Though Richard Muller has raised serious objections to the older claim that Reformed scholasticism represents a distortion of Calvin's original Reformation position, advocates of the new perspective on Calvin's doctrine of union with Christ typically argue that Calvin's treatment of the twofold grace of God represents a more biblical-theological treatment than the later scholastic formulations of an *ordo salutis*. Second, the "new perspective" on Calvin's doctrine of the twofold grace of God represents a kind of repristination of a nineteenth-century historiography that sought to identify a "central dogma" that formed the point of departure for Calvin's theology.[36] Third, Wenger notes that the "new perspective" authors tend to misread the *ordo docendi* that Calvin followed in Book III of his *Institutes* as though it expressed his conception of the relative order and priority of justification and sanctification.

The second major component of Wenger's critique of the "new perspective on Calvin" is his claim that its proponents have failed to make their case exegetically. Rather than a careful, textual reading of

---

35. Richard B. Gaffin, Jr., "Biblical Theology and the Westminster Standards," *Westminster Theological Journal* 65 (2003): 176–7.

36. In the older literature on Calvin, the "central dogma" of Calvin's theology was often identified as God's sovereign will or the doctrine of predestination. For a brief statement of this approach, see my *Accepted and Renewed in Christ*, 14–15.

Calvin's *Institutes* and commentaries, advocates of the new approach employ "erratic readings" of Calvin's writings. Proceeding from the presumption that union with Christ is the organizing principle of Calvin's soteriology, proponents of the new interpretation neglect to give particular attention to Calvin's own comments on the relative ordering of justification and sanctification. Since Calvin chose to treat sanctification before justification in his *Institutes*, it is wrongly concluded that he coordinated the two benefits of Christ's saving work in a manner quite distinct from the later scholastic *ordo salutis*.

Johnson: The Co-ordination of Justification and Sanctification

In a subsequent issue of the *Journal of the Evangelical Theological Society*, Marcus Johnson replies extensively to Wenger's criticisms of the "new perspective on Calvin." In his reply, Johnson offers some clarifications of the interpretation that Wenger opposes and defends the position that Calvin's doctrine of union with Christ constituted the basis for his unique emphasis on the coordination of the two benefits of justification and sanctification. He further argues that Calvin did not, by virtue of the role of union with Christ in his soteriology, order the relation between justification and sanctification in any kind of priority of "cause" and "effect" or of "ground" and "fruit."

Johnson begins his reply to Wenger by observing that a number of interpreters of Calvin's theology, in the older and more recent literature, have identified union with Christ as the central emphasis or theme of his soteriology. Contrary to Wenger's suggestion that this is a form of the "central dogma" approach to interpreting Calvin's theology, Johnson notes that it is a more modest claim, which asserts only that union with Christ is the primary emphasis in Calvin's view of the application of redemption to believers. The difference between Calvin's soteriology and that of later Calvinists, who articulated a more technical and sequential view of the relation between justification and sanctification, is evident at this point. Though Johnson acknowledges the significant influence of Philipp Melanchthon's *Loci Communes* on Calvin's ordering of his theology in the *Institutes*, he insists that "[u]nion with Christ is quite simply, the overriding presupposition of Calvin's understanding of the 'way in which we receive the grace of Christ.'"[37] For Calvin, union with Christ, not the

---

37. Johnson, "A Reply to Thomas Wenger," 550–1.

grace of free justification, is the basis for the believer's sanctification. Since both justification and sanctification are grounded in the believer's union with Christ, Calvin was able to treat sanctification before justification in Book III of the *Institutes*, and he was able to grant sanctification a prominence in the application of salvation that distinguished his soteriology from historic Lutheranism.[38] According to Johnson, "[j]ustification no more 'grounds' sanctification than sanctification grounds justification: both are grounded in, and proceed from, the believer's union with Christ."[39]

A Resolution of the Debate: Calvin's Understanding of the Order Between Justification and Sanctification

The debate between Wenger and Johnson regarding the order of Calvin's treatment of justification and sanctification illustrates the importance of stating clearly how Calvin viewed the relation of these two benefits of union with Christ.[40] Both Wenger and Johnson tend to exaggerate certain features of Calvin's view. Consequently, neither of them captures the fullness of Calvin's exposition of the interplay between justification and sanctification.

---

38. Ibid., 555.

39. Ibid. Rather than this representing an "erratic reading" of Calvin's writings, Johnson adduces Calvin's polemics with the Lutheran theologian, Osiander, and his sacramental theology of union with Christ, as further evidence for the centrality of the theme of union with Christ to Calvin's soteriology. In support of this claim, Johnson appeals to the study of Mark Garcia, "Life in Christ: The Function of Union with Christ in the *Unio-Duplex Gratia* Structure of Calvin's Soteriology with Special Reference to the Relationship of Justification and Sanctification in Sixteenth-Century Context" (Ph.D. thesis; University of Edinburgh, 2005), pp. 197–252.

40. The debate between Wenger and Johnson also illustrates the danger of an approach to Calvin's theology that is unduly influenced by contemporary debates. In his *Unaccomodated Calvin: Studies in the Foundation of a Theological Tradition* (New York: Oxford University Press, 2000), 4, Richard Muller observes that "Calvin's thought has been avidly deconstructed by [those] in search of a theological or religious ally or, occasionally, in search of a historical source for the theological trends of the present." It is difficult to suppress the impression that Wenger's criticism of what he terms the "new perspective on Calvin" is shaped by a desire to find more continuity between Calvin's position and the later orthodox Reformed doctrine of an *ordo salutis*. It is also apparent that advocates of the "new perspective" are motivated in part by a desire to find in Calvin something of an alternative to the *ordo salutis* position, one that is more congenial to a biblical-theological understanding of the dominant significance of the theme of "union with Christ" in the soteriology of the Pauline epistles.

For his part, Wenger downplays the fundamental importance of union with Christ in Calvin's understanding of these gospel benefits. It seems undeniable that Calvin did grant a kind of priority to the theme of union with Christ in his treatment of the twofold grace of God.[41] Though this theme is not to be construed as a kind of "central dogma" in Calvin's theology, it does constitute the principal theme and framework for Calvin's exposition of the believer's participation in Christ's benefits.

However, Johnson also tends to overlook the way Calvin granted a kind of priority to justification in the order of salvation in a manner that anticipated the later, more articulate doctrine of this order in orthodox Calvinism. Though Johnson correctly emphasizes the fundamental importance of union with Christ to Calvin's teaching about salvation, he does not adequately explain the reasons Calvin chose to treat sanctification before justification in his *Institutes*. In particular, Johnson glosses over Calvin's explicit teaching that sanctification properly "follows" or is an "effect" of justification.

The Significance of Calvin's Order of Teaching in the *Institutes*

In order to resolve this debate satisfactorily, therefore, it is necessary to consider the significance Calvin attached to his decision to treat sanctification before justification in the *Institutes*. It is also especially instructive to note how Calvin spoke of sanctification as an "effect" or "fruit" of justification. Calvin's keen awareness of the question regarding the relation between justification and sanctification is attested by his lengthy explanations in the *Institutes* as to why he chose to treat sanctification, the second aspect of the twofold grace of God, before justification, the first aspect.[42] In the recent discussion of the relation between union with Christ and the twofold grace of God in Calvin's theology, these explanations have not been adequately considered.

The first passage comes at the beginning of Calvin's treatment

---

41. See *Institutes* 3.1.2 (*OS* 4.1–54). For a treatment of Calvin's understanding of union with Christ in relation to the twofold grace of God, see my study, *Accepted and Renewed in Christ*, 83–94.

42. Calvin followed this order in every edition of the *Institutes* with the exception of the first (1536), where justification was treated, if at all, in the first chapter on the Law, and repentance was treated in the fifth chapter on the false sacraments. Justification was treated before repentance in his 1537 Catechism (*OS* I.393–5), however, and in his *Catechismus Ecclesiae Genevensis* of 1545 (*OS* II.93–6).

of the twofold grace of God in Book III, chapter 3, of the *Institutes*, and is remarkable for its thorough account of Calvin's purpose in his arrangement of the material:

> Now, both repentance and forgiveness of sins—that is, newness of life and free reconciliation—are conferred on us by Christ, and both are attained by us through faith. As a consequence, reason and the order of teaching demand that I begin to discuss both at this point. However, our immediate transition will be from faith to repentance. For when this topic is rightly understood it will better appear how man is justified by faith alone, and simple pardon; nevertheless, actual holiness of life, so to speak, is not separated from free imputation of righteousness. Now it ought to be a fact beyond controversy that repentance not only constantly follows faith, but is also born of faith.... [N]o one can embrace the grace of the gospel without betaking himself from the errors of his past life into the right way, and applying his whole effort to the practice of repentance.[43]

The second passage likewise comes at a transitional point, at the outset of Calvin's treatment of justification in Book III, chapter 11, of the *Institutes*:

> Of regeneration indeed, the second of these gifts, I have said what seemed sufficient. The theme of justification was therefore more lightly touched upon because it was more to the point to understand first how little devoid of good works is the faith through which alone we obtain free righteousness by the mercy of God; and what is the nature of the good works of the saints with which part of this question is concerned. Therefore we must now discuss these matters thoroughly. And we must so discuss them as to bear in mind that this is the main hinge on which religion turns, so that we devote the greater attention and care to it. For unless you first of all grasp what your relationship to God is, and the nature of his judgment concerning you, you have neither a foundation on which to establish your salvation nor one on which to build piety toward God.[44]

In these two passages, Calvin offered two distinct reasons for the odd order that he chose to follow. First, he believed that this order of treatment would convince his readers that justification is by

---

43. *Institutes* 3.3.1 (*OS* IV.5).
44. *Institutes* 3.11.1 (*OS* IV.182).

faith alone apart from works. In the first passage, this consideration was mentioned explicitly when Calvin noted that "when this topic [i.e., sanctification or regeneration] is rightly understood it will better appear how man is justified by faith alone, and simple pardon."[45] But it also was mentioned implicitly in the second passage when Calvin noted that this order would aid his readers when the topic of justification was taken up, since a clear picture would have emerged already as to "the nature of the good works of the saints, with which part of this question is concerned."[46]

Second, Calvin believed that this order of treatment would convince his readers that, though justification is not based on good works, it cannot be separated from its necessary accompaniment, repentance. Accordingly, in the first passage, Calvin identified a second consideration for adopting this order—that it would show how "actual holiness of life, so to speak, is not separated from free imputation of righteousness."[47] Similarly, in the second passage, he stated that this order of treatment would enable his readers to understand "how little devoid of good works is the faith through which alone we obtain free righteousness by the mercy of God."[48]

Thus, Calvin acknowledged in both passages that these two aspects of God's grace are inseparable, being conferred by Christ and obtained through faith. He also acknowledged that justification is the first and sanctification the second of these parts. In short, Calvin's order of teaching in the *Institutes* does not imply that he was indifferent to the distinction or theological relation between the benefits of justification and sanctification.[49]

Sanctification: An "effect" or "fruit" of justification
Within the framework suggested by his formula that justification and sanctification are distinct yet inseparable parts of God's grace in

---

45. *Institutes* 3.3.1 (*OS* IV.5): "...melius patebit quomodo sola fide et mera venia iustificetur homo...."

46. *Institutes* 3.11.1 (*OS* IV.182).

47. *Institutes* 3.3.1 (*OS* IV.5): "...neque tamen a gratuita iustitiae imputatione separetur realis (ut ita loquar) vitae sanctitas."

48. *Institutes* 3.11.1 (*OS* IV.182): "...et quam otiosa non sit a bonis operibus fides, qua sola gratuitam iustitiam, Dei misericordia obtinemus."

49. For a discussion of the extent to which "rhetorical" considerations may have played a role in Calvin's choice to follow this order, see my *Accepted and Renewed in Christ*, 135–7.

Christ, Calvin sometimes referred to sanctification as both an "effect" (*consequentia, effectus*) and an "inferior cause" (*causa inferior*) of justification. The question of the order, sequence, and inter-relation between justification and sanctification, therefore, is one that Calvin explicitly addressed, and for which he provided a distinct answer.

Calvin expressed his understanding of sanctification as the effect or consequence of justification in a variety of ways. To an extent, his designation of justification as the first or "principal" part, and of sanctification as the second part, of the gospel reflected this understanding. The same holds true for his analogy of the relation between the sun and its heat. Sanctification may no more be separated from justification than the heat, which necessarily and invariably accompanies it, may be separated from the sun's light.[50] Sanctification is by faith and follows it, not in any chronological sense, but in the sense that an effect follows its cause. As Calvin put it in a passage representative of this understanding:

> The righteousness of works...is the effect of the righteousness of faith, and the blessedness which arises from works is the effect of the blessedness which consists in the remission of sins.... We should consider here *the order of causes as well as the dispensation of the grace of God.*[51]

It is only in "consequence" (*effectus*) of God's free forgiveness that He "governs us by his Spirit, mortifies the lusts of our flesh, cleanses us from our corruptions, and restores us to the healthy condition of a godly and an upright life."[52] Though our adoption as God's children is free and "without repentance," the "earnest and seal" of that adoption is the Spirit of Christ in us, who brings about a confor-

---

50. Cf. e.g. Sermon on Galatians 2:17–18 (*CO* 50.438): "Ce sont deux choses coniointes comme d'un lien inseparable, comme la clarté du soleil ne peut point estre separee de sa chaleur. Ainsi ces deux graces (c'est à scavoir nostre iustice at la remission de nos pechez) sont inviolablement coniointes avec ce renouvellement qui est fait par l'esprit de sanctification."

51. *Commentary* on Romans 4:6 (*CO* 49.73, emphasis mine): "Ergo et operum iustitia effectus est iustitiae fidei: et beatitudo ex operibus effectus beatitudinis, quae sita est in peccatorm remissione.... Nempe consideranda est hic *tam series causarum, quam gratiaie Dei* dispensatio." This statement is one of the clearest indications in Calvin that he was aware of the question of the proper "order" of these benefits. Cf. *Commentary* on Romans 4:9–10 (*CO* 49.74); *Commentary* on 1 Timothy 1:5 (*CO* 52–253).

52. *Commentary* on Psalm 103:3 (*CO* 32.75).

mity between ourselves and Christ, such that God may recognize in us the genuine *insignia* of His children.[53] Within the context of the dispensation of God's grace in Christ, then, sanctification must be understood as the *telos* or *finis* of God's free pardon and the imputation of Christ's righteousness. God's gracious pardon is granted to us, "not to foster our sins, but to recall us to a desire to live in holiness and sanctification."[54] The "end" (*finis*) of Christ's atoning death is the service of God,[55] and the "end" (*finis*) of our calling is that God might make us holy in obedience.[56]

Because this order and sequence obtains between justification and sanctification within the dispensation of God's grace, Calvin also believed it is permissible to speak of good works as "inferior causes" (*causas inferiores*) of the believer's pardon.[57] This does not mean that

---

53. *Institutes* 3.17.6 (*OS* IV.259): "…quia in illis germana demum filiorm insignia agnoscit, qui Spiritu eius ad bonum reguntur." Cf. Sermon on Job 14:13–15 (*CO* 33.691): "…car le S. Esprit n'est point oisof en nous, mais plustost il nous declare qu'il habite en nous, afin que nous soyons enfans de Dieu: et nous ne le pouvons estre que quant et quant nous ne mettions peine de nous adonner à bonnes oeuvres, et suivre sa volonté." Also cf. *Commentary* on Ezekiel 3:20 (*CO* 40.96).

54. *Commentary* on Matthew 9:13 (*CO* 45.251).

55. *Commentary* on Hebrews 9:14 (*CO* 55.111).

56. *Commentary* on Hebrews 12:16 (*CO* 55.179). Cf. Sermon on Galatians 5:22–6 (*CO* 51.50): "Nous disons que Iesus Christ ne nous est pas seulement donné à fin que par son moyen nous obtenions remission de nos pechez devant Dieu: mais c'est à ce qu'estans regenerez par son sainct Esprit nous cheminions en nouveaté de vie." Sermon on Isaiah 28:16–17 (*SC* II.550): "…quelle est a fin de l'Evangile; c'est assavoir… que nous menions une vie sainte et telle qu'on puisse voir que la loy de Dieu domine sur nous." Eva-Maria Faber, *Symphonie von Gott und Mensch* (Neukirchen–Vluyn: Neukirchener Verlag, 1999), 460–1, notes that for this reason it is not enough to say that Calvin viewed sanctification as simply an "effect" of justification. Sanctification is a necessary and integral aspect of the renewed communion with the triune God that salvation bestows.

57. *Institutes* 3.14.21 (*OS* IV.238). Paul Helm, *John Calvin's Ideas* (Oxford: Oxford University Press, 2006), 406, offers a helpful comment regarding Calvin's use of the language "inferior cause" at this point: "Here, a different sense of 'condition' is to be understood from those considered earlier, the rather paradoxical sense in which a consequence may be said to be a condition. Note that Calvin distinguishes carefully between faith and works. Faith is a cause, the instrumental cause, of personal justification, while works are evidence of personal justification, an 'inferior cause,' and so are a consequence, a causal consequence of it which occurs later in time. We can say 'if no faith then no justification' just as we can say 'if no works then no justification' but if we do so we are using the if-thens very differently." Helms cites Calvin's subtlety on this point as an example of his positive use of scholastic distinctions in the formulation of his theology.

good works are the *originating cause* for our salvation and fellowship with God. Rather, it means that, because sanctification is the "effect" and "manner" (*modus*) of our free adoption by God, we may say that this adoption is granted to us only when we allow Him to govern us by His Spirit.[58] It is in this sense that we must interpret Scripture when it seems to describe repentance as the cause of our salvation:

> For it is an accustomed method of speaking in Scripture, to denote by the word that (*ut*) the consequence rather than the cause (*consequentiam magis notare quam causam*). For although the grace of God alone begins and completes our salvation; yet, since by obeying the call of God, we fulfill our course, we are said, also in this manner, to obtain the salvation promised by God (*dicimur etiam hoc modo salutem a Deo promissam consequi*).[59]

As the effect of our justification and its necessary accompaniment within the purpose of God's gracious action, sanctification, though not the cause or reason, describes the manner in which God delivers us from the power of sin.[60] Since the promise of salvation is perpetually joined to the doctrine of repentance, it is not possible to taste the goodness of God unless we abhor ourselves on account of sin, and renounce ourselves and the world.[61]

The burden of my comments on Calvin's handling of the relation between justification and sanctification is that he did offer a theological account of the relative order and priority between them. It is certainly true, as Johnson argues, that these benefits are "grounded"

---

58. *Commentary* on Acts 10:43 (*CO* 48.249–50): "…regenerationem spiritus sub fide comprehendi, sicuti eius est effectus. Nam ideo credimus in Christum, partim ut gratuita iustitiae imputatione restituat nos in patris gratiam; partim, ut nos spiritu suo sanctificet. Et scimus, hac lege nos adoptari a Deo in filios, ut spiritu nos suo gubernet."

59. *Commentary* on Genesis 18:19 (*CO* 23.259–60).

60. *Commentary* on Romans 8:2 (*CO* 49.137): "non…causam sed modum tradi duntaxat quo solvimur a reatu." This is but another way of saying, Calvin added, that the "grace of regeneration is never separated from the imputation of righteousness" (*regenerationis gratiam ab imputatione iustitiae nunquam disiungi*). Cf. Sermon on Job 22:1–8 (*CO* 34.280): "Car voila le seul moyen d'obtenir pardon de toutes nos offenses, c'est quand il plaist à Dieu de les couvrir et abolir par sa bonté, et nous en nettoyer par la vertu de son sainct Esprit." Also cf. *Commentary* on Romans 8:17 (*CO* 49.151).

61. *Commentary* on Isaiah 55:7 (*CO* 37.288): "Unde colligimus poenitentiae doctrinam cum promissione salutis perpetuo coniungendam esse: quia non aliter possunt homines gustare bonitatem Dei, quam si displiceant sibi in peccatis suis, sibique et mundo renuntient."

or "based" on the believer's union with Christ. The theme of union with Christ has foundational significance for Calvin's doctrine of grace, to be sure. For this reason, Wenger's claim that Calvin "grounded" sanctification on justification is rather misleading and unhelpful. However, within the broad framework of the doctrine of union with Christ, Calvin did speak of justification as the first or "principal" benefit and of sanctification as the second benefit of God's grace in Christ. When Calvin used this language, he was not simply offering an evaluative comment on the relative importance of these two benefits, justification being "the main hinge" of the Christian religion. He also was maintaining that justification is theologically prior to sanctification because it constitutes the framework within which the Christian life is one of "free" obedience. The Christian's obedience to God is set within the framework of an assurance of God's favor. It is an obedience born of gratitude, not the obedience of a mercenary. For its part, sanctification is the "end" or "goal"; the believer becomes righteous in a way that corresponds to his status as a righteous person. There is a remarkable balance and coordination in Calvin's understanding of these two gospel benefits. But this does not exclude a clear sense of the order or relation between them.

IMPLICATIONS OF CALVIN'S VIEW OF THE TWOFOLD GRACE OF GOD

At times, it might appear that my treatment of Calvin's doctrine of the two benefits of union with Christ is rather arcane, even a case of theological hairsplitting. What difference does it make how Calvin viewed the relation between justification and sanctification? Does it matter whether he ascribed any priority to justification in relation to sanctification, inasmuch as he viewed both benefits from the standpoint of union with Christ? These are legitimate questions, ones that Calvin himself answered at various points in his writings.

There are several important implications of Calvin's teaching regarding believers' participation in the benefits of Christ's saving work on their behalf. Though each of these implications has far-reaching theological and pastoral significance, I will conclude by simply identifying and offering a brief explanation of each of them.

First, Calvin claimed that a failure to distinguish justification and sanctification would lead inevitably to a doctrine and practice that would dishonor God's grace in Christ toward undeserving sinners. A clear and uncompromising insistence on justification by grace alone through faith alone, apart from works of any kind, is the only way to honor the sheer graciousness of the believer's acceptance into favor with God. If the believer's new obedience or sanctification is confused with justification, the perfection and sufficiency of Christ's saving work and righteousness suffer diminishment. When justification and sanctification are confused, the inevitable consequence is human pride before God and ingratitude for the free grace of justification in Christ. In Calvin's striking words, "why do we attempt, to our great harm, to filch from the Lord even a particle of the thanks we owe his free kindness?"[62]

Second, Calvin observed that a failure to distinguish justification and sanctification inevitably will undermine the basis for the believer's comfort and assurance before God.[63] The conscience of the believer will always suffer from anxiety and uncertainty in the presence of God's perfect holiness and righteousness when the believer rests any confidence whatever in his or her works. In Calvin's words, "[n]ow if we ask in what way the conscience can be made quiet before God, we shall find the only way to be that unmerited righteousness be conferred upon us as a gift of God.... For to have faith is not to waver, to vary, to be borne up and down, to hesitate, to be held in suspense, to vacillate—finally, to despair! Rather, to have faith is to strengthen the mind with constant assurance and perfect confidence, to have a place to rest and plant your foot."[64]

Third, contrary to the error of "antinomianism," Calvin offered an exposition of God's grace in Christ that properly included the renewal of the believer by the indwelling power and work of Christ's Spirit. As sharply as Calvin distinguished justification and sanctification, he held them together as the double benefit of Christ's work through His Spirit and Word. In Calvin's understanding of the fullness of Christ's gracious work for His people, the grace of sanctification

---

62. *Institutes* 3.13.1 (*OS* 4.216).

63. Cf. *Institutes* 3.13 (*OS* 4.215–220), which bears the title "Duo esse in gratuita iustificatione observanda." It is noteworthy that a recent study of Calvin's theology takes the theme of God's glory as a central motif in Calvin's thought. See Marijn de Kroon, *The Honour of God and Human Salvation* (Edinburgh: T. & T. Clark, 2001).

64. *Institutes* 3.13.3 (*OS* 4.217).

is strongly emphasized. To separate sanctification from justification would be tantamount to separating the Spirit, who ministers
Christ's benefits to us, from Christ Himself. Or, alternatively stated,
to diminish the work of sanctification would be to deny the threefold office of Christ, who is not only the believer's chief Prophet and
only High Priest but also his eternal King. Good works are necessary
in the salvation of believers, though this should not be understood
to mean that justification needs to be "completed" in sanctification.
Rather, the necessity of sanctification stems from the nature of the
gospel itself: sanctification is as much Christ's and the Spirit's work
as is justification. For this reason, the "motivation" for the believer's
sanctification is not simply "gratitude" for what has been received
in justification. The principal basis for the believer's sanctification
is that it belongs to God's gracious purpose in Christ to renew the
believer in holiness. Judged by Calvin's view, the popular slogan,
"I'm not perfect, just forgiven," presents a half-gospel and therefore
a half-truth. Calvin's summary of the gospel would be better stated,
"I'm not perfect, but I am forgiven and (am being) renewed." In other
words, Calvin offered a compelling antidote to antinomianism, but
without compromising the gospel of God's free grace in Christ.[65]

    Fourth, Calvin's treatment of the twofold grace of God provides
a helpful resolution of the question regarding the so-called "practical
syllogism" (*syllogismus practicus*). At the risk of oversimplification,
this question focuses on the role of the believer's good works in the
assurance of salvation. In Tridentine Catholicism, the faithful are not
able to have such assurance, but can obtain only a relative assurance based on a "moral conjecture." Only a few "saints" are granted
an assurance of their salvation by special revelation. Some students
of the Reformed tradition claim that later Calvinism reintroduced
a form of "moral conjecture" teaching by granting a role to good
works in the believer's obtaining of assurance of salvation. Though
this is not the place to sort out the historical aspects of this question,
it does seem clear that Calvin granted a limited role to good works

---

65. It should also be observed that, in Calvin's understanding of Christ's
work as Mediator, the holy law of God is upheld. Christ's "active" and "passive"
obedience to the law fulfills all of its obligations and constitutes the just basis for
the believer's justification. See my "Calvin's Doctrine of the Imputation of Christ's
Righteousness," 15–47.

as secondary confirmations of the genuineness of faith. Though the assurance of salvation is based or founded principally on the gospel promise of God's grace in Christ, the works of believers, which invariably accompany faith as the Spirit renews the believer in obedience, do constitute a kind of "aid" or, as Calvin put it, an *a posteriori* demonstration that the believer's faith is genuine and not a pretended, hypocritical faith.[66] The assurance that belongs to faith, in Calvin's view, is simply unable to thrive or flourish when it is unaccompanied by any tokens of the Spirit's work in sanctification.

Fifth, Calvin did speak of sanctification as an effect of justification in order to underscore the "freedom" of the believer from the law in its "first use," which is to condemn and expose the sinner to judgment.[67] When sanctification is made a partial cause for justification, those who are regenerate become "mercenary-minded by demanding something from God as their due."[68] When sanctification is placed within the framework of the believer's free justification, however, it represents the free, Spirit-authored life of a forgiven sinner in the presence of his gracious heavenly Father. If sanctification does not occur in the context of the believer's "prior" acceptance with God, it inevitably becomes tainted with the infections of "anxiety" before God ("Have I been sufficiently obedient?"), "pride" ("Surely my good works contribute something to my acceptance with God."), and a "mercenary" spirit ("No doubt, my obedience will prove valuable since God will 'repay' me in kind."). In Calvin's view, the Holy Spirit "enlivens" the law of God by working in the believer a kind of glad-hearted and spontaneous obedience and devotion to God.

In each of these respects, Calvin's handling of the delicate issue of the relation between justification and sanctification remains a helpful benchmark for Reformed believers today.

---

66. *Institutes* 3.4.37 (*OS* 4.129–30): "Est autem argumentum a posteriori, quo aliquid demonstrator a signis sequentibus." On this subject in general, see my *Accepted and Renewed in Christ*, 248–61; Joel Beeke, *The Quest for Full Assurance of Faith* (Edinburgh: Banner of Truth Trust, 1988), 65–72.

67. The priority of justification to sanctification in the order of salvation is similar to the priority of faith to the works faith produces. It is interesting that the Belgic Confession, Art. 24, declares that "it is by faith in Christ that we are justified, even *before* we do good works; otherwise they could not be good works, any more than the fruit of a tree can be good before the tree itself is good" (emphasis mine). This is precisely the point Calvin made.

68. *Commentary* on Romans 4:4 (*CO* 49.70).

CHAPTER 7

Calvin's View of Reprobation

Donald Sinnema

Calvin is well known for his doctrine of predestination, though it was not the central theme of his theology. He emphasized the positive side of predestination, election, which is God's eternal decision or decree to choose some people for salvation—a doctrine he viewed as the foundation initiating divine grace toward humanity and as a source of great comfort and consolation for believers. But for Calvin (and others) there was a shadow side of predestination—reprobation—which is God's eternal decree to send others to a destiny of punishment in hell. It was especially Calvin's teachings on this shadow side that drew criticism of his view of predestination.[1]

Calvin insisted this topic must be approached with utter humility, since we can never comprehend the mystery of God's sovereign choices.[2]

---

1. For Calvin's view of predestination, see C. Friethoff, *Die Prädestinationslehre bei Thomas von Aquin und Calvin* (Freiburg: St. Paulus-Druckerei, 1926); Paul Jacobs, *Prädestination und Verantwortlichkeit bei Calvin* (Neukirchen: Erziehungsvereins, 1937); Fred Klooster, *Calvin's Doctrine of Predestination* (Grand Rapids: Baker, 1977); Heinz Otten, *Prädestination in Calvins theologischer Lehre* (Neukirchen-Vluyn: Neukirchener Verlag des Erziehungsvereins, 1968); A. D. R. Polman, *De Praedestinatieleer van Augustinus, Thomas van Aquino en Calvijn* (Franeker: Wever, 1936), 305–92; Richard Muller, *Christ and the Decree* (Grand Rapids: Baker, 1988), 17–27; and Joel Beeke, "Election and Reprobation: Calvin on Equal Ultimacy," *The Banner of Truth* (June 2004): 8–19.

2. "Letter of Calvin and other Genevan pastors to the Ministers of Switzerland (November 14, 1551)," in *Selected Works of John Calvin: Tracts and Letters,* ed. Jules Bonnet (Grand Rapids: Baker, 1983), 5:325 (*CO* 8.207): "In the reprobate, whom God by his secret counsel passes over and abandons as unworthy, we are taught a clear lesson of humility." See also John Calvin, *Institutes of the Christian Religion,* ed. John T. McNeill, trans. Ford Lewis Battles (Louisville: Westminster John Knox, 1960), 3.21.1. Also, John Calvin, *Congregation sur L'Election Eternelle,* in Philip Holtrop, *The Bolsec Controversy on Predestination, from 1551 to 1555* (Lewiston: Edwin Mellon Press,

BACKGROUND TO CALVIN'S VIEW

Sources

Calvin's view of reprobation may be found wherever he addressed the issue of predestination. This appears largely in four types of his writings.

First, Calvin's most systematic treatment of reprobation occurs in his section on predestination in Book III of his *Institutes*. This section first appeared in his 1539 edition and reached its final form in the 1559 edition. Calvin's first formal treatment of predestination, however, was in his earlier, more popular *Instruction in Faith* of 1537 (chapter 13).

Second, Calvin developed his view of predestination especially in polemical writings in response to opponents who challenged his doctrine. His main polemical works on predestination were: *Congregation sur L'Election Eternelle*, written in 1551 against Jerome Bolsec; *De Aeterna Praedestinatione Dei*, written in 1552 against Albert Pighius and Georgius Siculus; and *Calumniae Nebulonis Cuiusdam de Occulta Providentia Dei*, written in 1558 against Sebastian Castellio.

Third, Calvin also developed his view in his exegetical writings, where he commented on biblical passages that related to predestination. On reprobation, his most important comments are found in his commentary on Romans 9 and 11 (1540) and his lectures on Malachi 1 (1559).

Fourth, Calvin sometimes also addressed reprobation in his sermons, but in a modest way. Of special interest are his thirteen sermons on Jacob and Esau in Genesis 25–27. These were first published in 1560, and appeared in a separate edition in 1562 as *Treze Sermons traitans de l'élection gratuite de Dieu en Iacob, et de la réiection en Esau*.[3]

Though predestination was not the center of Calvin's theology, in him one sees a new preoccupation with this issue, due in part to the influence of Augustine and Martin Bucer,[4] and in part to the

---

1993), 708, 709, 710 (*CO* 8.104, 105, 106, 107). Hereafter this work will be abbreviated as *Congregation*.

3. Wulfert De Greef, *The Writings of John Calvin, Expanded Edition* (Louisville: Westminister John Knox, 2008), 97. The English translation of 1579 has recently been republished as *Sermons on Election and Reprobation* (Audubon, N.J.: Old Paths Publications, 1996). Hereafter this work will be abbreviated as *Sermons*.

4. The topic of predestination shaped the whole of Bucer's theology. In his Romans commentary (1536), Bucer spoke not only of a predestination of saints but

pressure of pastoral concerns and controversy. Calvin presented the essential elements of his view as early as 1539 in the second edition of his *Institutes* and in his Romans commentary (on Romans 9), published the next year. After controversies on this issue with Bolsec, Pighius, Jean Trolliet, and Castellio in the 1550s, Calvin amplified his treatment of reprobation in the final 1559 edition of the *Institutes*.[5] Though Calvin's later writings treating reprobation are more developed, he maintained essentially the same view from the time of his early writings of 1539.

Based on Scripture

It was Calvin's firm conviction that what he taught about predestination, including reprobation, must be drawn only from what God has revealed in Scripture. He acknowledged that any inquiry into predestination penetrates the sacred precincts of divine wisdom. But God "has set forth by his Word the secrets of his will that he has decided to reveal to us. These he decided to reveal in so far as he foresaw that they would concern us and benefit us."[6] So, "let us allow ourselves to be ruled and taught by God, contented by his simple Word and wanting to know nothing more than is to be found there."[7] As for his own teaching, Calvin claimed that "nothing is taught by me concerning this matter that is not plainly declared by God to us all in the sacred scriptures."[8]

In this connection, Calvin warned of two dangers that apply also to reprobation. First, there is the danger of speculation. Much about reprobation is shrouded in mystery that we humans cannot under-

---

of a general predestination by which God destines all things from eternity to some fixed use. Hence, there is also a predestination of the wicked (*praedestinatio malorum*), whereby some are predetermined to perdition. The ultimate purpose (*finem ultimum*) of this is God's glory; its proximate purpose (*proximum finem*) is perdition. Willem van't Spijker, "Prädestination bei Bucer und Calvin," in *Calvinus Theologus*, ed. Wilhelm Neuser (Neukirchen, 1976), 85–111. Via Calvin, the emphasis on God's glory would become a prominent aspect of Reformed discussions of reprobation.

5. François Wendel, *Calvin* (London: Collins, 1972), 264, 269.

6. *Institutes* 3.21.1.

7. John Calvin, *Concerning the Eternal Predestination of God* (London: James Clarke, 1961), 61 (*De Aeterna Dei Praedestinatione*, ed. W. Neuser [Geneva: Librairie Droz, 1998], 26). Hereafter these editions will be abbreviated as *Predestination* and *De Praedestinatione*. Cf. *Commentary* on Romans 9:14; *Sermons*, 53 (*CO* 58.48).

8. *Predestination*, 68 (*De Praedestinatione*, 40); cf. *CO* 8.207.

stand. Hence, if we exceed the bounds of what is revealed in the Word and let our curiosity audaciously seek to search out and unravel the secrets of God, those things that He has willed should remain hidden in Himself, we enter a labyrinth from which we can find no exit. Such mysteries God would rather have us revere with wonder than to understand.[9] We should not be ashamed to be ignorant in these matters, wherein there is a certain "learned ignorance."[10]

Second, there is the danger of silence. Calvin also warned against avoiding the question of reprobation, insofar as it is taught in Scripture: "For Scripture is the school of the Holy Spirit, in which, as nothing is omitted that is both necessary and useful to know, so nothing is taught but what is expedient to know. Therefore we must guard against depriving believers of anything disclosed about predestination in Scripture."[11] Hence, Calvin aimed at a balanced approach, neither speculating where Scripture is silent nor remaining silent where Scripture speaks.

Misunderstandings

Before I examine Calvin's view of reprobation, it is worth addressing some misunderstandings of his position.

First, critics of Calvin have sometimes pointed out that the doctrine of reprobation is so noxious that Calvin considered it a "horrible decree" (*decretum horribile*). He does use this term in the *Institutes*, but *horribile* is better translated as "terrifying" or "dreadful" rather than "horrible." Moreover, it is incorrect that Calvin called reprobation a dreadful decree. Rather, it was God's decree concerning the fall, not His decree to reprobate, that Calvin called a *decretum horribile*.[12] He meant that the divine decree allowing the fall is surrounded by such unfathomable mystery that humans ought to view it with fearful awe.

Second, in his book *Calvin's Doctrine of Predestination*, Fred Klooster mistakenly sees in Calvin a distinction between preterition (the act of passing over) and condemnation as two aspects of reproba-

9. *Institutes* 3.21.1.
10. *Institutes* 3.21.2.
11. *Institutes* 3.21.3.
12. *Institutes* 3.23.7.

tion.[13] While it is true that Calvin implicitly distinguished preterition and (temporal) condemnation, the latter for him is not an aspect of reprobation.

Third, scholars sometimes confuse the crucial distinction between reprobation and condemnation that Calvin maintained. Ford Lewis Battles' translation of Calvin's *Institutes* often mistranslates *reprobare* as "condemn." Besides contributing to such confusion, this rendering of the term tends to obscure the role of reprobation in this translation of the *Institutes*.

Fourth, some scholars have tried to minimize the significance of reprobation for Calvin's theology. This tends to be the case, for example, with Edward Dowey, who argues that reprobation is subordinate and secondary to election in Calvin's theology, and that it is an isolated, fragmentary doctrine.[14] In a similar vein, Holmes Rolston III suggests that reprobation is inconsistent with the heart of Calvin's teaching.[15] Likewise, Robert Shank contends that Calvin is contradictory in asserting that God preordains the reprobate to damnation simply by His pleasure without regard to anything in them, and yet the cause of their perdition is in themselves.[16]

SPECIFICS OF CALVIN'S VIEW

Starting Point

From a systematic standpoint, it is noteworthy that Calvin began his treatment of predestination in the *Institutes* from an experiential starting point, rather than beginning with the divine decree. In Book III, within the context of soteriology, his discussion of the topic begins with the reality of the varied ways that preaching is received: "In actual fact, the covenant of life is not preached equally among all

---

13. Klooster, *Calvin's Doctrine of Predestination*, 59, 71, 76, 77.

14. Edward Dowey, *The Knowledge of God in Calvin's Theology* (Grand Rapids: Eerdmans, 1994), 211–9.

15. Holmes Rolston III, *John Calvin Versus the Westminster Confession* (Richmond: John Knox Press, 1972), 30. On this issue, see Tony Lane, "The Quest for the Historical Calvin," *Evangelical Quarterly* 55 (1983): 109–10.

16. Robert Shank, Appendix D: "Calvin's View of Reprobation, and his Erroneous Fundamental Assumption," in *Life in the Son* (Minneapolis: Bethany House, 1989), 345–57. Shank's critique also confuses the distinction between reprobation and condemnation.

men, and among those to whom it is preached, it does not gain the same acceptance either constantly or in equal degree."[17]

To explain this diverse response to the gospel, Calvin then rose to eternal election and reprobation:

> It comes to pass by God's bidding that salvation is freely offered to some while others are barred from access to it.... We shall never be clearly persuaded, as we ought to be, that our salvation flows from the wellspring of God's free mercy until we come to know his eternal election, which illumines God's grace by this contrast: that he does not indiscriminately adopt all into the hope of salvation but gives to some what he denies to others.[18]

Similarly, Calvin's first treatment of predestination in his 1537 *Instruction in Faith* began with the contrasting attitudes of believers and unbelievers to the call of the gospel and then rose to God's counsel. The seed of the Word takes root only in those whom the Lord predestined to be His children; to all others, "who by the same counsel of God are rejected [*reprouvez*] before the foundation of the world," preaching can be nothing but an odor of death unto death.[19]

Double Predestination

Calvin openly taught a doctrine of double predestination, consisting of election and reprobation. He described it as follows:

> We call predestination God's eternal decree [*decretum*], by which he compacted [*constitutum habuit*] with himself what he willed to become of each man. For not all are created in equal condition; rather, eternal life is foreordained [*praeordinatur*] for some, eternal damnation [*damnatio*] for others. Therefore, as any man has been created to one or the other of these ends [*finem*], we speak of him as predestined to life or to death [*ad vitam vel ad mortem praedestinatum*].[20]

Calvin was by no means original in advocating double predestination. Augustine taught a predestination to eternal life and to eternal death. In the seventh century, Isidore of Seville was the

---

17. *Institutes* 3.21.1.

18. Ibid.

19. John Calvin, *Instruction in Faith (1537)* (Philadelphia: Westminster Press, 1949), 36 (CO 22.46).

20. *Institutes* 3.21.5. This definition first appeared in the 1539 edition and remained unchanged in later editions. Cf. 3.21.1.

first to actually speak of "double predestination," and in the ninth century, Gottschalk presented a rigorous form of double predestination. Throughout the medieval period, single predestination of the elect alone was the prevalent view (including Aquinas); yet, at the same time, reprobation was also taught—alongside or opposite to predestination, rather than as part of it.[21] In the late medieval period, the Augustinian Thomas Bradwardine revived the concept of double predestination. Then, among the Reformers, Martin Luther and Bucer both taught forms of double predestination before Calvin did.[22] But it was especially Calvin's firm advocacy of double predestination that popularized the idea in Reformed circles.

Election Implies Reprobation

In Calvin's view, the act of election implies reprobation: "Election itself could not stand except as set over against [*opposita*] reprobation."[23] God cannot elect or choose some without rejecting others: "There is certainly a mutual relation between the elect and the reprobate, so that election...cannot stand, unless we confess that God separated out [*segregasse*] from others certain men as seemed good to him."[24] The French of this passage is even clearer: "God in choosing has separated [*separé*] his own from among others, so that he cannot elect without electing some and rejecting [*rejetté*] others."[25] Elsewhere Calvin asserted: "For just as God elected some, he rejected [*reietté*] all whom he pleased—and the one side entails [*emporte*] the other. For when there is an election, one does not take all, but elects a part."[26]

Though Calvin could thus present reprobation as a logical implication of election, his usual emphasis was that he simply taught

---

21. R. Scott Clark, in "Election and Predestination: The Sovereign Expressions of God," in *Theological Guide to Calvin's Institutes*, eds. David Hall and Peter Lillback (Phillipsburg: P&R, 2008), 91–5, overstates the prevalence of double predestination in the medieval period when he concludes that it was a catholic doctrine that was the common property since Augustine.

22. For a history of double predestination from Augustine to Calvin, see Donald Sinnema, "The Issue of Reprobation at the Synod of Dort (1618–19) in Light of the History of this Doctrine" (Ph.D. dissertation, University of St. Michael's College, Toronto, 1985), 8–59.

23. *Institutes* 3.23.1.

24. *Predestination*, 68 (*De Praedestinatione*, 40).

25. *De Praedestinatione*, 41.

26. *Congregation*, 712 (*CO* 8.109).

what Scripture teaches about the matter: "As Scripture, then, clearly shows, we say that God once established [*constituisse*] by his eternal and unchangeable plan [*consilio*] those whom he long before willed [*vellet*] once for all to receive into salvation, and those whom, on the other hand, he willed to devote to destruction [*devovere exitio*]."[27]

No Definition

Calvin did not offer a formal definition of reprobation, but its meaning is clear in the terminology he used in presenting this concept. He employed various terms and phrases such as to "reprobate" (*reprobare*),[28] "reject" (*reicere*),[29] "predestine to death" (*praedestinare ad mortem*),[30] "predestine to destruction" (*praedestinare ad interitum, praedestinare ad exitium*),[31] "predestine to punishment" (*praedestinare ad poenam*),[32] "predestine to damnation" (*praedestinare ad damnationem*),[33] "destine to death" (*destinare morti*),[34] "destine to destruction" (*destinare exitio, destinare ad interitum*),[35] "devote to destruction" (*devovere exitio*),[36] "preordain damnation" (*praeordinare damnationem*),[37] "pass over" (*praeterire*),[38] and "prepared for destruction" (*praeparata ad interitum, comparata in exitium*).[39]

---

27. *Institutes* 3.21.7; cf. 3.21.2; 3.23.1; *Predestination*, 56, 58 (*De Praedestinatione*, 18, 20).

28. *Institutes* 3.23.10: "God chooses [*eligere*] as sons those whom he pleases, according to the decision of his good pleasure, without any regard for merit, while he rejects [*reiectis*] and reprobates [*reprobatis*] others"; 3.24.12: "He leaves [*deserit*] in blindness those whom he once reprobated [*semel reprobavit*], deprived of participation in his light." The term *reprobare* occurs multiple times in Calvin's predestination writings.

29. *Institutes* 3.21.7: "God by his secret plan [*consilio*] freely chooses [*elegit*] whom he pleases, rejecting [*reiectis*] others"; 3.21.5; 3.22.11; 3.23.10; *De Praedestinatione*, 20, 178; *Commentary* on Romans 9:11.

30. *Institutes* 3.23.3; *Commentary* on Romans 9:19.

31. *Institutes* 3.21, title; 3.21.1; *De Praedestinatione*, 186.

32. *De Praedestinatione*, 38; *CO* 9.263, 297.

33. *Commentary* on Romans 9:11.

34. *Institutes* 3.23,3; *De Praedestinatione*, 144; *Commentary* on Romans 9:19.

35. *Institutes* 3.24.14; 3.24, title; *De Praedestinatione*, 12,16,70,140,194; *Commentary* on Romans 9:11.

36. *Institutes* 3.23.1; *De Praedestinatione*, 82, 166; *Commentary* on Romans 9:22.

37. *Institutes* 3.21.5.

38. *Institutes* 3.23.1; 3.23.10; *De Praedestinatione*, 18, 142; *Commentary* on Romans 9:11; *CO* 9.293.

39. *Institutes* 3.23.1; *De Praedestinatione*, 192, 212; *Commentary* on Romans 9:22, 23.

For Calvin, reprobation clearly involves a passing over of some in the election of others: "God in electing according to his own decision passes over [*praeterit*] others."[40] "Those whom God passes over [*praeterit*], he reprobates [*reprobat*]."[41] By his eternal plan, God distinguishes (*discernit*)[42] or separates (*segregat*)[43] the elect from the reprobate. But it involves more than a passing over. As the terms above indicate, reprobation is also a positive rejecting or predestining to eternal damnation or destruction.

Calvin included these aspects in a unified concept of reprobation without using the late medieval distinction between negative and positive reprobation, the decree to pass over (preterition) and the decree to condemn (predamnation). Beginning with Nicolas of Lyra, this distinction had become popular in late medieval Catholic theology, but Calvin and the early Reformers did not adopt the distinction. Only in the late sixteenth century was the distinction finally taken up by Reformed theology.[44]

Decree from Eternity

For Calvin, predestination involves a pure act of God's will expressed in an eternal plan—referred to as God's counsel (*consilium*), decree (*decretum*), plan (*propositum*), or decision (*arbitrium*)—concerning the destiny of the elect and the reprobate.[45]

Like election, reprobation is an act of God's will made from eternity: "God is said to have ordained from eternity [*ab aeterno ordinasse*] those whom he wills to embrace in love, and those upon whom he wills to vent his wrath."[46] For Calvin, "from eternity" meant before

---

40. *Institutes* 3.22.1.

41. *Institutes* 3.23.1; see also 3.23.10; *Predestination*, 56, 120 (*De Praedestinatione*, 18, 142); *Commentary* on Romans 9:11; CO 8.207.

42. *Institutes* 3.24.15; see also 3.22.4; 3.22.6; 3.22.7; 3.24.12; *Predestination*, 85, 120 (*De Praedestinatione*, 74, 142); *Commentary* on Romans 9:11.

43. *Institutes* 3.22.2; 3.22.6; *Predestination*, 68 (*De Praedestinatione*, 40).

44. On this late medieval distinction, see Sinnema, "The Issue of Reprobation," 32–40, 76–7, 87–8, 107–10, 112.

45. E.g., *Institutes* 3.21.5; 3.23.1; 3.24.15.

46. *Institutes* 3.24.17; cf. CO 8.210; CO 22.46: "*les autres, qui par mesme conseil de Dieu devant la constitution du monde sont reprouvez.*"

the creation of the world, following the language of Scripture (Eph. 1:4: "before the foundation of the world").[47]

Supralapsarian or Infralapsarian?

It is anachronistic to label Calvin's position either supralapsarian or infralapsarian, since this issue did not become clearly defined in terms of alternative formulations until later in the sixteenth century. His successor, Theodore Beza, was the first true supralapsarian.[48] Although Calvin sometimes spoke of God predestining man before he was created or fallen,[49] in some passages he spoke in a more Augustinian fashion of God electing or reprobating from the fallen mass of perdition.[50] Calvin can certainly not be called a supralapsarian or infralapsarian in the fully developed sense of these terms, for he did not formulate his position in either of the two classic ways in which this issue was later defined — in terms of an order of divine decrees or in terms of identifying the "object" of predestination to be man considered as fallen or man considered as not yet fallen or created. Nowhere in his writings did Calvin speak of an order of decrees; he did not speculate about whether in God's mind the decree to elect or to reprobate preceded or followed the decree of the fall.[51]

---

47. *Institutes* 3.22.1: "*ante mundi creationem*"; *CO* 8.18: "*ante mundi originem*"; *Commentary* on Romans 11:7: "*ante mundi creationem reprobati sunt a Deo*"; *CO* 8.96, 98: "*devant la creation du monde*"; *CO* 8.103: "*avant que le monde fust creé*"; *Commentary* on Ephesians 1:4; *Commentary* on Titus 1:2.

48. Donald Sinnema, "Beza's View of Predestination in Historical Perspective," in *Théodore de Bèze (1519–1605)*, ed. Irena Backus (Geneva: Librairie Droz, 2007), 225–9.

49. *Institutes* 2.12.5; 3.23.7; *Predestination*, 101, 121 (*De Praedestinatione*, 102, 104, 144).

50. For example, *Predestination*, 125 (*De Praedestinatione*, 150, 152): "God elected and reprobated out of the mass of perdition (*ex perdita massa*) those whom he willed"; "God elected out of the condemned race of Adam (*ex damnata Adae sobole*) those whom he pleased and reprobated whom he willed." See also *Institutes* 3.23.3; *Predestination*, 89, 101, 121 (*De Praedestinatione*, 82, 102, 144); *Congregation*, 700, 713 (*CO* 8.95, 109).

51. On this issue, see K. Dijk, *De Strijd over Infra- en Supralapsarisme in de Gereformeerde Kerken van Nederland* (Kampen: Kok, 1912), 12–13, 21–7, 30; Otten, *Prädestination*, 91–9; Klooster, *Calvin's Doctrine*, 33; Polman, *De Predestinatieleer*, 377; and J. Fesko, "Diversity within the Reformed Tradition: Supra- and Infralapsarianism in Calvin, Dort, and Westminster" (Ph.D. dissertation, University of Aberdeen, 1999), 81–139. Dijk mistakenly identifies as supralapsarian all who state that God predestined the fall and not just permitted it; hence he considers Calvin to be

Reprobation and Damnation

In Calvin's writings, it is very important to distinguish reprobation from damnation (*damnatio*), condemnation (*condemnatio*), or perdition (*perditio*), which involves some form of temporal judgment, such as the original condemnation of all men in Adam, temporal punishments, or final damnation to the punishments of hell.[52] Reprobation is God's decree to condemn, made in eternity before the foundation of the world; the actual damnation of the reprobate will occur at the end of history. Hence, Calvin said that God uses for good even evil things "to the damnation [*damnationem*] of those whom he had justly predestined to punishment [*praedestinavit ad poenam*]."[53] Likewise, he said, perdition depends on predestination.[54]

Calvin's references to God leaving (*relinquit*) or abandoning (*deserit*) the reprobate in their own destruction do not describe the eternal act of reprobating, but should be understood in the temporal sense of what happens to the reprobate in the course of history after the fall.[55] Thus, he asserted, God "leaves [*relinquit*] the world in its own destruction, to which it has been destined,"[56] and "he leaves [*deserit*] in blindness those whom he has once reprobated."[57]

Cause of Reprobation

Why does God reprobate some people? Calvin's fundamental answer was that the cause of reprobation is found in God's will alone:

> The reason [*causam*] why God elects some and reprobates others is to be found nowhere else than in his plan [*proposito*].[58]

> If, then, we cannot determine a reason [*rationem*] why he vouchsafes mercy to his own, except that it so pleases him, neither

---

supralapsarian. Fesko also mistakenly labels Calvin as supralapsarian, since he identifies as supralapsarian all who place the cause of election and reprobation solely in God's will apart from any consideration of human actions. Others consider Calvin to be infralapsarian, including Henri Blocher, "Calvin Infralapsaire," *La Revue Réformé* 31 (1980): 270–76; and Francis Turretin, *Institutes of Elenctic Theology* (Phillipsburg, N.J.: P&R, 1992), 1:349–50.

52. *Predestination*, 121 (*De Praedestinatione*, 144).
53. *Predestination*, 67 (*De Praedestinatione*, 38).
54. *Institutes*, 3.23.8.
55. *Predestination*, 102, 121 (*De Praedestinatione*, 104, 144).
56. *Institutes* 3.22.7.
57. *Institutes* 3.24.12.
58. *Commentary* on Romans 9:14 (*CO* 49.180).

shall we have another reason for reprobating [*reprobandis*] others, other than his will [*voluntatem*].[59]

God elects as sons those whom he pleases, according to the decision of his good pleasure [*secundum beneplaciti sui arbitrio*], without any regard for merit, while rejecting and reprobating others.... The fact that God therefore elects one man but rejects [*reiecto*] another arises not out of regard to the man but solely from his mercy.[60]

God, by his eternal good pleasure [*beneplacito*], which has no cause [*causa*] outside of itself, destined those whom he pleased to salvation, rejecting [*reiectis*] the rest.[61]

This is particularly true of that aspect of reprobation by which God distinguished the reprobate from the elect: "Those whom God passes over, he reprobates; and this he does for no other reason [*causa*] than that he wills to exclude [*vult excludere*] them from the inheritance which he predestines for his own children."[62] Such distinguishing or reprobating has an unknown reason hidden in God's will, Calvin said, and yet God is just in so doing:

The cause of discrimination [*causam discriminis*], which might otherwise be sought in the merits of each [Jacob and Esau], Paul assigns to the hidden counsel [*recondito consilio*] of God.[63]

The will of God, the cause [*causa*] of which neither appears nor ought to be sought outside of himself, distinguishes some from others.[64]

God had just causes [*iustas causas*] for reprobating part of mankind, though they are hidden from us.[65]

God reprobates them inasmuch as they are not chosen and elect. Nevertheless, we must recognize that God is just, even though

---

59. *Institutes* 3.22.11.

60. *Institutes* 3.23.10.

61. *Predestination*, 58 (*De Praedestinatione*, 20); cf. *Institutes* 3.23.2.

62. *Institutes* 3.23.1. See also 3.22.7; *Predestination*, 82, 85, 94, 120, 140 (*De Praedestinatione*, 66, 74, 90, 142, 178).

63. *Predestination*, 78 (*De Praedestinatione*, 58).

64. *Institutes* 3.22.4.

65. *Predestination*, 99 (*De Praedestinatione*, 100); cf. *Congregation*, 709–10 (*CO* 8.105–106).

we cannot comprehend the cause [*la cause*]. He does not have to give an account of himself to us.[66]

The rebellion of the others proves the latter were forsaken [*derelictos*]. No other cause [*causa*] of this fact can be adduced but reprobation [*reprobatio*], which is hidden [*abscondita*] in God's secret plan [*arcano consilio*].[67]

The Lord has created those whom he unquestionably foreknew would go to destruction. This has happened because he has so willed it. But why he so willed, it is not for our reason to inquire, for we cannot comprehend it.[68]

The cause of eternal reprobation [*aeternae reprobationis causa*] is so hidden from us, that we can do nothing else but wonder at the incomprehensible counsel of God.[69]

In the late medieval period, a common view, shared by Calvin's opponents Pighius and Castellio, was that the cause of reprobation was the evil that God from eternity foreknew in the reprobate, on which basis He decreed their condemnation.[70] But Calvin was insistent that God's distinguishing between elect and reprobate was not caused by sin or by a foreknowledge of their sin, since the elect and the reprobate are equally unworthy. If all are equally sinful, what is there in the elect to be foreknown by God that could at all distinguish them from the reprobate? God would not foresee anything in either of them that was not worthy of destruction.[71] For Calvin, God's foreknowledge is based on His decree, not vice versa.[72] To show that election and reprobation cannot be caused by human merit or demerit, Calvin also liked to appeal to Romans 9, where Paul pointed out that God distinguished between Jacob and Esau before they were born, before they did any good or evil.[73]

While Calvin's stress on God's sovereignty usually directed him

---

66. *Congregation*, 714 (*CO* 8.111); cf. 709–10 (*CO* 8.105–106).
67. *Institutes* 3.23.4.
68. *Institutes* 3.23.5.
69. *Commentary* on Romans 11:7; see also *Commentary* on Romans 9:14, 18, 22, and *Commentary* on Malachi 1:2–6 (*CO* 44.406–409); *Sermons*, 33 (*CO* 58.36).
70. *Predestination*, 55 (*De Praedestinatione*, 14).
71. *Institutes* 2.22.4; *Predestination*, 81, 115 (*De Praedestinatione*, 64, 130); *Commentary* on Romans 9:11.
72. *Institutes* 3.23.7.
73. *Commentary* on Romans 9:11.

to God's will as the cause of reprobation, his early 1540 commentary on Romans contained a reference, in his comment on Romans 9:11, to the curse inherited by all in Adam as the proximate cause of reprobation (*propinquam reprobationis causam*), whereas God has a just cause (*iustam causam*) for election and reprobation in His own will.[74] Calvin did not develop this idea of the proximate cause of reprobation in his later writings.[75]

Causes of Damnation

As Calvin distinguished reprobation from damnation, he also identified different causes of reprobation and damnation. While the sole cause of reprobation is hidden in God's will, the cause of damnation is twofold: human sin and God's will. Even though God from eternity reprobated some by His sovereign will, Calvin insisted that the reprobate themselves always deserve their damnation and God is just in condemning them:

> The cause of damnation [*damnationis causam*]...they are compelled to recognize in themselves.... But though I should confess a hundred times that God is the author [*authorem*] of it—which is very true—yet they do not promptly cleanse away the guilt [*crimen*] that, engraved upon their consciences, repeatedly meets their eyes.[76]

> The fact that the reprobate do not obey God's Word when it is made known to them will be justly charged against the malice and depravity of their hearts, provided it be added at the same time that they have been given over to this depravity [*in hanc*

---

74. *Commentary* on Romans 9:11 (*CO* 49.178). Likewise, commenting on Romans 11:7, Calvin again made use of the proximate-remote distinction to explain the causes of reprobation: "Indeed, the cause [*causa*] of eternal reprobation is so hidden from us, that we can do nothing else but wonder at the incomprehensible counsel of God.... It is foolishness to try to conceal beneath the garb of proximate causes [*propinquis causis*], as soon as we hear them mentioned, this first cause [*primam*] which is hidden from our notice, as though God had not freely decided before the fall of Adam to do what He thought best with the whole human race" (*CO* 49.216). Cf. *Commentary* on Malachi 1:2–6 (*CO* 44.407).

75. The English translation of *Predestination*, 160, incorrectly reads: "Paul indeed defines the proximate cause of reprobation [*primam reprobationis orginem*] as unbelief in the Gospel." Calvin does not actually refer to a proximate cause here (cf. *De Praedestinatione*, 220).

76. *Institutes* 3.23.3.

pravitatem addictos], because they have been raised up by the just but inscrutable judgment [*iudicio*] of God to show forth his glory in their damnation.... [Regarding Eli's sons,] it is not denied that their stubbornness arose out of their own wickedness; but at the same time it is noted why they were left [*deserti*] in their stubbornness,... because his immutable decree [*decretum*] had once for all destined them to destruction.[77]

Regarding the twofold cause of damnation, Calvin sometimes expressed this in a distinction between proximate and remote causes (*causae propinquae et remotae*). Though the remote and hidden cause of damnation lies in God's will, the proximate and evident cause is man's original corruption and sin:[78]

> The destruction they undergo by predestination is also most just. Besides, their perdition [*perditio*] depends on the predestination of God in such a way that the cause and occasion [*causa et materia*] of it are found in themselves.... Accordingly, we should contemplate the evident cause of damnation [*evidentem damnationis causam*] in the corrupt nature of humanity—which is closer [*propinquior*] to us—rather than seek the hidden [*absconditam*] and utterly incomprehensible cause in God's predestination.[79]

> I teach that a man ought rather to search for the cause of his condemnation [*la cause de sa damnation*] in his corrupt nature, than in the predestination of God.... I expressly state that there are two causes [*deux causes*]: the one *concealed* [*cachee*] in the eternal counsel of God, and the other open and *manifest* [*patente*] in the sin of man.... Here then, Messieurs, is the very core of the whole question: that I say that all the reprobate will be convicted of guilt by their own consciences, and that thus their condemnation is righteous, and that they err in neglecting what is quite

---

77. *Institutes* 3.24.14; see also 3.23.9; *Predestination*, 156 (*De Praedestinatione*, 210); *Commentary* on Romans 11:7; and *CO* 58.202.

78. Some scholars have mistakenly interpreted these passages, which refer to proximate and remote causes of temporal damnation, as referring to eternal reprobation. E.g., Klooster, *Calvin's Doctrine*, 70–1; Jacobs, *Prädestination*, 143. On Calvin's distinction between proximate and remote causality, see Donald Sinnema, "Calvin and Beza: The Role of the Decree-Execution Distinction in their Theologies," in *Calvinus Evangelii Propugnator: Calvin, Champion of the Gospel*, eds. David Wright, Anthony Lane, and Jon Balserak (Grand Rapids: Calvin Studies Society, 2006), 196–8.

79. *Institutes* 3.23.8. This passage first appeared in the 1539 edition.

evident [*evident*] to enter instead into the secret counsels [*conseil estroit*] of God, which to us are inaccessible.[80]

Calvin also used the remote-proximate distinction to explain how both God and Pharaoh could be the causes of the hardening of Pharaoh's heart:

> If the will of God is the highest or remote cause [*summa vel remota causa*] of the hardening, man himself, who hardens his own heart, is the more proximate cause [*propior causa*]. I everywhere distinguish the first or remote cause [*primam causam vel remotam*] from middle and proximate causes [*mediis et propinquis*].[81]

Objection

It is precisely on this issue of causality that Calvin encountered the most critical objection to his doctrine of reprobation. Pighius raised the objection: If God distinguished the elect from the reprobate before the fall of man, does it not follow that the reprobate are condemned not because they were lost in Adam but because before the fall they were devoted to destruction?[82] In other words, doesn't Calvin teach that the reprobate are condemned to eternal punishment simply because God decreed to reprobate them rather than because they deserved it as a just penalty for their sins?

In reply to such objections, Calvin emphasized that, though God from eternity reprobated some people by His sovereign will, the reprobate themselves always deserve their destruction and God is just in condemning them.[83] The reprobate are justly left in death, for in Adam they are dead and damned.[84] They deserve to be given over to a reprobate mind.[85] This solution shifted the focus of attention from the decree to the temporal damnation of the reprobate. It is on this level of actual damnation that Calvin insisted a distinction is to be made between proximate and remote causes. Though, indeed, the

---

80. Letter of Calvin to the Syndics of Geneva in the case of Jean Trolliet, Oct. 6, 1552, in *Selected Works*, 5:366–7 (CO 14.380).

81. Calvin, *Calumniae Nebulonis Cuiusdam de Occulta Dei Providentia* (CO 9.306). Calvin wrote this work on secret providence in 1558 to counter Castellio.

82. *Predestination*, 100 (*De Praedestinatione*, 102).

83. *Predestination*, 98, 120, 146, 156 (*De Praedestinatione*, 98, 142, 192, 212).

84. *Predestination*, 121 (*De Praedestinatione*, 144).

85. *Predestination*, 155 (*De Praedestinatione*, 210).

remote cause of damnation and destruction is God's will, its proximate cause is man's original corruption and sin. This distinction, Calvin asserted, Pighius failed to recognize:

> It is no wonder that Pighius should indiscriminately...confuse everything in the judgments of God, when he does not distinguish between causes proximate and remote [*causas propinquas et remotas*].... We cannot avoid concluding that the first origin of ruin [*prima interitus origo*] is in Adam and that we individually find the proximate cause [*proximam causam*] in ourselves. What can then prevent our faith from adoring from afar [*procul*] with due humility the hidden counsel of God by which the fall of man was foreordained, and yet acknowledging what appears closer [*propius*], that the whole human race in the person of Adam is bound to the penalty of eternal death and therefore subject to death? Therefore Pighius has not shattered, as he thought, the splendid and fitting symmetry [*symmetriam*] in which the causes proximate and remote [*causa propinqua et remota*] agree with one another.[86]

> The fault of our damnation [*damnationis culpa*] so resides in ourselves that it is forbidden to assemble extraneous pretexts with which to cover it. But it was permissible thus briefly to show how preposterously Pighius removes the remote cause [*remotam*] by bringing forward the proximate [*propinquae causae*]. He contends that the impious will be damned because they have provoked the wrath of God on themselves by their own misdeeds [the proximate cause]. From this he concludes that their damnation does not proceed from the decree of God [the remote cause].[87]

Since the proximate cause is their own sin, Calvin concludes that the blame for their destruction remains in the reprobate themselves, not in God. How God's decree could be the remote cause and yet not implicate Him as the author of sin was for Calvin a mystery known to God alone.[88]

---

86. *Predestination*, 100–101 (*De Praedestinatione*, 102).
87. *Predestination*, 116 (*De Praedestinatione*, 132).
88. *Predestination*, 124 (*De Praedestinatione*, 148).

OUTWORKINGS OF CALVIN'S VIEW

The Purpose of Reprobation

Like Bucer, Calvin saw the main purpose or end of reprobation as the revealing of God's glory: "The reprobate are raised up to the end [*finem*] that through them God's glory may be revealed."[89] Following Proverbs 16:4 ("The Lord hath made all things for himself; yea, even the wicked for the day of evil"), Calvin asserted that the wicked "have been created with the intent that they might perish [*destinato creatos ut perirent*]."[90] "The wicked were created for the day of destruction [*in diem exitii*] simply because God willed to illustrate his own glory in them; just as elsewhere he declares that Pharaoh was raised up by him that he might show forth his name among the Gentiles (Exod. 9:16)."[91] On the basis of this latter passage, Calvin also asserted that the "reprobate are set aside by the counsel of God to the end [*finem*] that in them he might demonstrate his power."[92] Moreover, he pointed out that the reprobate were created for destruction for the specific purpose of being instruments of God's wrath and examples of His severity:

> What of those, then, whom he created for dishonor in life and destruction in death, to become the instruments of this wrath and examples of his severity [*in vitae contumeliam et mortis exitium creavit, ut irae suae organa forent, et severitatis exempla*]? That they may come to their end, he sometimes deprives them of the capacity to hear his word; at other times he, rather, blinds and stuns them by the preaching of it.[93]

Later, in 1558, in response to criticism from Castellio, Calvin

---

89. *Institutes* 3.22.11; cf. 3.23.6.

90. *Commentary* on Romans 9:18 (*CO* 49.184); cf. *Institutes* 3.21.5; *Sermons*, 48 (*CO* 58.45).

91. *Predestination*, 97 (*De Praedestinatione*, 94).

92. *Predestination*, 84 (*De Praedestinatione*, 70); cf. *Commentary* on Romans 9:17.

93. *Institutes* 3.24.12. This passage is found already in the 1539 edition. Heinrich Bullinger quoted this passage in a March 3, 1553, letter to the early English Calvinist Bartholomew Traheron; he considered too harsh Calvin's statement that God created people for destruction (*CO* 14.489–90). Cf. *Commentary* on Romans 9:22: "He does so in order to demonstrate evidence of his severity, so that others may be stricken with terror at such fearful examples."

clarified his position by denying that he had ever stated that "the purpose [*finem*] of creation is eternal destruction."[94]

In Romans 9:22–23, Calvin found a second reason why God reveals His glory in the destruction of the reprobate: to confirm more clearly the fullness of divine mercy toward the elect. When they see how wretched are the reprobate, God's "infinite mercy toward the elect is more and more commended [*commendetur*]."[95] Reprobation makes the extent of His mercy toward the elect "better known and [makes it] shine with greater clarity"[96]: "Let us consider the reprobate, and learn to look at ourselves in their persons. We shall then say: 'It could be so with us, if God had not employed his fatherly goodness to separate us from them.'"[97]

Preaching and Reprobation

With Augustine, Calvin shared the fundamental assumption that we humans cannot identify the reprobate; only God knows who they are: "Since we do not know who belongs to the number of the predestined and who does not, it befits us so to feel as to wish that all be saved. So it will come about that, whoever we come across, we shall study to make him a sharer of peace."[98]

This view has a direct impact on preaching. So, for Calvin, the preaching of the gospel is shared by the elect and the reprobate.[99] There are two kinds of calling. By a general call (*universalis vocatio*), "God invites all equally to himself through the outward preaching of the Word"; by a special call, given for the most part to believers alone, God causes the preached Word to dwell in their hearts by the inward illumination of His Spirit.[100] The general call of the gospel "offers salvation to all.... All are equally called to penitence and faith; the same mediator is set forth for all to reconcile them to the Father."[101] But, Calvin asserts, the real question is whether the Lord in

---

94. *Calumniae, CO* 9.288.
95. *Commentary* on Romans 9:23.
96. *Commentary* on Romans 9:22.
97. *Congregation*, 715 (*CO* 8.112).
98. *Predestination*, 138 (*De Praedestinatione*, 176). This sentiment of Augustine Calvin repeated in *Institutes* 3.23.14.
99. *Institutes* 3.24.1.
100. *Institutes* 3.24.8; cf. *CO* 9.306.
101. *Predestination*, 103 (*De Praedestinatione*, 106).

His counsel destines salvation equally for all. Many are called by His external voice, but few believe.[102] Not all respond in belief "because not all were ordained to eternal life."[103] God effectively teaches only the elect, that He may lead them to faith.[104] Hence, God wills all to be saved, according to 1 Timothy 2:4, in the sense of all whom He mercifully invites by preaching to Christ.[105]

Calvin described the purpose of preaching and its effect on the reprobate in a number of ways. God's mercy is offered equally to both the elect and the reprobate, "so that those who are not inwardly taught are rendered only inexcusable."[106] Preaching of the Word is an odor of life to life for the elect, but for the reprobate it is an odor of death and the occasion for more severe condemnation.[107] The reprobate will receive a heavier judgment "because they reject the testimony of God's love; and God also, to show forth his glory, withdraws the effectual working of his Spirit from them."[108] Hence God sends His Word to many whose blindness He intends to increase; for example, to Pharaoh:

> Observe that he directs his voice to them but in order that they may become even more deaf; he kindles a light but that they may be made even more blind; he sets forth doctrine but that they may grow even more stupid; he employs a remedy but so that they may not be healed.... We cannot gainsay the fact that, to those whom he pleases not to illumine, God transmits his doctrine wrapped in enigmas in order that they may not profit from it except to be cast into greater stupidity.[109]

As for preaching the topic of predestination itself (including reprobation), Calvin followed Augustine in asserting that predestination ought to be forthrightly preached, as commended by Scripture, so "that he who has ears may hear of the grace of God and glory not in

---

102. Ibid.
103. *Predestination*, 104 (*De Praedestinatione*, 108).
104. *Institutes* 3.24.1.
105. *Predestination*, 109 (*De Praedestinatione*, 120).
106. *Predestination*, 103 (*De Praedestinatione*, 108); cf. *Sermons*, 59, 63 (*CO* 58.52, 54); *CO* 58.199.
107. *Institutes* 3.24.8; *Predestination*, 105 (*De Praedestinatione*, 110).
108. *Institutes* 3.24.2.
109. *Institutes* 3.24.13.

himself but in God."[110] But such preaching should be tempered and fittingly presented so as to avoid giving offence. He offered a couple of examples of blatantly offensive preaching of reprobation:

> If anyone addresses the people in this way: "If you do not believe, the reason is that you have already been divinely destined for destruction," he not only fosters sloth but also gives place to evil intention. If anyone extends to the future also the statement that they who hear will not believe because they are reprobate, this will be cursing rather than teaching. Augustine, therefore, rightly bids such men begone from the church, as foolish teachers or perverse and foreboding prophets.[111]

Proper preaching of predestination, Calvin insisted, must remember that we humans do not know who is elect and who is not, so we ought to wish that all men may be saved.[112] Calvin added that in such preaching there is a place for rebuke of both the elect and reprobate:

> A healthy and severe rebuke should be applied as a medicine to all that they may not either perish themselves or destroy others. It belongs to God, however, to make that rebuke useful to those whom he…has foreknown and predestined.[113]

In his sermons on Jacob and Esau in Genesis 25, we can see how Calvin actually preached reprobation. He did so in a way that placed emphasis on the election of Jacob as a source of consolation for believers and touched only very lightly on the reprobation of Esau.[114]

Conclusion

It is clear that Calvin developed the idea of reprobation much more than the other early Reformers. He was not content with Augustine's usual emphasis that those not elected are simply left in their ruin, but he vigorously maintained the side of Augustine that taught a

---

110. *Predestination*, 137, 135 (*De Praedestinatione*, 174, 170).

111. *Institutes* 3.23.14. Calvin repeated this warning in *Predestination*, 137–8 (*De Praedestinatione*, 174).

112. *Institutes* 3.23.14.

113. Ibid.

114. *Sermons on Election and Reprobation*. Of the thirteen sermons on Genesis 25–27, Calvin's modest references to reprobation are limited especially to sermons 2–5.

double predestination to life and to death. With his stress on divine sovereignty, Calvin's strong advocacy of unconditional election and reprobation based solely on God's will was to have a profound influence on the Reformed tradition, although later Calvinists tended to acknowledge that sin also has a place as a cause of reprobation.[115] Calvin did acknowledge the culpability of the reprobate in his distinction between proximate and remote causes of damnation, but his successor, Beza, and later Reformed theologians would drop the proximate-remote distinction and identify sin alone as the cause of damnation.[116] In these respects, Calvin's position on reprobation and damnation was more stringent than later Reformed orthodoxy, including its confessional expression in the Canons of Dort.[117] The canons, more so than Calvin, acknowledged human responsibility for reprobation.

---

115. Sinnema, "Issue of Reprobation," 112, 194–5, 379–82.
116. Sinnema, "Calvin and Beza," 206–207.
117. Sinnema, "Issue of Reprobation," 411–2, 432–3, 448–50.

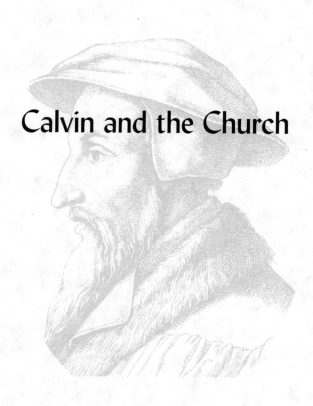

Calvin and the Church

CHAPTER 8

Calvin's Doctrine of the Church

Cornelis Pronk

A bout a month before he died, John Calvin dictated his last will and testament to a lawyer named Pierre Chenelat. The preamble reads:

> In the Name of God, I John Calvin, Minister of the Word of God in the church of Geneva, have decided to have my last will and testament drawn up. I have been brought down by so many sicknesses that I can come to no other conclusion than that God will soon take me out of this world.[1]

By referring to himself as "Minister of the Word of God in the church of Geneva," Calvin indicated what he believed to have been his most important life's work.

After a three-year period of forced exile in Strasbourg, he returned to Geneva in 1541 and devoted most of his gifts and energy to building up God's church in that city for the remaining twenty-three years of his life. This does not mean, however, that he lived there as on an island. Calvin looked upon all of Europe as his parish. Through many personal contacts and by maintaining an extensive correspondence with fellow pastors and other Christians, he kept abreast of what was happening in many countries. He especially kept close tabs on developments in France, his native country, where Protestants periodically suffered intense persecution.

Calvin also wrote letters to kings and emperors reminding them of their God-given duty to promote the reformation of the church in their domains. In the first edition of his *magnum opus*, the *Institutes of the Christian Religion* (1536), he included an appeal to the king of

---

1. Wim Moehn, "Calvijn en de kerk," *Reformatorisch Dagblad*, October 2008. Online: www.refdag.nl (accessed June 2009).

France, Francis I, to protect his fellow believers from their persecu-
tors. He warned the king not to close his ears or mind to the injustices
inflicted on his Protestant subjects, and he pointed out that a very
important question was at stake, namely, "how God's glory may be
kept safe on earth, how God's truth may retain its place of honour,
and how Christ's kingdom may be kept in good repair among us."[2]

THREE CONCEPTS OF THE CHURCH

By the time Calvin appeared on the ecclesiastical scene, three widely
differing concepts of the church were vying for dominance in sixteenth-century European Christendom.

The Roman Catholic View

According to Rome, the church was the divinely instituted body
of Christ headed by His vicar, the pope. Grace was dispensed via
sacraments administered by duly ordained priests. The church was
independent of state control but worked closely with it in order to
maintain and enforce religious hegemony in society.

The Lutheran View

Here the church was seen as the assembly of all who were united to
Christ by personal, justifying faith. This visible church, comprising
professing Christians and their children, focused on preaching the
gospel and administering the sacraments. The church was governed
by the state—the territorial prince or city council—which had the
authority to excommunicate delinquent members.

The Anabaptist View

Anabaptists viewed the church as a voluntary gathering of believers
who had experienced the new birth and testified to that experience
by being baptized and partaking of the Lord's Supper. Church discipline was strictly enforced as a means to keep the community of the
saints pure. Church and state were to be kept separate, and believers
could not participate in or cooperate with the civil government.

Although Calvin rejected all three views, he borrowed several key
elements from them in formulating his own doctrine of the church.

---

2. *Institutes*, vol. 1, p. 13.

He agreed with Martin Luther that the true church was the catholic or universal assembly of true Christian believers, known to God alone. But he also agreed with Rome that the church needed to work with the state to promote and preserve a Christian society. Being a child of his time, Calvin supported the concept of a Christian state. But like Rome and the Anabaptists, he believed that the state should not control the church and that discipline of delinquent church members was the prerogative of the church rather than the state.

CALVIN'S VIEW OF THE CHURCH

Calvin's view of the church, the state, and the relationship between them was fully developed in the *Institutes*, Book IV, and represented a major step forward in the development of Reformation theology. As N. R. Needham writes:

> It saved most of the Reformed churches from becoming merely departments of state…the condition into which the Lutheran Churches had drifted…. The Church once again stood forth as a divinely ordained, free, independent society, with its own God-given laws and officers. This time, however, the Church was a Protestant body, with no pope, acknowledging Christ as its only Head, submitting to Scripture alone, and teaching justification by faith alone.[3]

A very important part of Calvin's ecclesiology was the distinctive system of church government that he developed, based especially on Paul's letter to the Ephesians and the Pastoral Epistles. According to Calvin, the New Testament church was to be governed by Christ through four permanent offices, namely those of pastor, teacher, elder, and deacon. Those nominated for any of these four offices required the approval of the congregation, with input from the magistrates, before their election and ordination.

As a result of this embryonic democratic method of electing office bearers, "lay members of Reformed churches were far more active, and took more responsibility in congregational affairs than the Lutheran laity did in their state-controlled churches."[4] By devel-

---

3. N. R. Needham, *2000 Years of Christ's Power, Part Three: Renaissance and Reformation* (Darlington: Grace Publications Trust, 2004), 211.
4. Ibid., 212.

oping this well-thought-out system of ecclesiastical organization, Calvin enabled the Reformed churches "to function successfully in the most adverse conditions." Without having to rely on state support, they governed themselves and "spread their faith even when the political authorities were fiercely hostile."[5]

The Church's Origin

What made Calvin's view of the church so unique and important? According to Calvin, the church is of divine origin. However, this is not the same as saying the church is divine. This is the view of Rome, as R. B. Kuiper explains:

> By ascribing infallibility, whether to ecclesiastical councils or— since 1870—to the pope in his *ex cathedra* pronouncements in matters of faith and morals, Rome arrogates to itself a divine attribute. Rome regards the pope as Vicar of Christ and the church as the succession of the incarnate Son of God.... In absolution, Rome enters upon the role of Him who alone can forgive sin, and when it boasts of imparting saving grace to men in the administration of the sacraments, it equates itself in that respect with the Holy Spirit.[6]

Calvin emphatically rejected those claims. For him, the church is the communion of saints saved by grace through faith. This implies that the church consists of human beings who will continue to be human even in glory. Very important in this connection is that, with Cyprian and Augustine, Calvin insisted that while in the Apostles' Creed the believer professes faith *in* God the Father, *in* God the Son, and *in* God the Holy Spirit, he does not say "I believe *in*...the holy, catholic church" but "I believe...a holy, catholic church." Calvin wrote: "We testify that we believe in God because our mind reposes in him as truthful, and our trust rests in him. To say, 'in the church' would be as inappropriate as 'in the forgiveness of sins' or 'in the resurrection of the body.'"[7]

While for Calvin the church is not divine as to its essence, it has a divine and supernatural origin in that it is firmly rooted in God's

---

5. Ibid., 213.

6. R. B. Kuiper, "Calvin's Conception of the Church," *The Outlook,* 59, 2 (Feb. 2009): 13–18. Online: www.reformedfellowship.net.

7. *Institutes* 4.1.2.

sovereign election. This is the foundation of Calvin's ecclesiology. From eternity, God has chosen in Christ a people unto eternal salvation. In Book III of the *Institutes*, Calvin explained how these chosen ones are brought to faith in Christ by the "secret energy of the Spirit," whereby they are united to Christ by faith so that they come to enjoy Christ and all His benefits. However, in bringing them to faith, the Holy Spirit makes use of certain means, and here is where the church and its ministry come in. This subject is dealt with extensively in Book IV of the *Institutes*, which is titled, "The External Means or Aids by Which God Invites Us Into the Society of Christ and Holds Us Therein." Although "it is by faith in the gospel that Christ becomes ours," Calvin wrote:

> Since…in our ignorance and sloth (to which I add fickleness of disposition) we need outward helps to beget and increase faith within us, and advance it to its goal, God has also added these aids that he may provide for our weakness. And in order that the preaching of the gospel might flourish, he deposited this treasure in the church. He instituted pastors and teachers [Eph. 4:11] through whose lips he might teach his own....
>
> I shall start, then, with the church, into whose bosom God is pleased to gather his sons…that they may be guided by her motherly care until they are mature and at last reach the goal of faith…so that, for those to whom he is Father, the church may also be Mother.[8]

The Visible and Invisible Church

For Calvin, then, the visible church is an indispensable aid to the salvation of God's elect, who constitute the invisible church. Not that he saw the visible and invisible church as co-extensive. They are closely related, but they need to be distinguished from each other because not all members of the visible church are members of the invisible church. As he explained:

> Scripture speaks of the church in two ways. Sometimes by the term "church" it means that which is actually in God's presence, into which no persons are received but those who are children of God by grace of adoption and true members of Christ by sanctification of the Holy Spirit.... Often, however, the name "church"

---

8. *Institutes* 4.1.1.

designates the whole multitude of men spread over the earth who profess to worship one God and Christ.... In this church are mingled many hypocrites who have nothing of Christ but the name and outward appearance.[9]

Calvin based this teaching that the visible church is a mixed body, or *corpus permixtum*, on the parable of the wheat and tares recorded in Matthew 13:24–30. Following Augustine, Calvin interpreted this parable to mean that the church is made up of true believers and hypocrites who cannot be effectively separated until Judgment Day. In his commentary on this passage, he wrote:

> Although Christ cleanses the Church with his own blood so that it is without wrinkle or stain, yet he allows it still to labour under many faults.... [A]s soon as Christ collects his little flock, many hypocrites creep in, many perverse men infiltrate, even many wicked men find an entrance.... And so it happens that the holy assembly which Christ separated to himself is defiled by much filth.[10]

This interpretation of Matthew 13 was challenged by the Donatists in Augustine's time and by the Anabaptists in Calvin's day (as it is challenged by many people today, as well). They insisted that Christ Himself states in this parable that the field in which the evil one sows the bad seed is the world and not the church. Calvin admitted this but countered that "there can be no doubt that he [Christ] really wants to apply this name to the Church, about which, after all, he was speaking."[11]

Calvin's exegesis, controversial as it may be, is basically correct. As Kuiper wrote fifty years ago, in connection with the 450th anniversary of Calvin's birth:

> To infer, as is often done, from the sentence "The field is the world" that this parable has no reference to the church but teaches the inevitable co-existence of the righteous and the wicked in the world until the day of judgment, is truly simplistic. The parable refers unmistakably to the imperfect visible

---

9. *Institutes* 4.1.7.

10. John Calvin, *Calvin's Commentaries, A Harmony of the Gospels, Matthew, Mark and Luke*, ed. Thomas F. Torrance and David W. Torrance, trans. T. H. L. Parker (Grand Rapids: Eerdmans, 1972), 2:74.

11. Ibid., 75.

church. The field is indeed the world. Into that field the good seed is sown, and thus the church comes into being. But Satan sows tares among the wheat and thus introduces the children of the wicked one into the church. That is the presentation of this parable.[12]

One has to keep in mind that, like Augustine before him, Calvin was heavily involved with the issue of discipline, and the question at issue was how rigorously or leniently the church should deal with delinquent members.

Basically, there were two views. The Anabaptists held to a narrow view of the church; for them, the church consisted only of true believers, who, by the miracle of the new birth, were already as holy as the redeemed in heaven. From that holy fellowship, everything that was unholy or polluted had to be removed.

The Reformed were more realistic, seeing the church from a broader perspective. They believed the church comprised true believers and their seed, but mixed with them in the fold were many hypocrites whose lives were often far from holy. The latter were subject to ecclesiastical censure and excommunication, but—and this was the issue—one should never think that it was possible to remove all impurities from the church in this life.

Calvin has often been accused of being too lenient with the tares that are mixed with the wheat. But this charge is patently false. Church discipline, he knew, is not just desirable but absolutely necessary. He frequently made use of it in Geneva, where, especially during his first stay from 1536 until 1538, he ran into strong opposition to his efforts to raise the doctrinal and moral level of the congregation. Discipline, in his view, was a crucial indicator of the well-being but not of the essence of the church. Just "as the saving doctrine of Christ is the soul of the church," he wrote, "so does discipline serve as its sinews, through which the members of the body hold together, each in its own place."[13]

---

12. Kuiper, "Calvin's Conception of the Church," 13–18; see also Geerhardus Vos, *The Teaching of Jesus Concerning the Kingdom of God and the Church*, ed. John H. Kerr (New York: American Tract Society, 1903), 165–8.

13. *Institutes* 4.12.1.

Marks of the True Visible Church

Mixed assembly though she may be, this visible church, despite her many weaknesses, is the true church of Christ, which all believers should join and never leave because, Calvin insisted, outside her there is no salvation. This high view of the church raised the question as to which visible church came closest to the invisible church. Many people were convinced that Rome was not a true church. But how could they be sure which of the alternative churches that had come into being was her legitimate replacement?

Calvin addressed these concerns by pointing out that those who are looking for a true church may easily recognize her by two essential and objective criteria: the pure and faithful preaching of the Word and the proper administration of the two sacraments Christ instituted, namely baptism and the Lord's Supper. "From this the face of the church comes forth," Calvin wrote, "and becomes visible to our eyes. Wherever we see the Word of God purely preached and heard, and the sacraments administered according to Christ's institution, there, it is not to be doubted, a church of God exists [cf. Eph. 2:20]."[14]

Calvin did not mention discipline as a third mark of a church's soundness. The reason for this omission, according to Timothy George, was that for Calvin, "discipline pertained not so much to the essence of the church as to her constitution and organization. It belonged to the arena of visibility insofar as it too was a criterion of testing, both individually in self-examination and corporately in the public procedures of admonition, censure, and excommunication."[15]

In this respect, George points out, Calvin went beyond Luther and his disciples:

> In contrast to the unilateral accentuation of justification in the Lutheran confessions, Calvin gave precedence to sanctification in his systematic arrangement of the "benefits of Christ." The two are connected as distinct but interrelated "moments" in the grace of double cleansing…(*Inst*. 3.11.1). In this life the locus of sanctification is the congregation, the visible church, in which the elect participate in the benefits of Christ not as isolated individuals, but as members of a body in which "all the blessings

---

14. *Institutes* 4.1.9.

15. Timothy George, *Theology of the Reformers* (Nashville: Broadman & Holman, 1988), 235–6.

which God bestows upon them are mutually communicated to each other" (*Inst.* 4.1.3). In this way the visible church becomes a "holy community," an agent of sanctification in the large society where every aspect of life is to be brought within the orbit of Christian purposes and Christian regulations.[16]

Calvin's reluctance to make discipline a third mark of the church also had much to do with his aversion to the harsh way in which the Anabaptists enforced it, motivated as they were by an excessive zeal to keep the church as pure as they possibly could. Although Calvin also sought a pure-as-possible church on earth, he realized that this was an unattainable goal as long as we live in this broken and sinful world, and that by their harsh and untactful approach to discipline, the Anabaptists were driving sinners away from the church instead of bringing them back to Christ's sheepfold.[17]

All True Believers Have the Same Mother

As for Calvin's reference to the church as the mother of believers, this imagery may come across as strange to modern evangelical and Reformed Christians. It has a Roman Catholic ring to it. We are used to hearing the Roman Catholic Church described as "Mother Church," but Protestants, generally speaking, seldom make use of this term. Yet for Calvin, the word *mother* was an appropriate term to describe the church of Christ. He knew full well, of course, that Rome claimed to hold a monopoly on this title. But he was convinced that Rome had lost the right to call herself the mother of all believers because she was not fulfilling the tasks and responsibilities usually associated with mothers.

Calvin's use of the term *mother* to describe the church had an ancient precedent. Cyprian, a third-century bishop of Carthage, North Africa, said, "You cannot have God for your Father unless you have the church for your Mother."[18] Cyprian and Calvin meant that God has given us the visible church as our mother to minister His Word and sacraments to us under the direction of the Holy Spirit. Apart from this mother and her nurture and instruction, they said, there

---

16. Ibid., 236.

17. W. van't Spijker, *Gereformeerden en Dopers: gesprek onderweg*, ed. J. van der Graaf, C. den Boer, K. Exalto (Kampen: Kok, 1986), 60, 96–7.

18. *Institutes* 4.1.1, note 3.

is no salvation. Cyprian in his time and Calvin in his dared to make this strong statement out of concern for the unity of the church.

Cyprian, and Augustine after him, had to contend with the Donatists, who were causing the first major schism in the church. Likewise, the Reformer of Geneva saw Protestantism breaking up into all sorts of sects and cults. This was partly the result of Luther's doctrine of the priesthood of all believers, which many wrongly interpreted to mean that everyone was free to exegete Scripture as he or she thought fit.[19]

For Calvin, however, the spiritual unity of believers cannot exist without the visible unity of the church. This unity flows directly and logically from Calvin's doctrine of the mystical union between Christ and His people. In this union, which is based on faith and accomplished by the power of the Holy Spirit, we are engrafted into Christ's body so that we derive our spiritual life from Him alone.[20] Just as believers are joined to Christ their Head, they are joined to all fellow members of His body. Hence, there can be only one church. "There is only one spouse of Christ which consists of the whole body of the faithful," Calvin insisted.[21] Believers in Christ therefore should zealously guard and promote the unity of the church.

Calvin's Passion for Church Unity
Calvin labored long and hard to promote church unity. His goal was to bring together all true believers into one communion. He once wrote a letter to Archbishop of Canterbury Thomas Cranmer to propose an assembly of the most eminent men of learning from all the various churches that had embraced the pure doctrine of the gospel, in order that they might make careful study of the Word of God and then draw up a true and distinct confession to which all might subscribe.

Unity and unanimity, he said, are necessary if the church wants to persist in this world. Yet spiritual unity does not require uniformity. He understood that the unity Christ wants His people to pursue is

---

19. Alister E. McGrath, *Christianity's Dangerous Idea* (New York: Harper Collins, 2007), 63–70.
20. John Calvin, *Sermons on the Epistle to the Ephesians* (Edinburgh: Banner of Truth, 1973), 616–7.
21. *Commentary* on Psalm 45:10.

first of all a unity in the truth (John 17). Such unity, Calvin believed, was attainable even if some doctrinal differences continued to exist. As he explained:

> For not all articles of true doctrine are of the same sort. Some are so necessary to know that they should be certain and unquestioned by all men as the proper principles of religion. Such are: God is one; Christ is God and the Son of God; our salvation rests in God's mercy, and the like. Among the churches there are other articles of doctrine disputed which still do not break the unity of the faith.... First and foremost, we should agree on all points. But since all men are somewhat beclouded with ignorance, either we must leave no church remaining, or we must condone delusion in those matters which can go unknown without harm to the sum of religion and without loss of salvation.[22]

No Salvation Outside the Church

Since there is only one church, Calvin argued, there is no salvation outside of her. The reason for this is that God has entrusted to her alone the ministry of the Word and the sacraments as means of grace. This strong language was modified by the Westminster Confession of Faith in 1647, when it stated that outside of the church of Christ there is no *ordinary* possibility of salvation (Westminster Confession of Faith, 25.2).[23] There are exceptions, but these only prove the rule that we are dependent on the church as our mother for the dispensing of all the saving benefits that Christ has obtained for believers. Calvin explained the crucial importance of her ministry this way:

> *Let us learn even from the simple title of "mother" how useful, indeed how necessary, it is that we should know her.* For there is no other way to enter into life unless this mother conceive us in her womb, give us birth, nourish us at her breast, and lastly, unless she keep us under her care and guidance, until, putting off mortal flesh, we become like the angels in heaven (Matt. 22:30). Our weakness does not allow us to be dismissed from her school until we have been pupils all our lives.[24]

---

22. *Institutes* 4.1.12.

23. See A. A. Hodge, *The Confession of Faith, A Handbook of Christian Doctrine Expounding the Westminster Confession* (London: Banner of Truth, 1964), 310.

24. *Institutes* 4.1.4.

The logic here is striking. If God is our Father through regeneration, the church must be our mother, who not only gives birth to us, but nourishes and teaches us to spiritual life.[25]

The Two Jerusalems

In Galatians 4, the apostle Paul speaks of the church as the Jerusalem above, which is free, and as the mother of all believers (v. 26). He compares this heavenly city with the earthly Jerusalem, which, he says, is in bondage with her children. He means that only true Christians who are saved by grace are the true and legitimate offspring of their mother, the heavenly Jerusalem, while the Jews, who seek to be saved by the works of the law, are the children of their mother, the earthly Jerusalem.

In his sermons on Galatians, Calvin drew several analogies between these two Jerusalems and the churches of his own time, the Roman Catholic Church and the churches of the Reformation. Like the earthly Jerusalem, he said, Rome teaches salvation by works, while the Reformed churches, born from the Jerusalem above, proclaim the message of salvation by grace alone. The difference between these two churches, both claiming the honorable title of mother, is enormous. It is crucial, therefore, to know which mother has brought us to our spiritual birth:

> Therefore when we have God's Word preached unto us purely, without any mingling, so as there is no corrupting of the Gospel but we be led wholly unto God to seek all our welfare in him, and keep the way which is shown to us, which way is our Lord Jesus Christ, so that we being rid of all pride and overweening [high opinion], do allow ourselves to be clad with the clothing that is offered us in our Lord Jesus Christ and repose all our glory there, I say when we have the doctrine after that manner: then is it God's house and Sanctuary, then it is the true Church and our mother, and we may be well assured that God also avows and accepts us as his children.[26]

25. Cf. Gal. 4:8–22; Heb. 5:13–6:1.
26. John Calvin, *Sermons on Galatians* (Audubon, N.J.: Old Paths Publications, 1995), 627.

Calvin and the Anabaptists

As opposed as Calvin was to the errors of Rome, he was no less disturbed by the radical Anabaptists, who showed disdain for the Word of God and the offices of pastors and teachers, which they claimed they did not need. Relying on what they believed to be the immediate or direct operations of the Holy Spirit rather than the preaching and teaching of the Spirit-breathed Word by duly ordained ministers, many Anabaptists ended up in the morass of subjectivism and mysticism.

These were the people Calvin had in mind when, in a sermon on Ephesians 4:11–14, he wrote, "If they once get some saying of the gospel at their tongue's end, behold they are (in their own eyes), half way to becoming angels, and they never think of growing further in knowledge."[27] Calvin saw evidence of God's love for us in that He deals with us according to our small capacity. Citing Paul's statement that we see in part and know in part and therefore walk by faith (1 Cor. 13:9), he asked:

> Now where does this faith spring from? How is it nourished and increased? By the Word of God (Rom. 10:17). When we have preaching and are diligent to be edified by it, that is the first point by which and at which our faith begins, and that is the means by which it continues and increases from day to day until it is thoroughly perfected.[28]

APPLICATIONS FOR TODAY

Calvin's doctrine of the church is of great importance for us who live five hundred years after his birth, at a time that is different from his in many ways but that also bears many similarities to his day. God still has His visible church on earth, a church identifiable by the marks Calvin laid down.

Calvin, as we have seen, was keenly aware of the mixed composition of the visible church. He stressed that we are not members of the church by natural birth but become members by a spiritual rebirth.

---

27. Calvin, *Sermons on the Epistle to the Ephesians*, 377–8.
28. Ibid., 378.

But he also emphasized that rebirth to the heavenly life takes place in no way other than through the ministry of the church.[29]

The church's ministry is not only essential to the birth of those who by nature are dead in trespasses and sins (Eph. 2:1); that ministry remains necessary for the growth and development of the spiritual life of believers. "Those who neglect this means [i.e., the ministry of the church] and yet hope to become perfect in Christ are mad," Calvin writes, commenting on Ephesians 4:12. "Such are the fanatics, who invent secret revelations of the Spirit for themselves, and the proud, who think that for them the private reading of the Scriptures is enough, and that they have no need of the common ministry of the Church."[30]

These dangers are still with us. Not only in charismatic and evangelical circles, but also in certain sections of the Reformed community, there is a tendency to bypass the official ministry of the local church in favor of looking for spiritual food elsewhere. Many get their spiritual highs at conferences and retreats that feature unusually gifted speakers, who dazzle their audiences with eloquence and wit. Of course, there is nothing wrong with conferences or retreats as such. One can greatly benefit from them. But as Calvin insisted, our main spiritual food supply must come from the pastors and teachers God has given to His church. Believers are to be in regular attendance at the local church, even if the preacher is no Spurgeon but a man of average abilities.

Closely related to this is another danger facing the churches today—the way Bible studies are conducted. While it is obviously a good thing to study the Word in groups, this should be done within a church setting. Sound, Bible-based study guides by proven and duly authorized church leaders should be used. What sometimes happens is that the Scriptures are discussed without any guidance or authority as to the correct meaning of the Scripture passages. As a result, one hears statements like, "I think this passage means this," "I feel it means that," or "To me, it seems to say something like this."

There was a time when, in conservative Reformed churches, Bible studies were conducted only if the minister, an elder, or at least some knowledgeable church members were present. This was

---

29. *Commentary* on Psalm 87:5.
30. *Commentary* on Ephesians 4:12.

seen by some as too controlling, but after reading Calvin, I wonder whether this older approach was so wrong.

Another area of concern is the proliferation of Bible study guides that many young people and older people use. Some of these studies are not biblically sound and are certainly far from Reformed.

One mark of the true church is her apostolicity, which means that she adheres to the doctrines as set forth by the divinely appointed apostles who laid the foundations of the Christian church. This implies that if we wish to be part of this apostolic church, our understanding of Scripture must be in harmony with what the apostles taught. We are to "earnestly contend for the faith which was once delivered unto the saints" (Jude 3).

Understanding "apostolicity" means striving to understand the Word of God and the interpretation of it with the help of those who have taught and explained it throughout the history of the church. For Reformed believers, this means staying with those interpreters who follow the line of Augustine, Calvin, and the other Reformers, their successors, the Puritans, and those standing in their tradition—Jonathan Edwards, Charles Spurgeon, Charles Hodge, Benjamin B. Warfield, Wilhelmus à Brakel, Herman Bavinck, and many others. This is the best way to keep from falling into subjectivism and relativism. The teaching of the one visible church that displays the three marks of the true church is the standard by which we should measure everything pertaining to doctrine and life.

If God, in His gracious providence, has placed you in such a sound church, you should consider this a great and inestimable privilege. Be sure to be in regular attendance at the worship services and think of the church as your spiritual mother, who teaches you the apostolic truth by pastors called and equipped by our ascended and exalted Lord (Eph. 4:11). The same mother who gives us spiritual birth also lovingly feeds us, first with the milk of the Word and afterward with more solid food. Again, the same mother who teaches us the truth and nourishes us also disciplines us when necessary—and all this by means of faithful shepherds appointed by our heavenly Father.

If this is so—and who dares to deny it?—we need to receive these men and listen to them. As Calvin said:

> If our Lord is so good to us to have his doctrine still preached to us, we have by that a sure and infallible sign that he is near at

hand to us, that he seeks our salvation, that he calls us to himself as though he spoke with open mouth, and that we see him personally before us. We then cannot fail or be deceived in assuring ourselves that Jesus Christ calls us to himself, and that he holds out his arms to receive us, as often as the gospel is preached to us.... [So] if we desire our salvation, we must learn to be humble learners in receiving the doctrine of the gospel and in hearkening to the pastors that are sent to us, as if Jesus Christ spoke to us himself in his own person, assuring ourselves that he will acknowledge the obedience and submission of our faith when we listen to mortal men to whom he has given that charge.[31]

---

31. Calvin, *Sermons on the Epistle to the Ephesians*, 368.

CHAPTER 9

Calvin on Reforming the Church

Derek W. H. Thomas

It would be a tragedy if our commemoration of the five-hundredth anniversary of John Calvin's birth failed to highlight that he was a Reformer not only of doctrine but of the church. In assessing the influence for reform Calvin might exert on today's church, we are undoubtedly treading on difficult ground. Not all of us within the narrow confines of commitment to Reformed theology are agreed on the shape and contours of the church. To name but one obvious example, Calvin lived at a time when credobaptism was associated with sectarian and even heretical ideas, and some of Calvin's language in addressing the Anabaptists was, to say the least, colorful by today's standards. It is doubtful the Genevan Reformer would grasp the complexity of today's denominational and non-denominational churches, not to mention the variegated contours of the Emerging/ Emergent church movement of our time. However, that the church of the twenty-first century is in need of reformation at some important points is without question.[1] Identifying these points and suggesting the extent of reformation necessary is a more difficult challenge.

This chapter is therefore something of a potpourri of ideas without any necessary connecting thread apart from the fact that each idea represents an area where Calvin's theology and practice in sixteenth-century Geneva challenges us in significant ways in the twenty-first century. To be somewhat anachronistic as far as Calvin is concerned, I have chosen five points of discussion, well aware that Calvin would be a bit bemused by the significance of the numeral.

---

1. For evidence of how Calvin speaks to the need for reform in today's church, see the various essays in *John Calvin and the Church: A Prism of Reform*, ed. Timothy George (Louisville: Westminster John Knox, 1990).

CORPORATE WORSHIP

The first issue is public worship. Two important treatises come to mind when thinking of Calvin and church reformation. The first, written in 1543–44, just after Calvin had returned from exile in Strasbourg for the Diet of Spires, is called *The Necessity of Reforming the Church*.[2] Calvin was asked to write an *apologia* for the Holy Roman emperor, Charles V, in defense of the Protestant Reformation, and the result was one of the most important documents of the sixteenth century because it answered a fundamental question: Why was the Reformation necessary? Calvin began the treatise by saying:

> If it be inquired by what things chiefly the Christian religion has a standing existence among us, and maintains its truth, it will be found that the following two not only occupy the principle place but comprehend under them all the other parts, and consequently the whole substance of Christianity, and that is, first, of the mode in which God is duly worshipped.[3]

In his introduction to a recent republication of *Necessity*, Robert Godfrey writes: "Calvin stresses the importance of worship because human beings so easily worship according to their own wisdom rather than God's. Calvin insists, since medieval worship had become 'gross idolatry,'[4] that worship must be regulated by the Word of God alone."[5]

Calvin also mentioned, as we might have expected, the need for reformation in the understanding of justification, or what Calvin referred to as "the source from which salvation is to be obtained."[6] We might have expected him to major on this issue, given its importance to Martin Luther and Philipp Melanchthon. What could be more important than answering the question of how can sinners be right with God? But Calvin dug deeper and asked, having been made right with God through faith alone in Christ alone by the grace of God alone, what then? To what purpose are sinners saved? He

---

2. John Calvin, *The Necessity of Reforming the Church* (Audubon, N.J.: Old Paths Publications, 1994). This edition contains a valuable introduction by W. Robert Godfrey. See also *John Calvin: Tracts and Letters*, ed. and trans. Henry Beveridge, 7 vols. (1844; repr., Edinburgh: Banner of Truth, 2009), 1:123–236.

3. Calvin, *The Necessity of Reforming the Church*, 4.

4. Ibid., 27.

5. Ibid., vi.

6. Ibid., 4, 12ff.

answered that sinners are saved to give praise and worship to God. And how are they to do this? Does God provide us with instructions as to the right way to worship Him? Is there a *regulative principle* of worship? Calvin answered in the affirmative.[7] According to Calvin, the Reformation was necessary because both the manner and content of public worship needed to be reformed.

The second treatise came four years later, in 1547: *The True Method of Giving Peace to Christendom and Reforming the Church*.[8] In this treatise, Calvin called on the Reformers and the church to reject all Roman rites and ceremonies, and what he called "the lukewarm Nicodemites"—those whose zeal for reformation was half-hearted.

The treatise is significant because Calvin once again measured the relative importance of the doctrine of justification and the practice of worship:

> Those therefore, who not only postponing, but even abandoning the worship of God, urge the other head only [i.e. *justification*], have not yet learned what true religion is. If anyone objects, that a principal part of divine worship is comprehended in faith and its exercises, I admit it; but to debate about the mode in which men obtain salvation, and say nothing of the mode in which God may be duly worshipped, is too absurd.[9]

Calvin then proceeded to say that "no worship is legitimate unless it be so framed as to have for its rule the will of him to whom

---

7. Sadly, too much weight has been given to J. I. Packer's unfortunate statement: "The idea that direct biblical warrant, in the form of precept or precedent, is required to sanction every substantive item included in the public worship of God was in fact a Puritan innovation." J. I. Packer, *A Quest for Godliness* (Wheaton, Ill.: Crossway, 1990), 247. Others have followed Packer, including Ralph J. Gore, Jr., *Covenantal Worship: Reconsidering the Puritan Regulative Principle* (Phillipsburg, N.J.:P&R, 2002), 153. Many have disagreed with this point of view. Rowland Ward, for example, writes, "there is no fundamental difference between Calvin and the Westminster men on worship." See Rowland S. Ward, "The Directory for Public Worship Prepared by the Assembly of Divines at Westminster in the Year 1644," Westminster Assembly 2004: A Conference on the Westminster Standards, Westminster Theological Seminary, Philadelphia, Pa., Nov. 21–22, 2004 (unpublished manuscript dated Feb. 18, 2006). And Edmund Clowney, while granting a "legalistic" development in Puritanism, rejects the view that Calvin and the Puritans are fundamentally at odds with each other. See D. A. Carson, ed., *Worship: Adoration and Action* (Grand Rapids: Baker, 1993; repr., Eugene, Ore.: Wipf & Stock, 2002), 114.

8. *John Calvin: Tracts and Letters*, 3:240–358.

9. Ibid., 3:260.

it is performed." He condemned will-worship,[10] adding, "I deny that any worship of God is legitimate, save that which is required according to his will."[11]

Mention perhaps should also be given of a similar treatment of worship in this decade (1540s), sometimes referred to as "Calvin against the Nicodemites."[12] As early as 1537, Calvin published an open letter, *On Shunning the Unlawful Rites of the Ungodly*,[13] in which the Reformer argued for an outward practice that conformed to inward conviction. He distinguished *cowardice* and *dissimulation* — the latter involving outright duplicity. Adopting practices (attending the Mass, for example) designed to mislead others into thinking one was at ease with Romish ordinances when privately one was not drew the Reformer's ire. "Will it still be denied to me," Calvin asked, "that he who listens to the Mass with a semblance of religion, every time these acts are perpetrated, professes before men to be a partner in sacrilege, whatever his mind may inwardly declare to God?"[14]

Similar writings appeared in subsequent years. In 1541, Calvin wrote to the duchess of Ferrara.[15] As Carlos Eire points out, "The letter was designed to warn the Duchess against the dissembling attitude of her new almoner, François Richardot."[16] Among other matters, Calvin referred to the Mass as "a sacrilege, the most execrable that one can imagine."[17] The Mass, he said, should be avoided at all costs:

> Should someone object, that externals in religion are quite indifferent, that what is required is only that the heart within should be upright, to that our Lord answers, that he will be glorified in our body, which he has purchased with his blood, that he requires the confession of the mouth, and that all our prayers

---

10. Ibid., 3:263. Note the Greek *ethelothrēskia* and its use in Colossians 2:23. See also Calvin's use of this term in *The Necessity of Reforming the Church*, 7, 71, the Greek incorrectly spelled in both of these instances.

11. Ibid.

12. See Carlos M. N. Eire, *War Against the Idols: The Reformation of Worship from Erasmus to Calvin* (Cambridge: Cambridge University Press, 1986), 234–75; Wulfert de Greef, *The Writings of John Calvin (Expanded Edition): An Introductory Guide*, trans. Lyle D. Bierma (Louisville: Westminster John Knox, 2008), 122–6.

13. *John Calvin: Tracts and Letters*, 3:359–411.

14. Ibid., 3:386.

15. Ibid., 4:295–306.

16. Eire, *War Against the Idols*, 241.

17. *John Calvin: Tracts and Letters*, 4:300.

should be consecrated to his honour, without being any way contaminated or defiled by anything displeasing to him."[18]

In 1543, Calvin once more took up this theme with *A Short Treatise Setting Forth What the Faithful Man Must Do When He is Among Papists and He Knows the Truth of the Gospel*.[19] Once again, Calvin addressed those who distinguished inward and outward forms of religious worship in the interests of downplaying the importance of the latter:

> Since our body is bought with the precious blood of Jesus Christ, what point would there be in prostituting it before an idol? Since it is the temple of the Holy Spirit, how great an outrage would it be to pollute it by such sacrilege? Since it is destined to receive the crown of immortality, and to be a partaker of the glory of God, would it be fitting to corrupt and sully it in such garbage?[20]

Calvin's advice to those living in locations where no Reformed church was available was to emigrate if they could or retreat to private worship at home. He exhorted the timid to "seek every means of leaving this filth, and this poor and unhappy condition in which they dwell, and let them take the means that are offered them, showing that it was not hypocrisy on their part to ask God for deliverance."[21]

Documents of this nature continued in the 1540s, including *Answer of John Calvin to the Nicodemite Gentlemen Concerning Their Complaint That He is Too Severe* (1544).[22] The *Answer* (Fr. *Excuse*) identified four types of dissemblers:

- False preachers of the gospel who adopt some evangelical doctrines.
- Worldly people, courtiers, and refined ladies who are used to flattery and hate austerity.
- Scholars and literary men, who love ease and hope for gradual improvement with the spread of education and intelligence.

---

18. Ibid., 3:302.

19. See the English translations and introductory essay in *Come Out From Among Them: Anti-Nicodemite Writings of John Calvin* (Dallas: Protestant Heritage, 2001), 7–30, 45–96.

20. Ibid., 54.

21. Ibid., 95.

22. Ibid., 97–127. The French title is *Excuse à Messieurs les Nicodemites, sur la Complaincte qu'Ilz Font de Sa Trop Rigeur,* and it was published in Latin in 1549.

- Merchants and citizens who do not want their lives disturbed in any way.[23]

The *Short Treatise* and the *Answer* were published in German, Czech, English, Dutch, and Italian, leading to the influx (especially from France) of refugees into Geneva—more than five thousand in the decade 1549–1559.[24]

These writings demonstrate the importance to the Genevan Reformer of public worship. Calvin believed that God has ordered both the fact and the manner of public worship, and to worship God contrary to His will is to be guilty of idolatry. Calvin's reforms in worship reflected his overarching desire to "get back to the early church"—his use of the *sursum corda*, for example, reflected the second-century *Didache*.[25]

Much more could be said here, but Calvin's continuing importance as a Reformer addressing us in the twenty-first century is clear. Whether we agree with Calvin's positions on public worship (separation from idolatry or liturgical reform, to cite but two issues), our participation in the dialogue surrounding worship in our own time would benefit from the Reformer's input.

THE GOSPEL

A second feature associated with Calvin is his constant commitment to the gospel and the doctrine of justification. Calvin viewed the doctrine of justification as "the hinge on which the whole gospel turns."[26] In opposition to medieval Roman Catholic theology, a sacramental treadmill involving meretricious observance of the seven sacraments, Calvin emphasized that salvation is obtained in its entirety, here and now, through self-abandoning faith in the promises of God, as set forth in God's self-authenticating Word, the Scriptures. The gospel emphasizes five *solas* (Latin, "alone"): it is by *faith alone*, so the recipi-

23. Eire, *War Against the Idols*, 244–5.

24. De Greef, *The Writings of John Calvin*, 139. In addition to these treatises, Calvin preached and published four sermons under the title *Quatre sermons de M. Jehan Calvin, traictans des matieres fort utiles pour nostre temps* (*Four Sermons from John Calvin Treating Matters Which are Very Useful for Our Times*). See, *Come Out From Among Them*, 127–238.

25. See, Aaron Milavec, *The Didache: Text, Translation, Analysis, and Commentary* (Collegeville, Minn.: Michael Glazier Books, 2004).

26. *Institutes* 3.11.1.

ent is not obliged to work for it; it is by *grace alone*, so the recipient is not obliged to earn it in any way; it is by *Christ alone*, so there is no place for any other mediator, be that mediator a saint, a pope, or the virgin Mary; it is by *Scripture alone*, so there is no place for purgatory, pilgrimages, relics, or papal indulgences; and it is all to the *glory of God alone*, with credit being given to Him and none to ourselves.[27]

For Calvin, that meant emphasizing the doctrine of justification — the old perspective on justification, not the new perspective. At the heart of any view of justification other than the view of the Reformation lies the damning indictment of works and self-effort. According to recent opinion on justification, we are made right with God by joining the community of the faithful, aligning ourselves with the covenant people of God, and receiving the markers of separation, baptism and the Lord's Supper.[28] In essence, this is no different from what the medieval Catholic Church taught — that one becomes a Christian and identifies oneself as a Christian by joining the church, by joining the community of the faithful, and receiving its boundary markers.

There is this absolute contrast between the Reformation view of justification, which I am utterly convinced is a Pauline view and a biblical view of justification, and any other view, be it medieval Catholic or "new perspective." For Calvin, any view other than the Pauline and Reformation view, must receive a damning indictment, because if we introduce into justification the idea that somehow we are credited as believers in Jesus Christ by something that we *do*, we are altogether lost. Calvin believed we must be constantly addressing the issue of what I want to call the *gospel matrix* in order to ensure that at no place in our acceptance with God is there the intrusion of works. God set His love on us from before the foundation of the world, apart from any consideration of our works and any consideration of merit.

---

27. J. I. Packer, "Justification: An Introductory essay," in *Collected Shorter Writings of J. I. Packer*, Vol. 1, *Celebrating The Saving Work of God* (Carlisle, Cumbria: Paternoster Press, 1998), 138.

28. For an example of new perspective wrings on justification, see Tom Wright, *Justification: God's Plan and Paul's Vision* (London: SPCK, 2009). Examples of counter arguments are Guy Prentiss Waters, *Justification and the New Perspective on Paul: A Review and Response* (Phillipsburg, N.J.: P&R, 2004); J. V. Fesko, *Justification: Understanding the Classic Reformed Doctrine* (Phillipsburg, N.J.: P&R, 2008); Gary L. W. Johnson and Guy P. Waters, eds., *By Faith Alone: Answering the Challenges to the Doctrine of Justification* (Wheaton, Ill.: Crossway, 2006); John Piper, *The Future of Justification: A Response to N. T. Wright* (Wheaton, Ill.: Crossway, 2007).

Few defined the relationship between the indicative and the imperative, the relationship between justification and sanctification, clearer than did Calvin. His differentiation of the various "uses" of the law, particularly the so-called *tertius usus legis*[29]—the third use of the law—is masterful and particularly timely for us today.

For Calvin, it was important to distinguish between law and gospel. One thinks of the saying, attributed to Luther, that the person who can distinguish between the law and gospel can thank God and know himself to be a Christian. Calvin acknowledged that pejorative language is used concerning the old covenant, and this should be understood in at least two ways: first, that the redemptive significance of the coming of Christ and consequent coming of the Spirit at Pentecost following His death, resurrection, and ascension is so great as to put the old covenant in a shadow; and second, there is a great difference between using the law as a "bare letter" and using it through the power of the Holy Spirit. Jesus Christ is the end of the law—the law finds its focus and fulfillment in Christ—but that does not mean that we may become law-*less*. In union with Christ, we can do no other but joyfully obey the law.

Finding our way *to* justification and *onward* to sanctification remains for us, in our time, a difficult and controversial issue. The term *legalism* is over-employed, used more often to describe what we regard as irksome or inconvenient. Perhaps we should ban its utterance in Christian circles until we have grasped its true meaning! But what often lies at the heart of this misconstruction is a laudable instinct to preserve the *graciousness* of justification—a Spirit-given instinct that Calvin would recognize and accede to readily. Suggestions today that the Reformation (Calvin as much as Luther) completely misunderstood the doctrine of justification are silly and, more importantly, damning.

We need to be as passionate about the matrix of the gospel as Calvin was.

---

29. *Institutes* 2.7.12.

PREACHING

It is impossible to think about Calvin and the Reformation of the church without thinking of the importance of Calvin preaching the Word.[30] Theodore Beza, in his biography of Calvin written shortly after Calvin's death in 1564, gives us a little snippet and tells us what was more or less the later pattern of Calvin's ministry in Geneva.[31] Calvin preached two sermons on a Sunday and catechized between those two sermons; then one week he preached Monday, Tuesday, Wednesday, Thursday, and Friday, and the following week on Wednesday. That pattern changed a little, but basically, in the course of fourteen days, he preached ten sermons.[32]

In 1549, the Geneva authorities did a tremendously important thing. Understanding the importance of Calvin's preaching, they hired a stenographer, Denis Raguenier, to take down in shorthand every word Calvin spoke in public. Some 2,300 sermons were recorded in this way.[33] Only 1,500 of them have survived, the rest having been sold for the weight of paper to make room in the nineteenth-century European libraries in which they were kept. Lost in this culling were sixty-six sermons on 2 Corinthians, forty-six on 1 and 2 Thessalonians, and almost all of the sermons on the Minor Prophets.

Seven volumes of sermons (transcribed into longhand French) have emerged over recent decades, the *Supplementa Calviniana*.[34] Some of these have recently been translated into English, including sermons on 2 Samuel,[35] Acts,[36] Genesis,[37] and Micah.[38] Others were translated

30. T. H. L. Parker, *Calvin's Preaching* (Louisville: Westminster John Knox, 1992); Steven J. Lawson, *The Expository Genius of John Calvin* (Orlando, Fla.: Reformation Trust, 2007); Bruce Gordon, *Calvin* (New Haven: Yale University Press, 2009), 130–3.
31. Theodore Beza, *The Life of John Calvin* (Darlington: Evangelical Press, 1997).
32. Advocates of weekly communion, citing in their defense the Genevan Reformer, should bear in mind the relative weighting of sermons to Supper: 10–1.
33. Parker, *Calvin's Preaching*, 65–8.
34. *Supplementa Calviniana*, 7 vols. Sermons inédits (Neukirchen-Vluyn: Neukirchener Verlag Des Erziehungsvereins, 1936–81).
35. John Calvin, *Sermons on 2 Samuel*, trans. Douglas Kelly (Edinburgh: Banner of Truth, 1992).
36. John Calvin, *Acts of the Apostles, Chapters 1–7*, trans. Rob Roy McGregor (Edinburgh: Banner of Truth, 2008).
37. John Calvin, *Sermons on Genesis: Chapters 1–11*, trans. Rob Roy McGregor (Edinburgh: Banner of Truth, 2009).
38. John Calvin, *Sermons on the Book of Micah*, trans. and ed. Benjamin Wirt Farley (Phillipsburg, N.J.: P&R, 2003).

into English in Elizabethan times by Arthur Golding, including sermons on Deuteronomy, Job, the Pastoral Epistles, Ephesians, etc.[39]

Nothing signaled Calvin's commitment to preaching, and to *lectio
continua* preaching in particular, more than what he did upon returning to Geneva in 1542. Williston Walker records for us how Calvin
attended a meeting of the *Council Petite* on the morning of his return,
to deliver some papers, and then walked from the council to the Cathedral of St. Pierre, where he entered the pulpit at midday and picked
up his preaching at exactly the point where he had left off three years
before.[40] There was no more profound statement about what ministry
was and what reformation meant than what Calvin did that day. He
had come to preach the Word of God. He could have done anything
he wanted. They had asked him back, and when this happens, you
can ask for the moon. But Calvin gave himself to preaching because
he understood that it is through faithful expository preaching that
hearts are changed and the kingdom advanced.

For Calvin, commitment to the truth involves believing that the
Bible is inspired and inerrant, not just in its general details but in its
precise details, in its words, its nouns, its verbs, its prepositions. That
is why Calvin preached only after having studied the Hebrew and
Greek texts. He did not use a manuscript. He preached extemporaneous sermons. On mornings when he was scheduled to preach, he
would study the passage, walk to the pulpit, and expound the Scriptures. We search in vain for padding, for stories, or for illustrations in
his sermons. His was a commitment to the Word of God.

In his ninety-fifth sermon on Job, Calvin says: "What good would
it do if we were here [at St. Pierre] half a day, and I expounded half
a book, and without regard for you or for your benefit I had specu-
lated in the air, treated many things in a confused way? Everyone
would return to his house just as he had come to the church, and this
would be to profane the Word of God so much that it would have no
use among us."[41] Calvin believed preaching was about making the
Word of God clear.

---

39. Many of these volumes are currently in print and are available at discount
prices from www.heritagebooks.org.

40. Williston Walker, *John Calvin: Revolutionary, Theologian, Pastor* (Geanies,
Fearn: Christian Focus, 2005), 208.

41. The original Elizabethan text can be found in *John Calvin: Sermons on Job*,
trans. Arthur Golding (1574; repr., Edinburgh: Banner of Truth, 1993), 446.

His style of preaching was very simple. Calvin preached in simple French. There were few technical words, if any, in his preaching. He never quoted, or if he did, it was from memory. He never referred to his masterwork, the *Institutes of the Christian Religion.* That is shocking, isn't it? I have never seen any reference in any of his sermons to the *Institutes.* You don't find that. His sermons are direct speech, full of interrogatives. He was always asking and answering questions. He engaged the minds and the thinking of his hearers. He wanted them to understand the Word of God. His preaching was full of the most wonderful application. Calvin was committed to exposition, to the Bible, and to the God of the Bible.

One of my favorite quotations of all is in the very first sermon on Job. These Old Testament sermons were preached during the week. On the Lord's Day, he generally preached on the New Testament, and occasionally the Psalms. The sermons on Job began in February 1554 and went until April 1555. There were 159 of them, and in the first one he said, "God has such a sovereignty over his creatures, as he may dispose of them at his pleasure." Calvin went on to urge his listeners to be subject to the sovereignty of God.[42]

THE CHURCH

I recall finding Calvin a little difficult to swallow when I first encountered him. As a student for the ministry, I remember reading in Book Four of the *Institutes*: "those to whom he is Father the church may also be Mother."[43] I had come from an unchurched background. My ecclesiology was almost wholly undefined, and here I was immersed into what is in fact a statement from Cyprian. Calvin was talking about the importance of the church as the mother who nurtures the children of God. It is a vision of the corporate dimension of the church.

Calvin devoted one-third of the *Institutes* to the church (all of Book Four) and made evident from the very first line the direction he intended to follow. It was not simply a commitment to the church as a local gathered community, with its rites and ceremonies; it was also a commitment to the "catholic" or universal church (as in the Apostles' Creed: "I believe in the...catholic church"). As J. I. Packer

---

42. Ibid., 1.
43. *Institutes* 4.1.1.

puts it in a moment of autobiographical writing about how the *Institutes* affected him when he first encountered it:

> [Calvin] was observably formulating his Bible-led theology in conversation with the intellectual heritage of the early patristic and medieval Western church, and setting standards and limits and focusing ideals for the church of the future. Moreover, he saw that the church, the worldwide worshiping, witnessing, working fellowship of believers, embracing all gathered where Word and sacrament were biblically ministered, is central to God's whole plan of redemption, from eternal election to the perfecting of New Jerusalem. None of us may think of ourselves as the only pebbles on God's beach. As we are saved to serve in a benighted world, so we are saved to share in a corporate life. I took Calvin's point; my belief that honest, humble holiness and godliness must ever come first did not waver or wither in the least. But being the church and building the church became central concerns, alongside my other concern (his, too) never to let the centrality to the gospel of justification by faith be obscured.[44]

Given the stress in Geneva on church discipline and the role of the consistory,[45] Calvin's ecclesiology could be surprisingly accommodating. I was recently reading Calvin's letter to English (Anglican) exiles in Frankfurt in 1555. Calvin wrote: "In the Anglican liturgy, as you describe it to me, there are many silly things. However, if there lurked under them no manifest impiety, they are to be endured for a time."[46]

By any standards, Calvin's words are delicate and pastoral concerning aspects of a liturgy with which he was not in full agreement. In them, I think, we see a commitment to the corporate nature of the church—a church that in its universal aspect is fragmented and infantile. In an age that has become dominated by the importance of the individual (in church as much as in society generally), Calvin's

---

44. J. I. Packer, "Calvin, the *Institutes* and Me," in *Indelible Ink: 22 Prominent Christian Leaders Discuss the Books that Shape Their Faith*, ed. Scott Larsen (Colorado Springs, Colo.: WaterBrook, 2003), 83–4.

45. For an insight into the role of the consistory, see *Registers of the Consistory of Geneva in the Time of Calvin, Volume 1:1542–1544*, eds. Robert Kingdon, Thomas A. Lambert, Isabella M. Watt (Grand Rapids: Eerdmans, 1996).

46. *John Calvin: Tracts and Letters*, 6:121.

stress on the corporate nature of the church and its importance in Christian growth and maturity is a lesson for us to learn.

PIETY

My fifth point concerns Calvin's commitment to piety. It should be remembered that Calvin gave as a subtitle to the first edition (1536) of the *Institutes*, "...*concerning almost the whole sum of piety (pietas) and all that is necessary to know in the doctrine of salvation.*"[47]

From this we learn that, for Calvin, reform comes by a commitment to piety. One cannot help but think that he chose this subtitle with Thomas Aquinas's *Summa Theologia* in mind. However, he was writing not just a sum of theology but a sum of piety, a sum of how theology impacts the heart and the life.[48]

What does that mean? Let me give just one example. Calvin wrote to certain women who were facing martyrdom in Paris:

> How many thousands of women have there been who have spared neither blood nor their lives to maintain the name of Jesus Christ and announce His reign? Has not God caused their martyrdom to fructify? Have we not still before our eyes examples of how God works daily by their testimony and confounds His enemies in such a manner that there is no preaching of such efficacy as the fortitude and perseverance they possess in confessing the name of Jesus Christ?[49]

It is such a commitment—a commitment that may cost us our very lives—to which Christianity calls us. Calvin himself was acutely aware of the cost of what he wrote in the lives of those who listened to him and read his writings. There is a sense of urgency in what he says, an urgency born of the fact that he understood not only that we are to live for Jesus Christ, but we are also to die for Him. Perhaps there is no more important aspect of Calvin's theology for us to learn than this: that Christianity demands of us *everything*.

---

47. John Calvin, *Institutes of the Christian Religion (1536)*, trans. and ed. Ford Lewis Battles (Grand Rapids: Eerdmans, 1975).

48. See Joel Beeke, "Calvin on Piety," in *The Cambridge Companion to John Calvin*, ed. Donald K. McKim (Cambridge: Cambridge University Press, 2004), 125–52..

49. *John Calvin: Tracts and Letters*, 6:363.

CHAPTER 10

Calvin and the Missionary Endeavor of the Church[1]

Michael A. G. Haykin

It has often been maintained that the sixteenth-century Reformers had a poorly developed missiology and that overseas missions to non-Christians was an area to which they gave little thought. Yes, this argument runs, they rediscovered the apostolic gospel, but they had no vision to spread it to the uttermost parts of the earth.[2]

Possibly the first author to charge early Protestantism with failing to apply itself to missionary work was the Roman Catholic theologian and controversialist Robert Bellarmine (1542–1621). Bellarmine argued that one of the marks of a true church was its continuity with the missionary passion of the apostles. In his mind, Roman Catholicism's missionary activity was indisputable, and this supplied a strong support for its claim to stand in solidarity with the apostles. As Bellarmine maintained:

> In this one century the Catholics have converted many thousands of heathens in the new world. Every year a certain number of Jews are converted and baptized at Rome by Catholics who adhere in loyalty to the Bishop of Rome.... The Lutherans compare themselves to the apostles and the evangelists; yet though they have among them a very large number of Jews, and in

1. A version of this article appeared in the online journal *Reformation21*, 13 (September 2006). Used with permission.

2. See Kenneth J. Stewart, "Calvinism and Missions: The Contested Relationship Revisited," *Themelios*, 34, 1 (April 2009), especially the section "3. A Much Older Charge: The Entire Reformation Movement Neglected Missions" (http://www.thegospelcoalition.org/publications/34-1/calvinism-and-missions-the-contested-relationship-revisited/; accessed December 7, 2009).

Poland and Hungary have the Turks as their near neighbors, they have hardly converted so much as a handful.[3]

But such a characterization fails to account for the complexity of this issue. First of all, in the earliest years of the Reformation, none of the major Protestant bodies possessed significant maritime resources to take the gospel outside the bounds of Europe. The Iberian Catholic kingdoms of Spain and Portugal, on the other hand, which were the acknowledged leaders among missions-sending regions at this time, had such resources aplenty. However, their missionary endeavors were often indistinguishable from imperialist ventures. Also, it is noteworthy that other Roman Catholic nations of Europe that lacked seagoing capabilities, such as Poland and Hungary, evidenced no more cross-cultural missionary concern at that time than did Lutheran Saxony or Reformed Zurich. It is thus plainly wrong to make the simplistic assertion that Roman Catholic nations were committed to overseas missions while Protestant nations were not.[4]

Second, it is vital to recognize that, as Scott Hendrix has rightly said, the Reformation was the attempt to "make European culture more Christian than it had been. It was, if you will, an attempt to reroot faith, to rechristianize Europe."[5] In the eyes of the Reformers, this program involved two accompanying convictions. First, they considered what passed for Christianity in late medieval Europe to be sub-Christian at best and pagan at worst. As the French Reformer John Calvin (1509–1564) put it in his *Reply to Sadoleto* (1539):

> The light of divine truth had been extinguished, the Word of God buried, the virtue of Christ left in profound oblivion, and the pastoral office subverted. Meanwhile, impiety so stalked abroad that almost no doctrine of religion was pure from admixture, no ceremony free from error, no part, however minute, of divine worship untarnished by superstition.[6]

---

3. Robert Bellarmine, *Controversiae*, as quoted in Stephen Neill, *A History of Christian Missions* (Harmondsworth, Middlesex: Penguin, 1964), 221.

4. Stewart, "Calvinism and Missions."

5. Scott Hendrix, "Rerooting the Faith: The Reformation as Re-Christianization," *Church History*, 69 (2000): 561.

6. John Calvin and Jacopo Sadoleto, *A Reformation Debate*, ed. John C. Olin (Grand Rapids: Baker, 1976), 74–5.

Thus, the Reformers viewed their task as a missionary one: they were planting true Christian churches.[7]

The following brief examination of Calvin's missiology clearly shows the error of the perspective that the Reformation was, by and large, a non-missionary movement.[8] I develop Calvin's theology of missions by looking first at the theme of the victorious advance of Christ's kingdom that looms so large in his writings. I then examine statements from Calvin regarding the means and the motivations for extending this kingdom to show Calvin's concern for the spread of the gospel to the ends of the earth. Finally, I look briefly at the way Calvin's Geneva functioned as a missionary center.

The Victorious Advance of Christ's Kingdom

A frequent theme in Calvin's writings and sermons is the victorious advance of Christ's kingdom in the world. In his prefatory address to King Francis I of France in his theological masterpiece, the *Institutes of the Christian Religion*, Calvin said God the Father has appointed Christ to "rule from sea to sea, and from the rivers even to the ends of the earth." The reason for the Spirit's descent at Pentecost, Calvin noted in a sermon on Acts 2, was in order for the gospel to "reach all the ends and extremities of the world." In a sermon on 1 Timothy 2:5–6, one of a series of sermons on that chapter of the New Testament, Calvin underlined again the universality of the Christian faith: Jesus came, he said, not simply to save a few, but "to extend his grace over all the world."[9]

This global perspective on the significance of the gospel also gave Calvin's theology a genuine dynamism and forward movement. It has been said rightly that if it had not been for the so-called Calvinist wing of the Reformation, many of the great gains of that era would have died on the vine.[10]

---

7. Hendrix, "Rerooting the Faith," 558–68.

8. David B. Calhoun, "John Calvin: Missionary Hero or Missionary Failure," *Presbyterion: Covenant Seminary Review*, 5, 1 (Spring 1979), 17.

9. For the three quotes in this paragraph, see Calhoun, "John Calvin: Missionary Hero or Missionary Failure," 17.

10. Jean-Marc Berthoud, "John Calvin and the Spread of the Gospel in France," in *Fulfilling the Great Commission*, Westminster Conference Papers (London: Westminster Conference, 1992), 44–6.

Means for the Extension of Christ's Kingdom

Calvin was quite certain that the extension of Christ's kingdom is first of all God's work. Commenting on Matthew 24:30, he asserted that it is not "by human means but by heavenly power...that the Lord will gather His Church."[11] Likewise, in commenting on the phrase "a door having also been opened to me" (2 Cor. 2:12), he wrote:

> [The meaning of this metaphor is] that an opportunity of further-ing the gospel had presented itself. Just as an open door makes an entrance possible, so the Lord's servants make progress when opportunity is given them. The door is shut when there is no hope of success. Thus when the door is shut we have to go a different way rather than wear ourselves out in vain efforts to get through it but, when an opportunity for edification presents itself, we should realize that a door has been opened for us by the hand of God in order that we may introduce Christ into that place and we should not refuse to accept the generous invitation that God thus gives us.[12]

For Calvin, the metaphor of an "open door" spoke volumes about the way in which the advance of the church is utterly dependent on the mercy of a sovereign God.

In speaking this way, Calvin did not mean that Christians are to be passive in their efforts to reach the lost, and can sit back and wait for God to do it all. In his comments on Isaiah 12:5, Calvin dealt with this common misinterpretation of God's divine sovereignty:

> [Isaiah] shows that it is our duty to proclaim the goodness of God to every nation. While we exhort and encourage others, we must not at the same time sit down in indolence, but it is proper that we set an example before others; for nothing can be more absurd than to see lazy and slothful men who are exciting other men to praise God.[13]

As David Calhoun rightly observes, "The power to save [souls] rests with God but He displays and unfolds His salvation in our preaching of the gospel."[14] In short, while missions and evangelism

---

11. Cited in Calhoun, "John Calvin: Missionary Hero or Missionary Failure," 18.
12. *Commentary* on 2 Corinthians 2:12.
13. *Commentary* on Isaiah 12:5.
14. Calhoun, "John Calvin: Missionary Hero or Missionary Failure," 18.

are indeed God's work, He delights to use His people as His instruments.

The first major way in which God uses His people in missions is through our prayers for the conversion of unbelievers.[15] In Calvin's words, God "bids us to pray for the salvation of unbelievers,"[16] and Scripture passages such as 1 Timothy 2:4 encourage us not to "cease to pray for all people in general."[17] We see this conviction at work in Calvin's own prayers, a good number of which have been recorded for us at the ends of his sermons. Each of his sermons on Deuteronomy, for instance, ends with a prayer that runs something like this: "May it please him [God] to grant this [saving] grace, not only to us, but also to all peoples and nations of the earth."[18] In fact, liturgy Calvin drew up for his church in Geneva includes this prayer:

> We pray you now, O most gracious God and merciful Father, for all people everywhere. As it is your will to be acknowledged as the Saviour of the whole world, through the redemption wrought by your Son Jesus Christ, grant that those who are still estranged from the knowledge of him, being in the darkness and captivity of error and ignorance, may be brought by the illumination of your Holy Spirit and the preaching of your gospel to the right way of salvation, which is to know you, the only true God, and Jesus Christ whom you have sent.[19]

Calvin admonished believers not to be discouraged if they do not see immediate fruit as a result of their prayers. As he stated in his comments on Genesis 17:23:

> So, at this day, God seems to enjoin a thing impossible to be done, when he requires his gospel to be preached everywhere in the whole world, for the purpose of restoring it from death to life. For we see how great is the obstinacy of nearly all men, and what numerous and powerful methods of resistance Satan employs; so that, in short, all the ways of access to these principles are obstructed. Yet it behooves individuals to do their duty,

15. In this regard, see the masterful essay by Elsie McKee, "Calvin and Praying for 'All People Who Dwell on Earth,'" *Interpretation*, 63 (2009), 130–40, passim.

16. Calvin, cited in ibid., 133.

17. Calvin, cited in ibid., 138.

18. Calhoun, "John Calvin: Missionary Hero or Missionary Failure," 19, note 23; McKee, "Calvin and Praying," 139–40.

19. Cited in McKee, "Calvin and Praying," 139.

and not to yield to impediments; and, finally, our endeavors and our labors shall by no means fail of that success, which is not yet apparent.[20]

Second, God uses His people as they employ their strength to bring His salvation to others. In his sermon on Deuteronomy 33:18–19, Calvin argued that it is not enough to be involved in God's service. Christians need to be drawing others to serve and adore God.[21] Specifically, how does God use the strength of Christians? Calvin answered that it is by their words and deeds. Given Calvin's high appreciation of the Word of God, one would naturally expect that he would see this as a major means of witness. Thus, Calvin stated that whenever the Old Testament prophets foretold "the renewal of the Church or its extension over the whole globe," they always assigned "the first place to the Word."[22] Acting on this conviction, Calvin encouraged the translation and printing of the Scriptures in the work of reformation in Geneva. This belief also explains his own devotion to regular expository preaching and his penning of commentaries on all of the books of the New Testament (except for 2 and 3 John, and Revelation) and a goodly number of Old Testament books. Preaching is also central here, as Calvin noted: "God wants his grace to be known in all the world, and he has commanded that his gospel be preached to all people."[23]

Witness, though, is borne not only by the Word but by our deeds. Calvin established an academy in Geneva especially to train men to be missionaries for his native land, France. A significant number of those who studied there did indeed go back as missionaries, and some died as martyrs. For example, in the spring of 1552, five such missionaries—Martial Alba, Pierre Ecrivain, Charles Favre, Pierre Navihères, and Bernard Seguin—came from Lausanne to Geneva, where they got to know Calvin as they prepared to go back to France as missionaries in the region of Lyons. As they were on the road to Lyons, they met a man who asked whether he could travel with them. They had no suspicions of the man. He seemed very hospitable, and on arrival at Lyons, he urged them to stay with him. They did so,

20. *Commentary* on Genesis 17:23.
21. Calvin, sermon on Deuteronomy 33:18–19; CO 29:175. Trans. author.
22. Cited in Calhoun, "John Calvin: Missionary Hero or Missionary Failure," 22.
23. Cited in McKee, "Calvin and Praying," 134.

and he subsequently betrayed them into the hands of the authorities in April 1552. As soon as Calvin heard of their arrest, he began a letter-writing campaign seeking to bring pressure on the French king, Henri II, through a number of German Protestant allies. By the spring of 1553, however, it became obvious that he would not be able to obtain the missionaries' release. On May 15, 1553, Calvin wrote the five who were facing death by martyrdom (the students never saw this letter, for they were burned on May 16):

> Since it pleases him [God] to employ you to the death in maintaining his quarrel [with the world], he will strengthen your hands in the fight, and will not suffer a single drop of your blood to be spent in vain. And though the fruit may not all at once appear, yet in time it shall spring up more abundantly than we can express. But as he hath vouchsafed you this privilege, that your bonds have been renowned, and that the noise of them has been everywhere spread abroad, it must needs be, in despite of Satan, that your death should resound far more powerfully, so that the name of our Lord be magnified thereby. For my part, I have no doubt, if it please this kind Father to take you unto himself, that he has preserved you hitherto, in order that your long-continued imprisonment might serve as a preparation for the better awakening of those whom be has determined to edify by your end. For let enemies do their utmost, they never shall be able to bury out of sight that light which God has made to shine in you, in order to be contemplated from afar.[24]

Calvin saw the act of martyrdom as a powerful witness for the gospel, though it is one without words.

Calvin also was convinced that each and every Christian must be prepared to witness, by both word and deed, about God's grace and mercy in Christ to all whom they can. When it came to the spreading of the gospel, it is noteworthy that he made no distinction between the responsibility of pastors and of other Christians. All believers must be involved.[25]

Calvin and the Genevan pastors also helped further the work of Reformation evangelism in Europe through print media. In fact, by

---

24. John Calvin, *Letter 318*, in *Letters of John Calvin*, ed. Jules Bonnet, trans. Mr. Constable (1858 ed.; repr., New York: Lenox Hill, 1972), 2:406.

25. Calhoun, "John Calvin: Missionary Hero or Missionary Failure," 22.

Calvin's death, his interest in Christian publishing meant that there were no less than thirty-four printing houses in Geneva, which printed Bibles and Christian literature in a variety of European languages. Particularly in the 1550s, Geneva was a hive of biblical editions and translations. For example, there was Robert Estienne's Greek New Testament of 1551, which divided the text into verses for the first time; a new edition of the Vulgate; an Italian translation and a Spanish translation in 1555 and 1556 respectively; and at least twenty-two editions of the French Bible. In 1560, a complete English translation of the Bible was printed sometime between April 10 and May 30. This was the Geneva Bible, the bedrock of early English Puritanism.

There was one means that Calvin expected God to use in the spread of the gospel that we today in the West probably do not expect—evangelism through Christian rulers and magistrates. For example, when Elizabeth I (r. 1558–1603) came to the throne of England, Calvin saw it as a hopeful sign for the advance of the gospel in England. Over the years, he corresponded extensively with a number of French noblewomen, especially Jeanne d'Albret (1528–1572), queen of Navarre. This French noblewoman played a significant role in the French Reformation, and Calvin recognized his need of her support, and that of other nobility, if new territories were to be opened up to the spread of the evangelical faith.

Motivations for the Extension of Christ's Kingdom

What was to motivate the believer in bearing witness to the faith? First and foremost was the glory of God. As Calvin stated in his sermon on Deuteronomy 33:18–19: "When we know God to be our Father, should we not desire that he be known as such by all? And if we do not have this passion, that all creatures do him homage, is it not a sign that his glory means little to us?"[26]

In other words, a true passion for God's glory will result in witness. The Christian life, in all of its apostolic fullness, is marked by self-denial, the recognition that the Christian does not belong to himself or herself, but belongs totally to God and is to live for His glory. In Calvin's words:

Even though the law of the Lord provides the finest and best-

---

26. Calvin, sermon on Deuteronomy 33:18–19 (CO 29:175). Trans. author.

disposed method of ordering a man's life, it seemed good to the Heavenly Teacher to shape his people by an even more explicit plan to that rule which he had set forth in the law. Here [in Romans 12], then, is the beginning of this plan: the duty of believers is "to present their bodies to God as a living sacrifice, holy and acceptable to him"…we are consecrated and dedicated to God in order that we may hereafter think, speak, meditate, and do, nothing except to his glory.[27]

Moreover, bearing witness to the faith is pleasing to God. Consider in this regard Calvin's letter to a Christian landowner on the island of Jersey, written around the year 1553:

We praise God for having inclined your heart to try if it will be possible to erect, by your means, a small church on the place where you reside. And indeed, according as the agents of the Devil strive by every act of violence to abolish the true religion, extinguish the doctrine of salvation, and exterminate the name of Jesus Christ, it is very just that we should labor on our side to further the progress of the gospel, that, by these means, God may be served in purity, and the poor wandering sheep may be put under the protection of the sovereign Pastor to whom everyone should be subject. And you know that it is a sacrifice well pleasing to God, to advance the spread of the Gospel by which we are enlightened in the way of salvation, to dedicate our life to the honor of him who has ransomed us at so costly a price in order to bear rule in the midst of us.[28]

Compassion for the lost condition of people also should drive Christians to witness. "If we have any humanity in us," Calvin declared, "seeing men going to perdition,…ought we not be moved by pity, to rescue the poor souls from hell, and teach them the way of salvation?"[29] In fact, a Christian who is not involved in witness is really a contradiction in terms. As Calvin remarked in his commentary on Isaiah:

…the godly will be filled with such an ardent desire to spread the doctrines of religion, that everyone not satisfied with his own calling and his personal knowledge will desire to draw others

---

27. *Institutes* 3.7.1.

28. Calvin, *Letter 339*, in *Letters of John Calvin*, 2:453.

29. Calvin, sermon on Deuteronomy 33:18–19 (*CO* 29:175). Trans. author.

along with him. And indeed nothing could be more inconsistent with the nature of faith than that deadness which would lead a man to disregard his brethren, and to keep the light of knowledge choked up within his own breast.[30]

Finally, we are to evangelize because we have been commanded to do so by Christ.[31] Calvin declared that "God wants his grace to be known to all the world, and he has commanded that his gospel be preached to all creatures; we must (as much as we are able) seek the salvation of those who today are strangers to the faith, who seem to be completely deprived of God's goodness."[32]

Geneva as a Missionary Center

Geneva was not a large city. During Calvin's lifetime, it reached a peak population of slightly more than 21,000 by 1560, of whom a goodly number were religious refugees.[33] Nevertheless, it became *the* missionary center of Europe in this period of the Reformation. Calvin sought to harness the energies and gifts of many of the religious refugees so as to make Geneva central to the expansion of Reformation thought and piety throughout Europe. This meant training and preparing many of these refugees to go back to their native lands as evangelists and reformers.

Understandably, Calvin was vitally concerned about the evangelization of his native land, France. It has been estimated that by 1562, some 2,150 congregations had been established in France with around two million members, many of them converted through the witness of men trained in Geneva.[34] That two million comprised fifty percent of the upper and middle classes, and a full ten percent of the entire population. The growth is enormous when one reckons that at the time of Calvin's conversion, in the early 1530s, there were probably no more than a couple of thousand evangelicals in France.

Calvin was concerned not only for France but also for the ref-

---

30. *Commentary* on Isaiah 2:3.

31. Calhoun, "John Calvin: Missionary Hero or Missionary Failure," 20.

32. Calvin, sermon on 1 Timothy 2:8, cited in McKee, "Calvin and Praying," 134.

33. Alister E. McGrath, *A Life of John Calvin: A Study in the Shaping of Western Culture* (Oxford: Blackwell, 1990), 121.

34. W. Stanford Reid, "Calvin's Geneva: A Missionary Centre," *The Reformed Theological Review*, 42, 3 (Sept.–Dec., 1983), 69.

ormation of the church in places such as Scotland, England, Spain, Poland, Hungary, and the Netherlands. He even encouraged a mission to Brazil in 1555, which turned out to be a failure.[35] It is noteworthy that when the church in Geneva heard of this Brazilian opportunity, according to Jean de Léry, an eventual participant in the mission, the believers there "at once gave thanks to God for the extension of the reign of Jesus Christ in a country so distant and likewise so foreign and among a nation entirely without the knowledge of the true God."[36]

In light of all these missionary projects, there is little wonder that Calvin could write, "When I consider how very important this corner [i.e. Geneva] is for the propagation of the kingdom of Christ, I have good reason to be anxious that it should be carefully watched over."[37]

Conclusion

Of late, there have been assertions that the Christian tradition that comes down from Calvin is essentially uncomfortable with missionary zeal and is inherently anti-missionary. Some of those making this assertion are knowledgeable historians who are rightly esteemed in their respective schools. Possibly they are confusing biblical Calvinism with the hyper-Calvinism that frequently has developed on the fringes of the Reformed tradition. Every movement has its fringe element that no more represents the center than chalk resembles cheese. In this chapter, we have seen that the missionary zeal that marks biblical Calvinism—later espoused by men such as John Bunyan and John Eliot, Jonathan Edwards and David Brainerd, Andrew Fuller and William Carey, Horatius Bonar and Charles H. Spurgeon—is traceable back to one of its key sources, John Calvin himself.

---

35. See the story of this important mission in G. Baez–Camargo, "The Earliest Protestant Missionary Venture in Latin America," *Church History*, 21 (1952): 135–45; Amy Glassner Gordon, "The First Protestant Missionary Effort: Why Did It Fail?" *International Bulletin of Missionary Research*, 8, 1 (Jan. 1984): 12–18; and Stewart, "Calvinism and Missions."

36. Jean de Léry, *Journal de Bord de Jean de Léry en la Terre de Brésil 1557, présenté et commenté par M.R. Mayeux* (Paris, 1957), as quoted by R. Pierce Beaver, "The Genevan Mission to Brazil," in *The Heritage of John Calvin*, ed. John Bratt (Grand Rapids: Eerdmans, 1973), 61.

37. Calvin, in *Letters of John Calvin*, 2:227.

CHAPTER 11

Calvin on the Early Church

J. Ligon Duncan III

I was introduced to the early church fathers when I went to Covenant Theological Seminary after graduating with a history degree from Furman University. Having specialized in world history, I was already deeply interested in classical history. As I look back on my college career, I realize that the curriculum I followed in history and English was not unlike what the British would refer to as a "course in reading the classics."

In seminary, I studied under David Calhoun, a wonderful church historian who was also a brilliant and godly man. He had been a missionary and pastor, and was son-in-law of the famous J. Allen Fleece. Even during his years in seminary, Calhoun was marked as a man who would be especially useful for the Lord.

Upon his graduation, Calhoun learned that Covenant Seminary needed someone to teach Old Testament. The seminary asked Calhoun whether he would go to Princeton Theological Seminary for a master's degree in theology so he could teach at Covenant. Calhoun completed the program in eighteen months, but before he finished, Covenant filled the Old Testament teaching position. However, by then, Covenant needed someone to teach New Testament. Would Calhoun get a master's in New Testament so he could teach that at Covenant? By the time Calhoun finished that degree, Covenant again had filled the position, but the school wanted a teacher of church history. So Calhoun earned a Ph.D. in church history at Princeton under Edward Dowey, a Barthian/Calvin scholar of the twentieth century. Then Calhoun returned to Covenant Seminary, where he taught church history for about thirty years. He was my professor. His overview course on ancient and medieval history whetted my appetite for more.

While I was at Covenant, one of my professors gave me what I thought was the most spectacularly bad advice I had ever received. He said, "Go study something that you don't know anything about." I spent the next two years feeling like the stupidest human being on earth as I tried to catch up in the vast field of patristics, the study of the early church fathers of Christianity. Today, however, I bless the name of that professor of "bad advice" because I have come to see how important it is for us as evangelical and Reformed Christians to understand the early church fathers.

In His kindness, God gave me David F. Wright as my supervisor. He was the only evangelical on the faculty of the University of Edinburgh. He had a high view of Scripture, a total commitment to the gospel, and a massive knowledge of early Christianity. He was an expert both in Reformation history, having translated Martin Bucer's *Common Places*, and in the early church, especially of the theology of Augustine and other North African fathers.

For a year, I sat in on a course that Wright taught titled "The Origins of North African Christianity from the Beginnings to Augustine." Worlds exploded in my mind as I sat in that class. I still remember the day I learned about the early church father Irenaeus and his great work against heresy. Irenaeus had been taught by a man he referred to as "a certain elder," who probably was Tapius. Tapius had studied under John, who had leaned on Jesus' breast at the Last Supper and had written the fourth Gospel, three letters, and the book of Revelation. Here I was in Edinburgh, listening to a man who had studied under a person who had studied under the apostle John! The hair on my neck stood up. I will never regret the experience of studying the early church fathers.

In this chapter, I want to examine four ways in which the early church fathers were important in the ministry of John Calvin. I will be deliberately anecdotal to better draw you into the glory and the delight of this era of church history.

1. Calvin Knew the Church Fathers

I became interested in Calvin and the church fathers before I studied patristics. I was working on the development of covenant theology from the Reformation era to the time of the Westminster Assembly in the seventeenth century. For at least fifty years, Barthian scholars had claimed that Calvin and other Reformers did not embrace the covenant as a major theological category, especially in relation to their doctrine of the atonement as it was later stated in the Westminster Confession. It was just one more attempt to drive a wedge between Calvin and the Westminster Assembly.

Earlier, Perry Miller, a Puritan scholar, had made the same argument. He said the Puritans had invented covenant theology, and in doing so had departed from Calvin. Miller thought the departure was good, while Barthian scholars thought it was bad, but both argued a discontinuity between Calvin and the Westminster Assembly. So I began researching Calvin and the Westminster Assembly in the sixteenth and seventeenth centuries. As I did that, I began to wonder whether Calvin and other Reformers cited the early church fathers in writing about the covenant. I soon found out they did. In fact, Calvin and the other great Reformers of the sixteenth century, such as Heinrich Bullinger, Martin Luther, and Ulrich Zwingli, knew the church fathers well.[1]

Calvin was the product of a new type of learning that was sweeping across Europe. He studied under some of the most outstanding humanist scholars on the Continent. Even before he openly supported the Reformation and became a leader in Geneva, Calvin had his nose in the texts of the ancient classical world. He was stimulated by going back to those sources. He was in tune with the battle cry of the humanist revolution in education after the Renaissance: *ad fontes* — "to the sources" or "to the fountain." The idea was to go back to the original writings of the classical fathers, not just to the little *compendia* put together by medieval scholars. Scholars determined to go back to the original sources in the original languages and read them as they were meant to be read. The very heart of humanist

---

1. If you are a scholar or pastor looking for a book about Calvin and the church fathers, you might pick up Anthony N. S. Lane, *John Calvin: Student of the Church Fathers* (London: T&T Clark, 2007). Lane studied under T. H. L. Parker, one of the towering Calvin scholars of the twentieth century. Parker wrote two biographies of Calvin, a long and a short version. I also recommend Hughes Oliphant Old on this subject, because many years ago Old looked at Calvin's use of the fathers, particularly in his teaching on worship and preaching. Calvin learned from the church fathers what the Bible teaches about how to do corporate worship. Not many people in the world know that subject as well as Old, who, for many years, taught at the Center for Theological Inquiry in Princeton and is now in the Institute for Christian Worship at Erskine Theological Seminary.

learning was to go back to the original documents and discover what they meant in their time, not to understand them in terms of what fifteen centuries of church tradition said about them.

To do this, you had to be an exegete, and Calvin was an excellent exegete. His work was not inerrant or perfect. But when we look at his articulation of what he read, we have to say that he was one of the best exegetes in the history of Christianity. We especially see that in his exegesis of the writings of the early church fathers. This is quite amazing, for Calvin did not have easy access to the old writings. The books were expensive and hard to access, and Calvin had to travel around Europe to find what he needed. That meant that in quoting someone, he often had to recall from memory what he had read years earlier. But he clearly knew the church fathers well and had memorized much of their writings. We see this in three ways.

First, Calvin copiously cited church fathers such as Augustine, Chrysostom, and Bernard in *The Institutes of the Christian Religion*. He also cited Ambrose, Basil, Irenaeus, Tertullian, Justin Martyr, and Lactantius. What is more, when he cited the fathers in the *Institutes*, he cited them as authorities in his arguments against false teaching. In other words, he cited a father as if to say: "You see, we Reformers didn't make up this interpretation of Paul. We didn't make up this interpretation of the gospel. We agree with the church fathers against the medieval Roman Catholic Church about what the Bible says. We are reading the Bible just like the earliest Christians read the Bible."

In other words, Calvin appealed to the authority of the church fathers to make it clear that the Reformers' teachings were not novel. They were not liberal revisionist deconstructionists who disliked what they found in the Bible and made something up in its stead. No. They went back to the Bible as it was originally written and asked: "What did Paul mean? What was John saying? What does the book of Hebrews teach?" Calvin and other Reformers learned from the early church fathers, not because the fathers were inerrantly authoritative in their reading of Scripture, but because they offered what the earliest Christians thought about the Bible. That knowledge is still helpful to us today.

Today, a movement offers a so-called "new perspective on Paul." Its proponents say we have misread Paul for two thousand years, but *they* know how to read Paul better than the Reformers did. Now it is possible that the Reformers got Paul wrong at times, so how can you argue against this "new perspective"? One way is to say, "If this 'new perspective' is right, wouldn't you expect that someone among the early church fathers would affirm the 'new perspective's' reading of Paul as opposed to how the Reformers read Paul?"

You cannot properly understand the early writings of the church before reading a little work titled *Epistle to Diagnetus*. This little book interprets Paul's letter to the Romans exactly as the Reformers did. This epistle was written less than fifty years after Paul's death by an early church theologian who read Paul just like Calvin, F. F. Bruce, and Donald A. Carson read him. What early church writings are cited in the "new perspective on Paul"? None.

Second, when Calvin quoted the early church fathers in his Bible commentaries, he used them as conversational partners. He did not simply quote them as authorities. Sometimes we quote an authority because we feel feeble about our own interpretation. We want people to listen to us because Augustine, Calvin, Luther, George Whitefield, or Jonathan Edwards agrees with us. We appeal to an authority. Calvin, however, most often quoted the early church fathers as partners in interpretation. Even when he viewed their interpretation as faulty, he showed utmost respect to them as interpreters. He so esteemed their work that he didn't want anyone to trip over little points of difference. He batted ideas off the fathers' writings as he illuminated the meaning of Scripture for us.

Third, Calvin knew the major emphases of the fathers better than most patristic scholars and theologians today. Many modern patristic scholars who are not evangelical or conservative claim to know the field of patristics better than Calvin did, but few of them, if any, have his kind of judgment in understanding the great themes of the church fathers.

One thing that disappoints me when I read journals of patristic scholarship is the kind of trivial matters they focus on. Calvin would not fixate on such trivia; he went for the big stuff. He looked at what the fathers wrote on the Trinity, on grace, on sovereignty, and on justification. He looked at the big, hulking issues of the Christian life, asking, "What can I learn from the fathers about Scripture on this?" His judgment in selecting what to focus on was superb.

Furthermore, Calvin had a better working knowledge of the

church fathers than most evangelical scholars today. Sadly, few evangelical scholars know the church fathers as they should. Generally, you must consult Orthodox, Catholic, or Anglican writings to gain a working knowledge of the church fathers. Calvin knew the fathers better than most modern patristic scholars and theologians know them. He did not know them totally, but he knew them better. And he had better judgment. Calvin made it his business to know the writings of the church fathers, to read them, to interact with them, and to respect them.

2. Calvin Knew the Early Fathers Better Than His Roman Catholic Opponents

Early in Calvin's career, a meeting of proponents of Protestantism and Catholicism was set up. Calvin was invited as an observer, not as a participant. He could only listen to the debates between Protestants and Catholics about issues such as justification, authority in the church, the Lord's Supper, and the sacramental system. During the debates, Calvin heard one Roman Catholic proponent after another make claims based on writings of the church fathers. Calvin's colleagues were not prepared to stand up and refute the historical points that were being made.

Calvin had not come to the meeting with a stack of books; he only had his memory of the writings of the church fathers. But finally, in the midst of one discussion, Calvin stood up and began refuting the Roman Catholic scholars. Their mouths closed in astonishment as they heard him accurately cite from memory several works of the early fathers. Calvin had a better understanding of the meanings of the citations than any other person in the room. As Calvin biographer Bruce Gordon writes, "His formidable powers of recall, evident at this early point, became a hallmark of his career, much to the vexation of hapless opponents."[2]

Similarly, a debate between one of my professors and the Barthian scholar Thomas Forsyth Torrance, from Scotland, proved the value of truly understanding the work of the early fathers. Torrance was trying to make various points in the debate, backing them with quotes in English from Cyril of Alexandria, Basil, or one of the other Cappadocian fathers. Most people in the room were not familiar

---

2. Bruce Gordon, *Calvin* (New Haven, Conn.: Yale University Press, 2009), 67.

with the citations, and I am sure they were exceedingly impressed by the professor's ability to cite the early church fathers.

My professor, however, responded to one point by saying that he had been meditating on the work of that particular church father that very morning in his devotions. He then began to quote from memory, in Latin, the quote *around the quote* that Torrance had given, showing that Torrance had completely reversed the meaning of the church father. Everyone in the room then knew who *really* understood what that church father was saying.

I remember another such exchange at the University of Edinburgh. That evening, Gerald Bonner, an upper-crust, British professor of theology at Durham who wrote *Augustine: His Life and Controversies*, gave a paper on Augustine and the Pelagian controversy. Present at that lecture was Father O'Donohue, an Irish Catholic Carmelite monk who taught theology at Edinburgh.

Father O'Donohue was a kind of Augustinian expert himself, except that as an Irish Catholic Carmelite monk, he did the most Pelagian reading of Augustine that I have ever heard. He could turn Augustine into a Pelagian by the way he read Pelagius. For his part, Bonner was no warm-hearted evangelical believer, and he hated the doctrine of predestination. He was an excellent scholar who would not say Augustine taught something that he *did not* teach or deny something that Augustine *did* teach. But at one point during the lecture, Bonner stopped to basically rip Augustine to shreds for his horrific doctrine of total depravity and predestination.

One glorious thing about British scholarship is the question-and-answer session after a paper is given. Anyone can read a paper, but it takes a true scholar to stand up to the questions that follow. During the question-and-answer session that followed Bonner's paper, Father O'Donohue asked two questions. The first was about the origin of Pelagius. He said some scholars thought Pelagius came from Ireland and could actually name the clan he came from because of the etymological roots of his name and how they corresponded to Irish names of that day. O'Donohue asked Bonner what he thought of the theory. "It is poppycock!" Bonner said.

A few minutes later, Father O'Donohue dared to ask another question: "Professor Bonner, don't you think there is at least a hint of the Pelagian in the early Augustine?" He then quoted a long section from one of Augustine's earlier writings. I must say that as he cited the words in English, they sounded a bit Pelagian to me. What would Bonner say?

In British scholarship, you never answer a question with a yes or no. There must always be nuance. You respond to a question with various viewpoints, saying, "On the one hand," then "on the other hand," always giving your questioner some credit.

Bonner's response to the monk was anything but politic. Instantaneously, emphatically, and without qualification he exploded, saying: "Absolutely not! It's rubbish!" He went on to say, "Augustine was *terrifyingly consistent* on predestination." He then quoted *in Latin* the rest of the passage that O'Donohue had quoted to him, then translated it, making it absolutely clear that Augustine could not in any way be accused of being Pelagian.

That is precisely what Calvin did as he debated his Roman Catholic opponents. He revealed himself as a master of key patristic texts in a polemical context. And that leads to the third point.

3. Calvin Used the Fathers in Polemics
Roman Catholics believed that the Bible, church tradition, and the *Magisterium* (teachings or doctrines) of its councils and ultimately the pope were coordinate authorities in the Christian life. They held they could cite from any of those sources because ultimately all three coalesced as expressions of the Holy Spirit's authority. They believed they could cite any of those sources as the ultimate appeal to authority. According to the *Catechism of the Catholic Church*, "Both Scripture and Tradition must be accepted and honored with equal sentiments of devotion and reverence. . . . The task of giving an authentic interpretation of the Word of God, whether in its written form or in the form of tradition . . . has been entrusted to the bishops in communion with the successor of Peter, the Bishop of Rome."[3]

The Reformers might have responded by saying, "Who cares what the church fathers think; I want to know what the *Bible* says." But they did not. They refrained from taking that stand not because they did not believe in the supreme authority of Scripture; they believed that the opinions of the church fathers, church councils, and

---

3. *Catechism of the Catholic Church* (Liguori, Mo.: Liguori Publications, 1994), Q&A 82, 85.

doctrines of the greatest theologians in church history were subservient to Scripture and its authority. But they also believed that though the early church fathers were not authoritative in themselves, their writings could help them understand how the earliest Christians interpreted the Bible.

They also believed that studying the church fathers would help them understand the Bible without limiting their interpretation to the context of their own situation and culture. They wanted to understand what the fathers thought the Bible taught, not because that determined what the Bible meant but because the fathers helped them make sure that they were accurately reading the Bible. They could make mistakes, and the fathers could make mistakes, but studying the fathers allowed them to transcend their time and culture by asking: "What did the earliest Christians think Paul meant here? What did the earliest Christians think John meant here? What did they think Jesus meant here?"

So the Reformers quoted the early church fathers in debates against the Roman Catholics, saying, "You say that the fathers of the church are authoritative, but in the main, the fathers of the church agree with us, not with you." Luther, Bullinger, and Zwingli all could do this—but not as well as Calvin. Calvin knew the early church fathers so well that he could constantly press home the point that the balance of the church fathers' writings, with all their imperfections and weaknesses, agreed with the Protestants, not the Roman Catholics.

Calvin thus cited the church fathers in debating the Roman Catholics, saying: "They unjustly set the ancient fathers against us (I mean the ancient writers of a better age of the church) as if in them they had supporters of their own impiety. If the content were to be determined by patristic authority, the tide of victory—to put it very modestly—would turn to our side."[4] He was saying: "Those of us who are committed to Protestantism, to Reformed theology (or who believe in evangelicalism) are the gospellers. We agree with the Bible and the church fathers, not because the fathers are equal in authority to the Bible, but because the fathers, in the main, read the Bible like we read the Bible."

---

4. *Institutes* 1:18.

4. Calvin Mined the Riches of the Church Fathers
to Understand the Covenant

Until I got involved in the study of the early church fathers, I won-
dered whether they wrote at all about the covenant. I found only
one dissertation and one article published on that topic in the last
fifty years. When I called my professor to ask whether he thought
my proposal to write a thesis on the covenant and the early church
fathers had any merit, I mentioned that one of the pieces I had read
to write my proposal was written by Everett Ferguson. His response
was, "Oh, Everett is a dear friend of mine." He trusted Ferguson's
work, even though he himself had not worked in this area, and was
thus ready to approve my proposal.

So I began to research how early Christianity regarded the covenant. I wanted to make sure I did not carry the Reformation debate
into the patristic era, imposing its questions and debates on patristic
writings. I wanted to read the fathers for themselves, asking how
they viewed the covenant, if at all, and how they used it.

I studied eight theologians in four geographic areas, covering a
span of about 250 years in the early church, from the days of the
apostolic fathers to the Council of Nicea. I found that the covenant
was important to them in the following ways.

First, the covenant was important in their discussions with Jewish opponents. The Jews whom the earliest Christians debated said
only Jews were heirs of the Abrahamic promises. The early church
fathers used the covenant to argue that Christians are, by grace, heirs
to the promises that God gave to Abraham in Genesis 12.

Second, they used the covenant to dispute the arguments of the
Gnostics. Gnosticism was a mind-boggling labyrinth in early Christianity; even defining what it consisted of is difficult today. Yet all
forms of Gnosticism shared contempt for the material world, contempt for the God of Israel, and contempt for the Old Testament.
Consequently, Gnostics attempted to sever every possible connection between Christianity and the Old Testament. The early fathers
used the covenant to solidify that connection.

For many years, early Christians had evangelized their Jewish
friends by quoting Old Testament passages demonstrating that Jesus
was the Messiah predicted in the Old Testament. In their debates with
the Gnostics, the earliest church fathers took that technique (*demon-
stratio evangelica*) and reversed it. Justin Martyr, then Irenaeus, said

to Gnostic teachers of their time: "If Jesus and the New Testament writers quoted the Old Testament to prove Jesus was the fulfillment of Old Testament prophecy, then the God and Father of our Lord Jesus Christ is the same God who inspired Old Testament prophets to prophesy about Jesus in the first place. That vindicates Him."

The early fathers showed the continuity of the Old Testament and the New Testament, using the covenant to show God's plan of redemption throughout Jewish and Christian history. They used the covenant to show that the Christian story hangs together from Old to New Testament.

We have lost many of the writings of the early church fathers. We know from Eusebius of Caesarea that Melito of Sardis wrote a book titled *The Covenant*, probably before the middle of the second century. How I wish we had that book today!

About a hundred years ago, we discovered a Cyriac translation of *The Demonstration of the Apostolic Preaching*, a book written by Irenaeus. In that book, Irenaeus walked through all of the covenants of the Old Testament, from Adam to Noah to Abraham to Moses to David, and finally to Christ. He showed the big picture of God's plan of redemption throughout the Bible, from the Old Testament through the New.

As I studied the writings of the early church fathers, I asked whether the Reformers were aware of these writings. How much of the fathers' teachings had they integrated into their own perspective on the covenant? I went back to Calvin and other Reformers and found that, time after time, the Reformers cited passages not just from Augustine but from Irenaeus, Tertullian, and Cyprian. They went back from Justin Martyr to the apostolic fathers and forward to Ambrose. They even cited passages from Lactantius, highlighting what the early church had learned about the covenant.

Calvin knew the writings of the early church fathers. He knew those writings better than his Roman Catholic opponents did. He used the writings in polemics, but he also mined the writings of the fathers to develop his understanding of the covenant. Though later theologians would develop these ideas in greater detail, Calvin and the other Reformers showed by their study of and interaction with the early church fathers that their theology was not only consistent with the Bible but was a more faithful interpretation of it than what their Roman Catholic opponents taught.

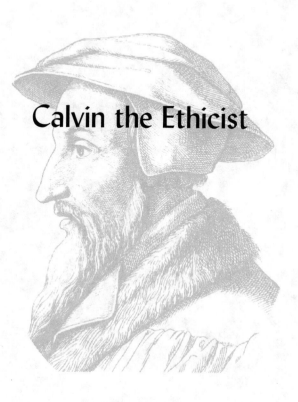

Calvin the Ethicist

CHAPTER 12

Calvin on Ethics

Nelson D. Kloosterman

A t least two difficulties attend the writing of something meaningful on the subject of John Calvin and Christian ethics. The first
is that, like other Reformers, Calvin's treatment of morality was dis-
persed throughout all of his writings, so that his ethical views were
interwoven with his doctrinal expositions. However, the challenge
of systematizing Calvin's moral thought has been met very compe-
tently by several recent surveys or compendiums of his thinking on
ethics.[1] The second challenge, which flows from the first, is that of
selecting a theme by which to organize Calvin's ethical teaching into
a system he never gave us. A number of students have focused on
concepts close to the center of Calvin's moral understanding that can
help illumine its inner relationships, such as the concepts of equity,
the kingdom of God, or the covenant.[2] Others have argued that there

---

1. Included among these surveys would be Georgia Harkness, *John Calvin: The
Man and His Ethics* (New York: Abingdon, 1931); Ronald S. Wallace, *Calvin's Doctrine
of the Christian Life* (Edinburgh: Oliver and Boyd, 1959; repr., Tyler, Texas: Geneva
Divinity School Press, 1999); John H. Leith, *John Calvin's Doctrine of the Christian Life*
(Louisville: Westminster John Knox, 1989); W. H. Velema, "Calvin's Ethics and Its
Validity Today," *Free Reformed Theological Journal* 8 (Fall 2004): 52–87; H. G. Stoker,
"Calvin and Ethics," *John Calvin—Contemporary Prophet*, ed. Jacob T. Hoogstra
(Grand Rapids: Baker, 1959), 127–47; Nelson D. Kloosterman, "Calvinist Ethics,"
Living for God's Glory: An Introduction to Calvinism, ed. Joel R. Beeke (Orlando, Fla.:
Reformation Trust, 2008), 374–83; William Edgar, "Ethics: The Christian Life and
Good Works According to Calvin (3.6–10, 17–19)," *A Theological Guide to Calvin's
Institutes: Essays and Analysis*, ed. David W. Hall and Peter A. Lillback (Phillipsburg,
N.J.: P&R, 2008), 320–46; Jeannine E. Olson, "Calvin and Social-Ethical Issues," *The
Cambridge Companion to John Calvin*, ed. Donald K. McKim (Cambridge, England:
Cambridge University Press, 2004), 153–72; and Guenther H. Haas, "Calvin's
Ethics," *The Cambridge Companion to John Calvin*, ed. Donald K. McKim (Cambridge,
England: Cambridge University Press, 2004), 93–105.

2. Examples of such thematic treatments include Guenther H. Haas, *The Concept*

is no single basic doctrine from which to derive the whole of Calvin's theology. Similarly, it could be argued that Calvin's moral teaching has no single basic concept that determines the whole.

In the face of these two challenges, I would appeal to the theme of this book: "Calvin for the Twenty-First Century." Embedded in this theme is the quest for relevance, for contemporizing Calvin, for using him today. I believe that this provocative theme both excuses me from providing a comprehensively systematic survey of Calvin on ethics and permits me to select a concept within Calvin's teaching that can function usefully as a heuristic tool, serving to stimulate interest as a means of furthering investigation.

A number of students of Calvin have identified the notion of order as one that supplies texture and fiber to his moral thinking. I have in mind particularly the studies of Ronald Wallace,[3] Susan Schreiner,[4] Lucien Richard,[5] and M. Eugene Oosterhaven.[6] One of these, Richard, has gone so far as to claim that "the concept of order was a fundamental category in Calvin's theology," a key to understanding his teaching on Christian spirituality.[7]

In this essay, I first will explain the role of order in Calvin's teaching by briefly tracing it in connection with the doctrines of creation, the image of God, sin, and redemption. Second, I will look at the nature of Christian living as living within order restored. Third, I will suggest a few points of contact between Calvin's teaching on

of Equity in Calvin's Ethics (Waterloo, Ontario: Wilfrid Laurier University Press, 1997); Haas, "Calvin, the Church and Ethics," *Calvin and the Church: Papers Presented at the 13th Colloquium of the Calvin Studies Society, May 24–26, 2001,* ed. David Foxgrover (Grand Rapids: CRC Product Services, 2002), 72–91; G. Brillenburg Worth, "Calvin and the Kingdom of God," *John Calvin—Contemporary Prophet,* ed. Jacob T. Hoogstra (Grand Rapids: Baker, 1959), 113–26; and W. Stanford Reid, "Calvin and the Political Order," *John Calvin—Contemporary Prophet,* ed. Jacob T. Hoogstra (Grand Rapids: Baker, 1959), 243–57.

3. Wallace, *Calvin's Doctrine of the Christian Life,* Part III, The Restoration of True Order, 103–192.

4. Susan E. Schreiner, *The Theater of His Glory: Nature and the Natural Order in the Thought of John Calvin,* Studies in Historical Theology (Durham, N.C.: The Labyrinth Press, 1991; repr., Grand Rapids: Baker, 1995).

5. Lucien Joseph Richard, *The Spirituality of John Calvin* (Atlanta: John Knox, 1974).

6. M. Eugene Oosterhaven, "John Calvin: Order and the Holy Spirit," *Reformed Review* 32, 1 (Fall 1978): 23–44.

7. Richard, *The Spirituality of John Calvin,* 112.

order and concerns being raised in the twenty-first century by post-modernism.

THE ROLE OF ORDER IN CALVIN'S TEACHING
Among the terms Calvin used to denote this concept of order were *ordination, mandate, counsel, command,* and *integrity*. For Calvin, the notion of order entailed "proper being, correct arrangement, beauty, harmony, symmetry, a situation as it ought to be; in a word, perfection, or…the presence of the Holy Spirit."[8] We might summarize this idea as "divinely proportioned harmony and integration" (captured well by the Latin word *integritas*).

We note immediately, then, that order begins with God as the source and pattern of true order. The person of God, the inter-Trinitarian relationships between Father, Son, and Holy Spirit, and all the works of God *ad extra* display an arrangement of harmony, integration, beauty, and order.

This feature of the divine life was embedded in the creation of the world and in God's continuing providential maintenance of the creation. The act of divine creating was the act of imparting proportioned harmony and integration to all of created reality. Such harmony and integration characterized every human relationship, with God, with creation, with others, and with self.

Most prominently, the image of God in humanity expresses itself through order, as human beings live in response to divine grace and in dependence on divine provision. Living in Paradise with rectitude and integrity, human beings were called to follow the law of their Creator and creation, and live within the genuine order. As Wallace indicates, meditation on the future life (*meditatio futurae vitae*) and the life of faith that depended on divine grace belonged to the original order at creation. Living the rightly ordered, harmoniously proportioned life in relation to God, to others, and to the creation constituted humanity imaging God. For Adam and Eve, to reflect the image of God meant to live in an ordered integrity and a dependent righteousness before God in creation with others. Wallace writes: "For man to have been made in the image of God does not mean for Calvin that he had some static impress on his soul, or some inherent

---

8. Oosterhaven, "John Calvin: Order and the Holy Spirit," 25.

faculty or endowment which can be neatly defined. Man possessed the image of God by living continually by the Word of God and by constantly responding to the grace of God for which he was created."[9] This is how Calvin expressed it in his commentary on the creation account in Genesis:

> That he made this image to consist in "righteousness and true holiness," is by the figure *synecdoche*; for though this is the chief part, it is not the whole of God's image. Therefore by this word the perfection [*integritas*] of our whole nature is designated, as it appeared when Adam was endued with a right judgment, had affections in harmony [*compositos*] with reason, had all his senses sound and well-regulated [*sanos et ordinatos*], and truly excelled in everything good. Thus the chief seat of the Divine image was in his mind and heart, where it was eminent: yet was there no part of him in which some scintillations of it did not shine forth. For there was an attempering in the several parts of the soul, which corresponded with their various offices [*Erat enim in singulis animae partibus temperatura quae suis numeris constabat*]. In the mind perfect intelligence flourished and reigned, uprightness attended as its companion, and all the senses were prepared and moulded for due obedience to reason; and in the body there was a suitable correspondence with this internal order [*ad illum ordinem proportio*].[10]

Note the emphasis on the image of God as the perfection, integration, and harmony of all of Adam's senses and faculties. The mind, will, and affections, together with the body, shared an internal order. As Calvin put it: "But here the question is respecting that glory of God which peculiarly shines forth in human nature, where the mind, the will, and all the senses, represent the Divine order [*divinum ordinem repraesentant*]."[11]

The supreme Old Testament example of such order was Job, described by God Himself as perfect and upright. In his first sermon on Job, Calvin explained Job's character this way:

> Now this word [*perfect*] in Scripture is taken as a general term when there is neither falsehood nor hypocrisy in a man, but

---

9. Wallace, *Calvin's Doctrine of the Christian Life*, 105.
10. *Commentary* on Genesis 1:26.
11. Ibid.

what is inside is shown outside, and that he does not keep a shop in the rear to turn himself away from God, but he displays his heart, and all his thoughts and affections, he asks only to consecrate himself to God and to dedicate himself entirely to Him. This word has been rendered "perfect" by both the Greeks and the Latins; but because the word "perfection" was later improperly expounded, it is much to be preferred that we should have the word "integrity."... Here then is Job who is called "entire."[12]

Such integrity, such proportioned wholeness, consists in pure and simple affection, emptied of all pretense and hypocrisy, wholly devoted to God. The head and hands, the eyes and feet, are all co-ordinated (an important verb!) by the heart. In addition, Job was described as upright and one who feared God, which features serve to identify how integrity and order come to expression, namely, toward the neighbor and toward God.

Humanity's fall into sin, therefore, constituted nothing less than the inversion of divine order embedded in creation. Turning from dependence on God to dependence on themselves, human beings began to display the fruit of infidelity or faithlessness by ascribing to themselves what belongs to God alone, and applying to God what applies only to the creature. Disorder and confusion replaced order and harmony, and disintegration replaced integration, through all of creation, among human beings, and within individuals themselves. Within the human heart, there is no moderation but "perpetual disorder and excess,"[13] where "all affections with turbulent impetuosity exceed their due bounds."[14]

If humanity's fall into sin consisted of disorder coming in the place of order, then for Calvin, salvation consists, as Wallace has shown, of the restoration of true order: "That our lives should be conformed to the image of God is therefore a most important aspect of Calvin's conception of the Christian life and of his ethics. This image as the pattern of which we are to be reformed has been set before us in Jesus Christ who is the 'living image of God His Father.'"[15]

Therefore, let us briefly consider the nature of Christian living

---

12. John Calvin, *Sermons from Job*, trans. Leroy Nixon (Grand Rapids: Eerdmans, 1952), 10.

13. *Institutes* 3.3.12.

14. *Institutes* 2.16.12.

15. Wallace, *Calvin's Doctrine of the Christian Life*, 107.

as living with the divinely proportioned harmony and integration restored through Jesus Christ.

CHRISTIAN LIVING AS LIVING WITHIN ORDER

Calvin's discussion of the Christian life in the *Institutes* is found at 3.6–10. As he opened this discussion, Calvin identified the goal of the new life in Christ wrought by the Holy Spirit to be the manifestation of harmony and order between God's righteousness and our obedience. He wrote: "The object of regeneration, as we have said, is to manifest in the life of believers a harmony and agreement between God's righteousness and their obedience, and thus to confirm the adoption that they have received as sons [Gal. 4:5; cf. 2 Pet. 1:10]." He added immediately that "[t]he law of God contains in itself that newness by which his image can be restored in us."[16]

Notice the place and role of the law in its relation to the restoration of order (divinely proportioned harmony and integration) in the Christian's life: "Even though the law of the Lord provides the finest and best-disposed method of ordering a man's life, it seemed good to the Heavenly Teacher to shape his people by an even more explicit plan to that rule which he had set forth in the law."[17] Thereupon, Calvin set forth to exposit the significance of Romans 12:1, with its teaching about not conforming to the world and being transformed by the renewal of the mind. With His law, God is not seeking merely an outward order, but inward spiritual order and true integrity of heart. Through the law, God is seeking to possess us entirely in the integration of body, soul, and spirit.[18]

As Richard observes, piety, which may be called the predominant category of Calvin's spirituality, is "the attitude of a person integrated within God's order: a pious person is one who has taken his place within God's order."[19] To take one's place within God's order is to live by faith in God's goodness and obedience to His will. Christian living, indeed all of Christian spirituality, begins at the point of call-

---

16. *Institutes* 3.6.1.
17. *Institutes* 3.7.1.
18. Wallace, *Calvin's Doctrine of the Christian Life*, 118.
19. Richard, *The Spirituality of John Calvin*, 114.

ing upon God, denying ourselves, and aiming at God's glory, apart from which we pervert all order.

The Christian life as a life of order is closely related to the life of the Trinity. The Father is the source of order, Christ is the pattern of order, and the Holy Spirit is the restorer of order. It is God's program, or desire, that His own harmony and perfection be displayed among all people on earth; such was His purpose at creation and now in redemption. In his commentary on Ephesians 1:10 ("he might gather together in one all things in Christ"), Calvin observed:

> The Vulgate has *instaurare* (restore). Erasmus has added *summatim*. I have preferred to keep the strict meaning of the Greek word, ἀνακεφαλαιώσασθαι, because it is more agreeable to the context. For to my mind, Paul wants to teach that outside Christ all things were upset, but that through Him they have been reduced to order.... Such an ἀνακεφαλαίωσις as would bring us back to regular order, the apostle tells us, has been made in Christ. Formed into one body, we are united to God, and mutually conjoined with one another. But without Christ, the whole world is as it were a shapeless chaos and frightful confusion. He alone gathers us into true unity.[20]

As Oosterhaven has shown, this restoration to order occurs only through the work of the Holy Spirit in regenerating, bestowing faith to, sanctifying, and preserving believers. The Spirit does this through the instrument of the Word, which includes the Word Incarnate, Jesus Christ, and the Word inscripturated, Holy Scripture, as well as the Word proclaimed in preaching.[21] Through the internal testimony of the Holy Spirit, the self-authenticating power of Scripture supplies both the objective ground and the subjective cause for the restoration of order.

One of the most important Scripture passages teaching the character and elements of divinely proportioned harmony and integration within the life of the believer is Titus 2:11–14. Calvin introduced his exposition of this passage in the *Institutes* with these words: "In another place, Paul more clearly, although briefly, delineates the individual parts of a well-ordered life." He continued:

---

20. *Commentary* on Ephesians 1:10.
21. Oosterhaven, "John Calvin: Order and the Holy Spirit," 30–4.

For, after he proffered the grace of God to hearten us, in order to pave the way for us to worship God truly he removed the two obstacles that chiefly hinder us: namely, ungodliness, to which by nature we are too much inclined; and second, worldly desires, which extend more widely. And by ungodliness, indeed, he not only means superstition but includes also whatever contends against the earnest fear of God. Worldly lusts are also equivalent to the passions of the flesh [cf. I John 2:16; Eph. 2:3; II Peter 2:18; Gal. 5:16; etc.]. Thus, with reference to both Tables of the Law, he commands us to put off our own nature and to deny whatever our reason and will dictate. Now he limits all actions of life to three parts: soberness, righteousness, and godliness. Of these, soberness doubtless denotes chastity and temperance as well as a pure and frugal use of temporal goods, and patience in poverty. Now righteousness embraces all the duties of equity in order that to each one be rendered what is his own [cf. Rom. 13:7]. There follows godliness, which joins us in true holiness with God when we are separated from the iniquities of the world. When these things are joined together by an inseparable bond, they bring about complete perfection.[22]

The establishment within human society of relationships that involve superiority and subjection belongs to the restoration of order as the goal of redemption. This mutuality is not only necessary for preserving order in society, but is a means whereby the image of God can be reflected within human life.[23] The ordered harmony to be promoted and protected by the earthly magistrate can be described well by identifying him as "the father of his country, the pastor of the people, the guardian of peace, the president of justice, the vindicator of innocence."[24] Earthly parenthood especially serves to represent the order and harmony of God Himself, as family relationships reflect the mutual submission and order of the divine Trinity. Marriage gives expression to companionship within mutual subjection. Calvin occasionally summarized the duties of those in authority by referring them to the law of mutual subjection, which demands that both those in authority and those under authority be subject to one another.[25]

---

22. *Institutes* 3.7.3.
23. Wallace, *Calvin's Doctrine of the Christian Life,* 160.
24. *Institutes* 4.20.24.
25. *Commentary* on 1 Peter 5:5.

The consolidation of this divinely proportioned harmony and integration may be understood as the essence of the kingdom of God. When we pray in the Lord's Prayer for the coming of God's kingdom, we are in fact praying that God will cause order, symmetry, harmony, and integrity to govern every relationship within creation and among His creatures. In expositing the meaning of the second petition of the Lord's Prayer (Matt. 6:10), Calvin observed that we are praying "that God will show His power both in Word and in Spirit, that the whole world may willingly come over to Him. The opposite of the Kingdom of God is complete ἀταξία (disorder) and confusion: nor is anything in the world well-ordered unless He arranges its thoughts and feelings by His controlling hand. So we conclude, that the beginning of the Kingdom of God in us, is the end of the old man, the denial of self, that we may turn to newness of life."[26]

In Calvin's understanding, the restoration of history and of society is linked inseparably to the renewal of the elect, according to Schreiner. She goes so far as to say that "the efforts and activity of the elect directly contribute to the restoration of the world's order, [and] Calvin believed that Christians are called to a well-ordered life in the world, not only to guarantee the survival of society but for the glory of God and the upbuilding of the church."[27] This ordered life contributes to the gradual restoration of an ordered world. United to Christ as the divine manifestation of genuinely ordered humanity in the world, believers understand the revealed law of God as providing coherence within the order of nature. Most helpful is Schreiner's observation that "in Calvin's thought, the ordered life of the church bears a social and ecclesiastical dimension which includes, but also goes beyond, the restraint of evil imposed by natural law. The life of charity and justice helps to restore society to order and to the praise of God."[28] Here we find a clue in Calvin for the relationship between the church and the world, for, as Schreiner observes, "Calvin's doctrines of predestination, the certainty of salvation, spiritual combat, and sanctification directed Christians outward toward the world. The elect are turned toward creation for the good of the neighbor, the upbuilding of the church, and the restoration of society. Concepts

26. *Commentary* on Matthew 6:10.
27. Schreiner, *The Theater of His Glory*, 110.
28. Ibid.

of order, stewardship, service, charity, equity, and justice governed
Calvin's ethic and demonstrate the high evaluation he placed on the
active, ordered, and sanctified activity of Christian life."[29] Calvin saw
the church as the organ that led the renewal of both the cosmos and
society. Christians are restored by Jesus Christ to be active in the
ordering of society, not because this world can offer salvation or fulfillment, but because these activities express the glory of God within
His created order.[30]

CALVIN'S TEACHING ON ORDER
AND POSTMODERNISM

The question before us is that of relevance. How can this concept of
order as divinely proportioned harmony and integration, a concept
interwoven throughout Calvin's thought, serve the church in the
twenty-first century?

Let me suggest two points of contact between Calvin's teaching
on order and concerns being raised in the twenty-first century by
postmodernism. The first is ecclesiology and the second is vocation.

I do not presume to offer a comprehensive definition of postmodernism or to probe its many deep complexities.[31] In simple terms,
postmodernism rejects the idea of a universe in which unified truth is
embedded in favor of a universe that is historical, relational, and personal, one where all truth is historically and culturally conditioned,
and therefore relative. All truth is social truth, more a construction of
the human personality than an objective phenomenon.

Among its sympathetic critics is Stanley Grenz, who urges evangelicals to reflect on ways to meet the concerns of postmodernism
with the heritage of biblical Christian thought, to see postmodernism
as a *cri de coeur*, a genuine cry from the heart. Grenz has encour-

---

29. Ibid., 111.

30. Ibid., 114, 122.

31. Valuable surveys and evaluations of postmodernism include *The Challenge
of Postmodernism: An Evangelical Engagement*, ed. David S. Dockery (Wheaton: Victor
Books / SP Publications, 1995); D. A. Carson, *The Gagging of God* (Grand Rapids:
Zondervan, 1996); Millard J. Erickson, *Postmodernizing the Faith: Evangelical Responses
to the Challenge of Postmodernism* (Grand Rapids: Baker, 1998); F. G. Oosterhoff,
Postmodernism: A Christian Appraisal (Winnipeg: Premier Publishing, 1999); and *The
Challenge of Postmodernism: An Evangelical Engagement*, ed. David S. Dockery, 2nd ed.
(Grand Rapids: Baker Academic, 2001).

aged evangelical theologians to articulate the gospel in terms that are post-individualistic, post-rationalistic, post-dualistic, and post-noeticentric.[32]

The Church

As we consider the contribution of Calvin's emphasis on redemption as the restoration of order in relation to the church, recall our suggestive definition of order as divinely proportioned harmony and integration. The unity, harmony, and order of the church of Jesus Christ were very important to Calvin. These features constituted not merely the external attributes of an association of believers, but formed the essence of the communion of saints in Christ Jesus. Put another way, God's people are redeemed and called to actively unify, harmonize, and integrate every spiritual blessing received from God the Father through the Son by the Spirit.

Far from being a set of externally imposed rules, any biblical church order gives expression to the church's identity as the new humanity in Christ, the restored *imago Dei*. Wallace writes: "It is within the Church that the mutual communication of offices which... is that aspect of the order of nature which is the basis of human society, finds its truest and best expression in the service of one member for another within the body of Christ—this 'beautiful order' and 'symmetry' of the Church being a true reflexion of the order and symmetry of man's original creation in the image of God."[33] Calvin saw such divinely ordered symmetry in the distribution of spiritual gifts in the church.[34] Love among the saints is the bond of unity, the fiber of harmony, and the texture of symmetry in the church. The bond of faith and unity is created by the Holy Spirit, first between Christ and His people, and then among the saints themselves. We have no access to God in prayer, no union with Christ as our Head, and no hope for a future inheritance without such divinely proportioned harmony and integration among believers. Moreover, such order and harmony within the church places the liberty believers

---

32. See his *Revisioning Evangelical Theology: A Fresh Agenda for the 21st Century* (Downers Grove, Ill.: InterVarsity, 1993) and *A Primer on Postmodernism* (Grand Rapids: Eerdmans, 1996), esp. 161–74.

33. Wallace, *Calvin's Doctrine of the Christian Life*, 244.

34. *Commentary* on Romans 6:6.

have in Christ in service to love toward fellow believers. Solicitude and care must be shown particularly toward the weak in the faith, who might be led astray by the example of the strong.

In sum, we must value the welfare of the church above our own welfare, realizing that no individual member can flourish without the entire body flourishing.

Listen for a moment to similar notes being sounded among post-modernists. "At the heart of a postmodern Christian ecclesiology," Grenz writes, "is the concept of the church as community."[35] True humanness is found only in relationships with a personal being out-side oneself. Postmodernism is working with an understanding of community that includes the features of shared identity, integrated diversity rather than uniformity and unanimity, and personal focus. The human self is dependent on the group; the human person is socially produced, formed by a "tradition." Personal identity is shaped by the community in which the person is a participant.

Taken as a whole, the Bible teaches that God's program is directed to the goal of bringing about a community whose origin lies in God Himself, patterned after the Lord Jesus Christ, and empowered by the Holy Spirit. The integrative relationship between the identity of the triune God and the identity of the church lies at the heart of the church's relationship to the world. "The church's identity as a community must emerge out of the identity of the God it serves and in whom its life is hidden...." At the heart of the biblical narra-tive is God's program of restoring humanity as the *imago Dei*, as the reflection of His own character. Because the Holy Trinity exists in relationship, the *imago Dei* does as well, extending to the church-as-*imago Dei*. "The church is to be a people who reflect in relation to each other and to all creation the character of the Creator and thereby bear witness to the divine purpose for humankind.... This determines the church's proclaiming, reconciling, sanctifying, and unifying mission in the world."[36] The source of the church's existence is in its union with Christ, the *imago Dei* par excellence (2 Cor. 4:4; Col. 1:15; Heb. 1:3). Being in Christ is the source of the church's true identity in the

---

35. Stanley J. Grenz, "Ecclesiology," *The Cambridge Companion to Postmodern Theology*, ed. Kevin J. Vanhoozer (Cambridge: Cambridge University Press, 2003), 257.

36. Grenz, "Ecclesiology," 267.

world as the fellowship of those who participate in the life of the triune God by grace through faith. To live as the church is to live the ordered life as a testimony to the world of the power of grace and of the purpose of the gospel. True humanness flowers in the church of Jesus Christ as the ordered new humanity.

Vocation

A second point of contact between Calvin's emphasis on order as divinely proportioned harmony and integration is the postmodern search for personal identity. As those related to all other creatures in the universe by virtue of being created in God's image, human beings have a special calling or vocation within the matrix of relationships. But what, really, does it mean to live according to the "calling" the Lord gives us? In commenting on Calvin's teaching about *vocatio*, or "calling," John Webster notes:

> What is his "calling"? It is not mere designation to a location in a social or metaphysical scheme. Rather, it is to a "kind of living" characterized by both integration (what Calvin later calls "harmony") and a "path" or movement toward a "goal." "Looking to" this calling is, moreover, very far from passivity, mere occupation of a space; it is engagement "in all life's actions" in "a particular way of life." The Trinitarian setting of Calvin's sketch of calling to a human way of life is implicit; but it would not be difficult to fill out. Created by the Father for the active life of fellowship, the creature is reconciled by the Son and renewed by the Spirit, impelled into true human living. The grace of the triune God is thus the ground, healing, and quickening of life.[37]

In contrast to the subjectivization of human identity, where the self is supposed to create its own identity, Christian theology insists that "nature and destiny can be construed as 'role' or—as some classical theology might have put is—as 'office.' Role and office are the shape of the self and its activity; like 'calling' they are not mere 'placing' but the form and direction bestowed upon human life through participation in a historically structured set of relations. In those relations, the

---

37. John Webster, "The Human Person," *The Cambridge Companion to Postmodern Theology*, ed. Kevin J. Vanhoozer (Cambridge: Cambridge University Press, 2003), 230.

human subject encounters calls, invitations, corrections, and blessing which enable identity and which undergird purposive action."[38]

Let me state the matter this way: in Calvin, with his emphasis on the Trinitarian source, on the Christomorphic pattern, and on the Spirit's energizing perfection of order as divinely proportioned harmony and integration, the "ecclesial self" (Grenz[39]) meets the "responsible self" (to borrow only the title of H. Richard Niebuhr's work[40]). The Reformers in general, and Calvin in particular, stressed that as believers live before the face of God, both the active life (daily labor) and the contemplative life (special service) are equally spiritual, integrated, and harmonized in Christ through the Spirit. Their recovery of the biblical notion of office both liberated life and assigned value to its various activities. Father, mother, servant, citizen, artisan, craftsman, merchant, and noble—all could now live and labor *in this world* as children of God. Every vocation is carried out under God and His Word, and alongside others.

Conclusion

In 2009, God gave us a welcome opportunity to reflect together on the life and labor of his servant, John Calvin. Whether Calvin himself would have personally enjoyed all the attention cannot be determined but only surmised. I think not. But he surely would have enjoyed the reflection on biblical truth, on churchly identity in society, and on Christian engagement with living before God in our modern world. With the passing of the centuries, the legacy of Calvin has remained as richly textured as ever, rewarding any serious attempt to follow his lead in thinking God's thoughts after Him.

In a real sense, Calvin's life and labor remain perhaps the strongest testimony to the significance in his theology of the concept of order as divinely proportioned harmony and integration. Calvin exhibited the harmony and integration of thinking and doing, of prayer and work (*ora et labora*), of theology and life. He championed the ordered and integrated spirituality of the Father's original cre-

---

38. Ibid., 231.
39. See Stanley Grenz, *The Social God and the Relational Self: A Trinitarian Theology of the* Imago Dei (Louisville: Westminster John Knox, 2001), esp. 304–336.
40. H. Richard Niebuhr, *The Responsible Self: An Essay in Christian Moral Philosophy* (New York: Harper & Row, 1963).

ation, made accessible in Christ Jesus to the redeemed church, and cultivated by the Holy Spirit within the renewed believer—*in that order!* There are not three spiritualities, but one, because undergirding all of these, and common to all of these, is the spirituality of the triune God Himself as source, pattern, and power of all genuine human living.

CHAPTER 13

Christian Marriage in the 21st Century: Listening to Calvin on the Purpose of Marriage

Michael A. G. Haykin

In the final decade of the second century A.D., an African Christian by the name of Septimius Florens Tertullianus[1]—we know him simply as Tertullian—penned one of the loveliest descriptions of Christian marriage in the literary corpus of the ancient church:

> How shall we ever be able adequately to describe the happiness of that marriage which the Church arranges,…upon which the blessing sets a seal, at which angels are present as witnesses, and to which the Father gives his consent?… How beautiful, then, the marriage of two Christians, two who are one in hope, one in desire, one in the way of life they follow, one in the religion they practice. They are as brother and sister, both servants of the same Master. Nothing divides them, either in flesh or in spirit. They are, in very truth, two in one flesh; and where there is but one flesh there is also but one spirit. They pray together, they worship together, they fast together; instructing one another, encouraging one another, strengthening one another. Side by side they visit God's church and partake of God's Banquet; side by side they face difficulties and persecution, share their consolations. They have no secrets from one another; they never shun each other's company; they never bring sorrow to each other's hearts. Unembarrassed they visit the sick and assist the needy. They give alms without anxiety;…they perform their daily exercises of piety without hindrance…. Psalms and hymns they sing to one another, striving to see which one of them will chant

---

1. This is the name given to him by medieval manuscripts. See T. D. Barnes, *Tertullian: A Historical and Literary Study* (Oxford: Clarendon Press, 1971), 242.

more beautifully the praises of their Lord. Hearing and seeing this, Christ rejoices. To such as these he gives his peace.[2]

Building on the biblical given that marriage is a one-flesh union (Gen. 2:24; Matt. 19:4–6; 1 Cor. 6:16–17), Tertullian detailed what such a union entails with regard to Christian privileges and responsibilities. It is noteworthy that Tertullian assumed that a Christian marriage is one that has the blessing of the church, a perspective that can be traced back at least to Ignatius of Antioch at the beginning of the second century.[3]

Tertullian's high view of marriage was also particularly significant in light of the church's battle at the time with the Gnostics, who despised marriage and rejected it as a legitimate choice for one seeking to lead a spiritual life. In the words of one Gnostic, Saturninus, "marriage and procreation are of Satan."[4] The church's general response to this Gnostic disparagement of marriage was shaped by biblical texts such as 1 Timothy 4:1–4, which stress that marriage is a good estate and one ordained of God. Subsequent Christian thought has never explicitly departed from this key truth. As John Chrysostom (345–407), one of the leading preachers of the late fourth century, argued: "How foolish are those who belittle marriage! If marriage were something to be condemned, Paul would never call Christ a bridegroom and the Church a bride."[5]

LATE PATRISTIC AND MEDIEVAL BACKGROUND

Yet, there have been writers within the parameters of Christian orthodoxy who have sounded significantly different notes from those of Tertullian and Chrysostom on the vital institution of marriage. The latter's fourth-century contemporary Jerome (d. 420), for instance, who was responsible for the Latin translation of the Bible known as the Vulgate, vigorously defended the view that celibacy was a vastly superior state to marriage, more virtuous and more pleasing to God.

---

2. Tertullian, *To His Wife* 2.8, in *Treatises on Marriage and Remarriage*, trans. William P. LeSaint (1951 ed.; repr., Ramsey, N.J.: Paulist Press, n.d.), 35–6.

3. See Ignatius, *Letter to Polycarp*, 5.

4. Cited in Irenaeus, *Against Heresies* 1.24.

5. John Chrysostom, *Homily 20 on Ephesians 5:22–23*, in *On Marriage and Family Life*, trans. Catharine Roth and David Anderson (Crestwood, N.J.: St. Vladimir's Press, 1986), 54–5.

Jerome was convinced that all of those who were closest to God in the Scriptures were celibate. In fact, Jerome argued, sexual relations between spouses was a distinct obstacle to leading a life devoted to the pursuit of genuine spirituality.[6]

Augustine (354–430), another Latin-speaking theologian from the same era, whose thought provided the foundation for much of the thinking of the Middle Ages, similarly maintained that the individual who devotes himself or herself to Christ in order to live a celibate lifestyle is like the angels. He or she experiences a foretaste of heaven, for in heaven there is no marriage.[7] Why, then, did God ordain marriage? In Augustine's eyes, it was given for the sake of fidelity, that is, the avoidance of illicit sex, and as a symbol of the unity of those who would inherit the heavenly Jerusalem, but primarily for the procreation of children.[8] Commenting on Genesis 2, Augustine declared that Eve would have been no use to Adam if she had not been able to bear children. What, then, of the biblical idea, found in this very chapter of Genesis, that the woman was made to be a delightful companion to the man, a source of comfort and strength? And what of the man as this for the woman? These ideas receive scant attention in Augustine's theology.[9]

Exaltation of Celibacy

These positions of Jerome and Augustine were largely embraced by the medieval Roman Catholic Church, which affirmed the goodness of marriage but argued that celibacy was a much better option for those wanting to pursue a life of holiness and serve God vocationally.[10] Not surprisingly, by the High Middle Ages—the Second Lateran Council (1139), to be specific—the Roman Catholic Church legislated that only those who were celibate were to be ordained. But it was precisely here that reality collided with theological legislation,

---

6. J. N. D. Kelly, *Jerome: His Life, Writings, and Controversies* (New York: Harper & Row, 1975), 183, 187.

7. James A. Mohler, *Late Have I Loved You: An Interpretation of Saint Augustine on Human and Divine Relationships* (New York: New City Press, 1991), 71.

8. Ibid., 68. See also the summary of Augustine's position in John Witte, Jr., *From Sacrament to Contract: Marriage, Religion and Law in the Western Tradition* (Louisville: Westminster John Knox Press, 1997), 21–2.

9. Edmund Leites, "The Duty to Desire: Love, Friendship, and Sexuality in Some Puritan Theories of Marriage," *Journal of Social History*, 15 (1981–1982): 384.

10. Witte, *From Sacrament to Contract*, 24–5.

for many of those who were technically celibate priests in the High and Late Middle Ages were not able to live chastely. As John Calvin once noted, "virginity...is an excellent gift; but it is given only to a few."[11] One of the major scandals of the late medieval church was the household of the parish priest, who was celibate but not chaste, his so-called "cook" or "housekeeper" actually serving as his concubine.[12] For Calvin, the Roman Catholic requirement of celibacy for its priests was thus a "diabolical system," "a modern tyranny—in sum, a doctrine of devils."[13] So it was that for many in Western Europe, the Reformation in the sixteenth century was not only a rediscovery of the heart of the gospel and the way of salvation, but also a recovery of a fully biblical view of marriage.

After the death of his wife, Idelette, in March 1549, Calvin (1509–1564) wrote to his fellow Reformer and confidant, Pierre Viret (1511–1571): "I am deprived of my excellent life companion, who, if misfortune had come, would have been my willing companion not only in exile and sorrow, but even in death."[14] This simple statement from one of the central figures in the Reformation, who was normally very discreet about his personal feelings, reveals a view of marriage poles apart from that of medieval Roman Catholicism. According to the Reformers and those who followed in their stead—such as the Puritans of the seventeenth century and the Evangelicals of the eighteenth and nineteenth centuries—marriage has an innate excellence, is vital for the development of Christian affection and friendship, and is one of God's major means for developing Christian character and spiritual maturity.

In what follows, I explore this perspective on Christian marriage through Calvin's experience of wedded life, interweaving some theological reflection from Calvin on the institution of marriage. I should note that Calvin, drawing on his legal training, was

---

11. Cited in J. Graham Miller, *Calvin's Wisdom: An Anthology Arranged Alphabetically by a Grateful Reader* (Edinburgh: Banner of Truth, 1992), 206.

12. Susan C. Karant-Nunn, "Reformation Society, Women and the Family," in *The Reformation World*, ed. Andrew Pettegree (New York: Routledge, 2000), 437–8.

13. Cited in Miller, *Calvin's Wisdom*, 206, and Scott Brown, *Family Reformation: The Legacy of Sola Scriptura in Calvin's Geneva* (Wake Forest, N.C.: Merchant Adventurers, 2009), 114. I am deeply indebted to Brown for sending me a copy of his book and to Joel Beeke for drawing my attention to it.

14. Cited in Richard Stauffer, *The Humanness of John Calvin*, trans. George H. Shriver (Nashville: Abingdon, 1971), 45.

instrumental in crafting a comprehensive body of law surrounding marriage and divorce, but I will not directly treat this area of Calvin's thought here.[15]

THE COURTSHIPS OF CALVIN

There is no evidence that Calvin seriously entertained getting married prior to his sojourn in Strasbourg.[16] As he wrote around this time: "I have never married, and I do not know whether I ever will. If I do, it will be in order to be freer from many daily troubles and thus freer for the Lord. Lack of sexual continence would not be the reason I would point to for marrying. No one can charge me with that."[17] It was not that Calvin was opposed to marriage. His embrace of Reformation doctrine certainly entailed approval of marriage. As he noted in his sermon on Ephesians 5:31–33: "Marriage is not a thing ordained by men. We know that God is the author of it, and that it is solemnized in his name."[18] In his commentary on the minor prophet Malachi, Calvin put it even more succinctly: "God is the founder of marriage."[19] It was simply that there was no need in his life pushing him in that direction. As he said on another occasion, "I shall not belong to those who are accused of attacking [the Church of] Rome, like the Greeks fought Troy, only to be able to take a wife."[20] If he did enter into the estate of marriage, he confessed in the above-cited text, it would be so that he could be freed from the concerns of daily life and thus freer to give himself more wholeheartedly to the work of Christ.

But if Calvin was not eager to get married, a number of his friends

---

15. For details on this subject, see especially John Witte Jr. and Robert M. Kingdon, *Sex, Marriage, and Family in John Calvin's Geneva. Vol. 1: Courtship, Engagement, and Marriage* (Grand Rapids: Eerdmans, 2005), 97.

16. Ibid., 87.

17. Cited in ibid., 97.

18. Cited in John Witte Jr., "Marriage and Family Life," in *The Calvin Handbook*, ed. Herman J. Selderhuis, trans. Henry J. Baron, Judith J. Guder, Randi H. Lundell, and Gerrit W. Sheeres (Grand Rapids: Eerdmans, 2009), 457. This important overview of Calvin's thinking about marriage will henceforth be cited as Witte, "Marriage and Family Life."

19. Cited in Miller, *Calvin's Wisdom*, 204

20. Cited in William J. Petersen, "Idelette: John Calvin's Search for the Right Wife," *Christian History*, 5, 4 (1986): 12.

were anxious to see him wed, among whom the chief were Martin Bucer (1491–1551) and Guillaume Farel (1489–1565).

Bucer was at the forefront of a sweeping reform of marriage, both institutionally and conceptually, in Strasbourg and various other cities in Switzerland and Germany. A former Dominican monk who had been converted through the preaching of Martin Luther (1483–1546), Bucer had married his first wife, a former nun by the name of Elisabeth Silberstein, in 1522, and had come to view love as the indispensable qualification of marriage. Where love was absent, he even reasoned, there was sufficient ground for divorce.[21] (This was not a ground for divorce that Calvin would later sanction, though; in harmony with other Reformers, he would reject the Roman Catholic doctrine of the indissolubility of marriage as it had been defined in the Middle Ages.) Bucer was especially convinced that a gospel minister was rarely able, given the stresses and strains of ministry, to fulfill his calling without a faithful companion. Machiel van den Berg rightly suggests that "Bucer may well be called the founder of the Protestant parsonage."[22]

Calvin's Hopes for a Bride

Only a few months after Calvin arrived in Strasbourg in 1538, Bucer had found a woman for Calvin to consider marrying. Things seem to have been proceeding toward an actual wedding, for Calvin wrote to Farel in February 1539 to ask whether he could come to Strasbourg "to solemnize and ask a blessing upon the marriage."[23] Calvin told Farel that he expected the bride to arrive shortly after Easter, and there is a distinct possibility that he was to meet her then for the first time.[24] As it turned out, the marriage did not take place, but there is no surviving literary evidence to indicate why.

---

21. Witte and Kingdon, *Sex, Marriage, and Family in John Calvin's Geneva*, 98.

22. Machiel van den Berg, *Friends of Calvin*, trans. Reinder Bruinsma (Grand Rapids: Eerdmans, 2009), 125.

23. John Calvin, "Letter to Guillaume Farel, February 28, 1539," in *John Calvin: Tracts and Letters*, ed. Jules Bonnet, trans. David Constable (Edinburgh: Banner of Truth, 2009), 4:110. This translation of Calvin's correspondence will henceforth be simply cited as *Tracts and Letters*, with the appropriate volume and page. In tracing the various attempts by Calvin's friends to get him married, Witte and Kingdon, *Sex, Marriage, and Family in John Calvin's Geneva*, 97–100, has been very helpful.

24. Calvin, "Letter to Guillaume Farel, February 28, 1539," *Tracts and Letters*, 4:110.

It was then Farel's turn to play matchmaker. By the following May, he had found a woman whom he thought might suit his
friend. When he wrote to ascertain Calvin's level of interest, Calvin
responded with details as to what he was seeking in a wife:

> I am not one of those insane kind of lovers who, once smitten
> by the first sight of a fine figure, cherishes even the faults of his
> lover. The only beauty that seduces me is of one who is chaste,
> not too fastidious, modest, thrifty, patient, and hopefully she
> will be attentive to my health.[25]

This is an important text, for in it Calvin laid out what was most
vital for him in a potential spouse, namely character and such inner
qualities as modesty, self-control, and patience. In other words, in
Calvin's view, a Christian seeking a wife or a husband must consider
genuine piety as the thing most needful.[26]

In other texts, Calvin revealed that he did not altogether discount
the place of physical beauty in the choice of a spouse. As he pointed
out in 1554 in his commentary on Genesis 6:2, "Moses does not condemn men for regarding beauty in their choice of wives, only lust."[27]
And in the same work, when he came to comment on Jacob's love for
Rachel, he noted:

> A man who is induced to choose a wife because of the elegance
> of her form will not necessarily sin, provided reason always
> maintains the ascendancy, and holds the wantonness of passion
> under control.... For it is a very culpable lack of self-control
> when any man chooses a wife only for her beauty. Her excel-
> lence of disposition ought to be deemed the most important.[28]

Calvin was well aware how a man can be bedazzled by a beautiful
woman and forget that "excellence of disposition" is all-important,
hence his emphasis that "reason...maintains the ascendancy" over
the passions set in motion by the eyes.

25. Calvin, "Letter to Guillaume Farel, May 19, 1539," *Tracts and Letters*, 4:141,
following the amended translation by Witte and Kingdon, *Sex, Marriage, and Family
in John Calvin's Geneva*, 109.
26. Witte, "Marriage and Family Life," 461–2.
27. *Commentary* on Genesis 6:2 (cited in Witte and Kingdon, *Sex, Marriage, and
Family in John Calvin's Geneva*, 108).
28. *Commentary* on Genesis 29:18 (cited in Witte and Kingdon, *Sex, Marriage, and
Family in John Calvin's Geneva*, 108).

Farel's potential spouse for his friend soon disappeared, only to be replaced by two more the following year. In February 1540, Calvin wrote to Farel that a woman of considerable wealth had been proposed to him as a possible wife. Calvin told his friend that he had "the audacity to think of taking a wife." But he had concerns about the woman's suitability. First, the woman was German and apparently could not speak French, and when Calvin had asked whether she was willing to learn French, she had asked for time to think about it—not a good sign! Calvin also seems to have been concerned that she might find it difficult living with someone like himself, whose standard of living was below what she was accustomed to.

At the same time, Calvin had his brother Antoine (d. 1573) approach another woman, who was highly regarded by those who knew her, about marriage. Again Calvin asked Farel to be ready to come to conduct a wedding, which, he hoped, would be held before March 10 of that year. He would look quite foolish, he added, if this marriage also failed to transpire.[29] He must have been embarrassed indeed, for this courtship also fell through.

When it did, the family of the wealthy woman who spoke no French began to try to rekindle Calvin's interest in this woman. But Calvin told Farel plainly that the only way he would ever consider marrying her was if the Lord altogether took away his wits![30] That summer he told Farel, "I have not yet found a wife," and painfully admitted that he was on the verge of resigning himself to a life of celibacy.[31]

But two months later, everything had changed. Calvin had married a widow whom he had known for a number of years, Idelette van Buren (d. 1549).[32]

---

29. Calvin, "Letter to Guillaume Farel, February 6, 1540," *Tracts and Letters*, 4:173–4.

30. Calvin, "Letter to Guillaume Farel, March 29, 1540," *Tracts and Letters*, 4:175.

31. Calvin, "Letter to Guillaume Farel, June 21, 1540," *Tracts and Letters*, 4:191.

32. For studies of Idelette, who is often named by the French version of her surname, "de Bure," see especially Willem Balke, *Calvin and the Anabaptist Radicals*, trans. William Heynen (Grand Rapids: Eerdmans, 1981), 133–8; Petersen, "Idelette: John Calvin's Search for the Right Wife," 12–15; van den Berg, *Friends of Calvin*, 123–33. For further studies, see the articles and books listed by Balke, *Calvin and the Anabaptist Radicals*, 133–4, n.46, and Van den Berg, *Friends of Calvin*, 124, n.1.

Marriage to Idelette

Idelette's roots were in the Netherlands. Van den Berg suggests that she may have come from the province of Gelderland, where there is a town called Buren.[33] Be this as it may, her first husband, Jean Stordeur, was a Walloon from Liège, today in Belgium. For a time, Jean and Idelette were convinced Anabaptists. It was as a prominent Anabaptist that Jean first met Calvin in Geneva in March 1537, when Jean came to the city for a discussion between the Anabaptists and the Reformed pastors. Two years later, Calvin had succeeded in showing Jean and Idelette the error of their distinct Anabaptist views, and they became members of the French congregation that Calvin was pastoring in Strasbourg.

Jean died of the plague in the spring of 1540. Calvin obviously had gotten to know Idelette through the discussions she and her husband had had with him about the Reformed faith. Then, when Jean was dying, Calvin likely saw more of Idelette when he made pastoral visits to their home. What he saw of her made such a deep impression on him that by August 27, 1540, Calvin had married her. Idelette had two children, a boy and a girl, from her first marriage, and thus Calvin inherited a ready-made family, as it were. Although Calvin had rightly emphasized that external beauty was not to be a key determinant in marriage, Idelette was, according to Farel, very pretty.[34]

THE PURPOSES OF MARRIAGE

Compared to the marriages of other famous Reformers, we know comparatively little about Calvin's marriage to Idelette. Luther's famous marriage to Katharina von Bora, for example, became something of a public exemplar for Protestants. Not so Calvin's marriage, which was very much in line with Calvin's habitual reticence to go public about his personal affairs. However, he did reveal snippets about his relationship with Idelette, and in the process, he left us important clues about his ideas as to the purposes of marriage.

---

33. Van den Berg, *Friends of Calvin*, 128.
34. Ibid., 129.

Companionship

First, Calvin believed companionship was a chief purpose of marriage. Following Idelette's death on March 29, 1549, he stated in
his little tract *Concerning Scandals* (1550) that Idelette was "a rare
woman" (*singularis exempli femina*, literally, "a woman of matchless
type").[35] This briefest of statements matches what we learn about
Idelette from a letter Calvin wrote after her death. It was addressed
to Viret and written on April 7, 1549. In it, Calvin stated:

> Although the death of my wife has been exceedingly painful
> to me, yet I subdue my grief as well as I can...you know well
> enough how tender, or rather soft, my mind is. Had not a pow-
> erful self-control, therefore, been vouchsafed to me, I could not
> have borne up so long. And truly mine is no common source
> of grief. I have been bereaved of the best possible companion
> of my life, of one, who, had it been so ordered, would not only
> have been the willing sharer of my indigence, but even of my
> death. During her life she was my faithful co-labourer in my
> ministry.[36]

Here, in the space of a few lines from his sorrowing heart, Calvin
summed up the Reformed understanding of marriage: it is a union
of intimate allies. Idelette had been the "best possible companion" of
his life (*optima socio vitae*), one who had been a "faithful co-labourer"
in his ministry (*fida ministerii me iadjutrix*).

Behind this understanding of marriage lies Genesis 2:18–24,
where we are told that being alone was not "good" for Adam, which
is striking in view of the fact that everything else God had made to
that point is said to have been good. So God made Adam a "helper"
(*'ezer*), a word, according to Calvin's commentary on this text, that
goes to the heart of his understanding of marriage:

> Now, since God assigns the woman as a help to the man, he...
> pronounces that marriage will really prove to men the best
> support of life.... The vulgar proverb, indeed, is, that she is a
> necessary evil; but the voice of God is rather to be heard, which

---

35. Balke, *Calvin and the Anabaptist Radicals*, 136.
36. Calvin, *Tracts and Letters*, 5:216, alt.

declares that woman is given as a companion and an associate to the man, to assist him to live well.[37]

But the fallenness of humanity—which, in Calvin's day, had issued in the unbiblical perspectives on marriage, celibacy, and sexuality promoted by Roman Catholic theologians—has deeply disfigured God's intentions for the holy estate of marriage. As Calvin went on to delineate:

> I confess, indeed, that in this corrupt state of mankind, the blessing of God, which is here described, is neither perceived nor flourishes; but the cause of the evil must be considered, namely, that the order of nature, which God had appointed, has been inverted by us. For if the integrity of man had remained to this day such as it was from the beginning, that divine institution would be clearly discerned, and the sweetest harmony would reign in marriage; because the husband would look up with reverence to God; the woman in this would be a faithful assistant to him; and both, with one consent, would cultivate a holy, as well as friendly and peaceful intercourse.[38]

It was this conviction about marriage, rooted as it was in solid reflection on Scripture, that led Calvin to make such wide-ranging statements about marriage as that it is "the sacred bond," "a holy fellowship," "a divine partnership," "a loving association," "the best support of life," and "the holiest kind of company in all the world."[39]

Having Children

A second purpose of marriage for Calvin was the procreation of children. Thus, Calvin argued that those who were incapable of having sexual relations should not marry, for such marriages "completely obviate the nature and purpose of marriage."[40]

In July 1542, during their first summer back in Geneva, Idelette

---

37. Cited in Brown, *Family Reformation*, 131–2. On companionship as the central purpose of marriage, see Rousas J. Rushdoony, "The Doctrine of Marriage," in *Toward a Christian Marriage. A Chalcedon Study*, ed. Elizabeth Fellersen (2nd ed., Vallecito, Calif.: Ross House, 1994), 12.

38. Cited in Brown, *Family Reformation*, 132.

39. This selection of phrases is taken from Witte, *From Sacrament to Contract*, 109, and Brown, *Family Reformation*, 97–114, 131–2.

40. Cited in Witte, "Marriage and Family Life," 462.

gave birth prematurely to a boy, whom they named Jacques.[41] By
mid-August, though, the child had died. Viret's wife wrote a con-
solatory letter to Idelette, for which Calvin thanked her on behalf of
his wife. He noted that Idelette was so overcome with grief that she
could not even dictate a letter in reply. "The Lord," he told Viret,
"has indeed inflicted a severe and bitter wound in the death of our
infant son. But he is himself a Father, and knows best what is good
for his children."[42] Here Calvin drew strength from his conviction
that God always acts out of goodness with regard to His children.

In 1544, Idelette became pregnant again and this time bore a
daughter, who also soon succumbed to death.[43] Yet a third child
eventually was born to Calvin and his wife, but this child, too, was
taken away soon after birth.

A few years before Calvin's death, one of Calvin's former co-
workers, François Bauduin, who had become estranged from Calvin
and penned a bitter biography of him, stated that God had punished
him for his misdeeds by not giving him any children. Calvin tersely
replied, "I have myriads of sons throughout the Christian world," as
was indeed the case.[44]

Despite the early deaths of his children, we have a picture of what
Calvin would have been like as a father from a letter he wrote to a
Dutch couple who were among his closest friends, Jacques de Bour-
gogne (d. 1556) and Yolande van Brederode.[45] In 1547, he wrote to
them shortly after the birth of one of their children: "I am sorry that I
cannot at least spend half a day there with you to laugh together with
you, trying to make the little child laugh also, at the risk of having to
experience how it would start to weep or cry."[46] Here is a rarely seen
side of the Reformer, one that reveals a man who delighted in the
joys of family life and who recognized that children were an essential reason for the institution of marriage.

But procreation was not the sole reason for marriage; thus, Calvin

---

41. Calvin, "Letter to Pierre Viret, July, 1542," *Tracts and Letters*, 4:335.
42. Calvin, "Letter to Pierre Viret, August 19, 1542," *Tracts and Letters*, 4:344.
43. Calvin mentions an illness of his daughter in a letter to Guillaume Farel,
May 30, 1544. *Tracts and Letters*, 4:420.
44. Calvin, *Tracts and Letters*, 4:344, n.3.
45. On Calvin's friendship with this couple, as well as the rift that developed
between them and Calvin, see van den Berg, *Friends of Calvin*, 185–95.
46. Cited in ibid., 193.

refused to countenance divorce on the grounds of sterility or barrenness. Neither did he agree with surrogate motherhood, as found in the story of Abraham, Sarah, Hagar, and their children. Those who cannot have children, Calvin emphasized, need to recognize that, in his words, "we are fruitful or barren as God imparts his power."[47] Here we see a concrete display of the theological conviction that undergirded all of Calvin's theology, namely, the sovereignty of God. Also, an inability to bear children opens a door to adopt orphans, and to nurture and care for relatives such as nephews and nieces.[48] Above all, husband and wife are to continue to be devoted to each other in mutual companionship and continue to engage in marital relations as an aspect of that companionship.[49]

It is noteworthy that Calvin encouraged husbands and wives to continue to enjoy one another sexually, even after the childbearing years were past. "Satan dazzles us," he preached in one of his sermons on Deuteronomy, "to imagine that we are polluted by intercourse," referring to a common Roman Catholic belief. But, he continued, "when the marital bed is dedicated to the name of the Lord, that is, when parties are joined together in his name, and live honourably, it is something of an holy estate."[50] Apart from the Pauline recognition in 1 Corinthians 7 that there may be certain seasons when a husband and his wife forgo sexual intimacy for spiritual reasons, Calvin emphasized in two of his sermons that a husband and his wife should not withhold sexual intimacy from the other.[51]

Conclusions

The depth and profundity of Calvin's theology of marriage exercised an enormous influence for good on his contemporaries and successors. In the words of John Witte, "Calvin's covenant theology of marriage proved to be a powerful Protestant model for marriage that exercised an enormous and enduring influence on the Western tradition."[52] Here are six conclusions derived from Calvin's view of marriage:

---

47. Cited in Witte, "Marriage and Family Life," 463.
48. Ibid.
49. Ibid.
50. Cited in Ibid.
51. Ibid.
52. Witte, *From Sacrament to Contract*, 109.

1. Christian marriage is an institution ordained and sealed by God. But we live in a world that is retreating rapidly from this rigorously biblical vision of the married estate. Ours is a day of sexual chaos, when there is massive confusion about marriage and gender, and why sexuality exists.[53] As the political philosopher Slavoj Žižek (1949–) has rightly summed it up, ours is a day of "ordained transgression, in which the marital commitment is perceived as ridiculously out of step."[54] But Calvin's day was also a day of confusion, with competing visions of marriage and unbiblical views of sexuality. If we listen, his wisdom can help guide our footsteps into ways pleasing to the One who designed marriage in the first place.

2. It is an exclusive heterosexual union between one man and one woman.

3. It is not to be entered into lightly, for a critical determining factor in choosing a spouse has to be character: Is he or she godly? Will he or she help me grow in Christ? Will our temperaments complement one another? While external attractiveness is not to be ignored, our culture's preoccupation with it has proven to be utterly foolish.

4. At its heart, marriage is an intimate alliance and companionship of two glorious bearers of the image of God, which finds expression in sexual intimacy.

5. Such a marriage is *the* divinely sanctioned context for the procreation and raising of children.

6. One final perspective of Calvin on marriage remains to be mentioned—the all-important Christological dimension. The Lord Jesus Christ designed Christian marriages—and here Calvin surely was thinking about Ephesians 5:25–32—to be "an image of his sacred union with the Church. What greater eulogy could be pronounced on the dignity of marriage?"[55]

---

53. Mark Noll, "Calvin's Battle for Marriage: Studying Geneva's sexual reformation has lessons for today," *Christianity Today*, April 1, 2006 (http://www.ctlibrary.com/ct/2006/april/20.104.html; accessed August 28, 2009).

54. "The Thrilling Romance of Orthodoxy," in Creston Davis, John Milbank, and Slavoj Žižek, eds., *Theology and the Political: The New Debate* (Durham, N.C.: Duke University Press, 2005), 53.

55. Cited in Brown, *Family Reformation*, 106.

Calvin and His
Contemporary Impact

CHAPTER 14

The Resurgence of Calvinism in America

J. Ligon Duncan III

A Reformed resurgence is happening today. It is young and vast, and stretches across the English-speaking world. You can see this resurgence in Australia, North America, Britain, and other parts of the world where conferences on Calvin are held, not only in old-line Calvinist denominations, but also in Baptist churches, independent churches, and charismatic churches. A fever for the glory of God has gotten into the bloodstream of a new generation. Even *Time* magazine noted this trend in the past year, calling "New Calvinism" one of ten key ideas sweeping the Western world today.[1]

What is going on? Where did this resurgence of Calvinism come from?

I first read William Cunningham's *Introduction to Historical Theology* about twenty-five years ago. It said that in the year 1800, weakness, slumber, and death reigned in the Church of Scotland. Pulpits that had proclaimed the glories of God and the crown covenant rights of the Lord Jesus Christ had become cold and moralistic.

God did three things to change this situation. The first was to prompt the publication of a book by Thomas McCrie titled *The Life of John Knox*. Within a matter of years, that book was in the home of every godly layperson in Scotland. Reading what God had done through the life and ministry of Knox restoked the fire of evangelicalism.

Second, a minister was converted. This preacher had been more interested in mathematics than the gospel, but when he thought he was about to die, he was brought to God by saving grace and faith in

---

1. David Van Biema, "Ten Ideas Changing the World Right Now," *Time*, March 12, 2009, http://www.time.com/time/specials/packages/article/0,28804,1884779_1884782_1884760,00.html (accessed Jan. 9, 2010).

Christ. That man was Thomas Chalmers. Under his teaching, a new evangelical revival in Scotland blossomed into full flower.

Third, boys born from 1801 to 1810 with names such as McCheyne, Bonar, and Buchanan grew up under the evangelical influence of Chalmers. That led to the revival of Reformed Christianity in Scotland. It also influenced the entire English-speaking world from that time to today.

I believe a similar resurgence is under way today, and I believe there are similar factors behind it. In fact, I see at least nine factors that have contributed specifically to the resurgence of Calvinism in America. But before I go into those factors, let me explain a few things.

First, the new Calvinism is not the full-orbed confessional Calvinism of the Three Forms of Unity or the Westminster Standards. The new Calvinism draws from the rich deposit of truth that has been bequeathed to us from older and wiser theologians, and it appreciates the *soteriology* of the older confessional Calvinism. But it does not adequately appreciate the *ecclesiology* that goes with it. In short, the new Calvinism is not identical to the old Calvinism. That is important for us to understand.

Second, the new Calvinism is a mixed theology. Every work on earth is a mixture. If you see slow but sure spiritual growth in your congregation due to the operation of the Holy Spirit and to the faithful administrations of the means of grace, is that work in your congregation pure and without sin? No, it is not. Every church in this world has some impurity. Likewise the new Calvinism contains considerable impurity.

In every factor that I list, we could find something to criticize. So I suggest, especially if you have drunk deeply from the pristine well of confessional Calvinism, that you appreciate what God is doing in a work that is mixed in character, and glorify Him by shepherding this awakening to a fuller appreciation of the glorious doctrine of the church as revealed in Scripture.

That said, here are nine factors that have contributed to this resurgence of Calvinism in America.

1. Three Preachers

Three key preachers have contributed to this new Calvinism: Charles

Haddon Spurgeon in the nineteenth century; David Martyn Lloyd-Jones in the middle of the twentieth century; and John MacArthur, who is still preaching today. One preacher was Baptist, one a Presbyterian/Independent Congregationalist, and one a dispensationalist. God certainly showed His sovereignty in choosing three such disparate men to revive an appreciation for Calvinism!

Spurgeon's fifty-seven-volume set of sermons preached at the Metropolitan Tabernacle has been commended by ministers as diverse as W. A. Criswell, Billy Graham, Stephen Olford, John Wolvoord, R. G. Lee, Charles Feinberg, Jack Hyles, and D. James Kennedy. Some of those men were avid anti-Calvinists, yet all heartily recommended the work of the great Calvinistic Baptist preacher Spurgeon to a generation of unsuspecting evangelicals, who swallowed his teachings hook, line, and sinker.

Spurgeon said, "I have my own private opinion that there is no such thing as preaching Christ and Him crucified unless you preach what is nowadays called *Calvinism*."[2] He consistently introduced generation after generation of Bible-believing preachers to the Word of God via the teachings of Calvinism in a grand vision of the display of God's grace in the work of salvation.

D. Martyn Lloyd-Jones, whom J. I. Packer says is the greatest man he has ever known,[3] also has had a staggering impact on twentieth-century evangelicalism. He towered like a giant in Britain in influencing Tyndale House, InterVarsity Fellowship, the International Fellowship of Evangelical Students, the Christian Medical Society, and the Evangelical Library. He also inspired many leaders in the United States. His sermons spoke powerfully to men such as my boyhood pastor, who had never read anything like Lloyd-Jones's exposition of the Sermon on the Mount. My pastor was completely caught up with that exposition and passed on the essence of those great sermons to me and others.

In his *Preaching and Preachers*, Lloyd-Jones encouraged a generation of expositional evangelical ministers. In his *Spiritual Depression*,

---

2. Charles H. Spurgeon, *The Autobiography of Charles H. Spurgeon* (Chicago: Curts and Jennings, 1898), 1:172.

3. Mark Dever, "Where'd All These Calvinists Come From? Part 2 of 10," 9Marks Ministries blog post, July 2, 2007, http://blog.9marks.org/2007/07/whered-all-thes.html (accessed Jan. 9, 2010).

he encouraged numerous hurting saints by providing comfort from the gospel.

Donald A. Carson said that he once slipped into a service at Westminster Chapel in London to hear Lloyd-Jones. After one sermon, Carson thought: "What's all the fuss about? He's just preaching the Bible." Eight weeks later, Carson realized that he was sitting under the most masterful expositor of Scripture ever.

Leader after leader can testify about Lloyd-Jones's impact. In short, Lloyd-Jones had a massive impact on his generation.

Lloyd-Jones was a Calvinist. He didn't wear that label on his sleeve and didn't use Calvinistic theological jargon, but he was emphatically a Calvinist. From the Welsh Methodist Church, which is Presbyterian, Lloyd-Jones brought sound Reformed theology into every sermon he preached. Lloyd-Jones would preach an evangelistic sermon every Sunday evening. Three hundred of those sermons were recorded on tape. Tim Keller, pastor of Redeemer Presbyterian Church in New York City, has listened to all of those sermons. He credits Lloyd-Jones with teaching him how to preach the gospel.

The third key preacher of the new Calvinism, John MacArthur, is still preaching today. MacArthur was raised in a dispensational Bible church, but he was so committed to the Word of God that he was willing to go wherever the Word took him. It led him to the glory of the sovereign God and the doctrines of grace. MacArthur's preaching, which was enriched by the doctrines of Calvinism, is heard in many languages by millions of people all over the world today.

I will never forget the story MacArthur told at one of his conferences about a young girl from a Muslim country who was attending the Master's College. She had come to faith in Christ by listening to a broadcast of MacArthur's sermons read by a man in her own language. She was from a Muslim family in a Muslim country, but she came to faith by listening to a radio-broadcast sermon.

Her father was a mid-level official in government. He loved his daughter so much that he allowed her to pursue her dream of going to the Master's College in California. She majored in computers and technology because her country would not allow her to study anything that included Christianity or the Bible. But along with her studies in computers, she began to study Greek, Hebrew, and related languages because she wanted to translate the Scriptures into the language of her people.

When she flew home, she was met at the airport by secret service agents of her country, who interrogated her for two hours, then released her. When she got home, her uncle was waiting for her. He asked, "Are you a Christian?"

She said, "Yes, I am." He said, "You have shamed our family and you will pay the price." He picked up a chair, broke it over her back, then took a leg and began beating her. When she feared for her life, her father walked in and rescued her. He drove her to the airport, put her on a plane, and told her not to come back. She arrived back in California at the Master's College, and just a few days later met with MacArthur.

MacArthur asked the young woman, "What were you thinking as your uncle was beating you to death?" She responded, "I was thinking that this man has a religion that he would kill for, but I have a Savior that I would die for."

I was humbled to the dust that this young woman knew so much of the glory of God's grace, the power of the Savior, and the sovereignty of God that she was willing to lay down her life for her Savior. She learned that from MacArthur, who teaches the doctrines of grace and the sovereignty of God.

2. Books

The second factor in the Reformed resurgence has been books. The grandfather organization that influenced this movement is the Banner of Truth Trust. Lloyd-Jones, Iain Murray, and others met in the late 1950s to establish a trust to republish Puritan literature. In those days, you could find Puritan literature only on the dusty shelves of neglected libraries or antiquarian bookstores in Britain and New England. The Banner of Truth Trust began to systematically and carefully publish Puritan literature as well as a magazine, to whet an appetite for sound, spiritual books.

Students in the 1970s who were used to shallow spiritual reading, suddenly had access to Thomas Brooks' *Precious Remedies Against Satan's Devices* and Stephen Charnock's massive *The Existence and Attributes of God*. These books, and scores of others, led to a deepening

grasp of biblical truth. All of these books, of course, were Calvinistic
and exalted the sovereignty of God in grace and salvation.

This, then, encouraged other publishers, such as Reformation
Heritage Books, to produce more sound, Calvinistic books.

3. Evangelists

Evangelists were another factor in the resurgence of Calvinism. The
idea of a Calvinistic evangelist would not have struck anyone as surprising in the sixteenth through nineteenth centuries, for the greatest
evangelists of those days were Calvinistic preachers. However, in the
twentieth century, perhaps because of the deleterious effects of the
Second Great Awakening and the pragmatic revivalism of Charles
Finney and D. L. Moody, Calvinism became disassociated with evangelism.

Calvinism birthed the modern missions movement and fed the
fires of evangelical preaching for decades. To help him preach 28,000
sermons during the Great Awakening, for example, George Whitefield read four times a day on his knees the writings of Matthew
Henry, the great English Calvinist. Yet one of the great charges levied
against Calvinism in the twentieth century was that it killed the gospel, diminished evangelicalism, and was deficient in evangelism.

D. James Kennedy changed that viewpoint. Kennedy, who
developed the Evangelism Explosion outreach method, was a passionate Calvinist and a passionate evangelist. We may fault some
of his methods as high-pressure sales tactics and decision-based,
but no one could question this man's commitment to the doctrines
of grace, to passionate evangelism, and to the public proclamation
of the gospel. After Kennedy became well known, it became difficult for people who listened to him to say that Calvinists couldn't
evangelize because of their theology. In Kennedy's wake, many more
helpful and biblical Calvinistic presentations of both the gospel and
of how one shares the gospel have been developed. Kennedy was a
pioneer for evangelism who dispelled the myth that Calvinism was
anti-evangelistic.

4. The Battle for the Bible

The fourth influence on the Reformed resurgence was the battle for
the Bible. This theological controversy of the late twentieth century

stretched across denominations of modern evangelicalism in North America and Britain.

Though many prominent non-Calvinists took a brave stand for the inerrancy of Scripture during the battle for the Bible, the most well-known people who defended Scripture through the International Council on Biblical Inerrancy were Packer, R. C. Sproul, James Montgomery Boice, and Roger Nicole.

In the late 1970s, a committee was asked to draft a document for the International Council on Biblical Inerrancy listing the affirmations and denials that would be debated at its next gathering. When the committee met, however, the draft was not finished. So Packer and Sproul sat up all night to draft that document.

It is almost impossible to calculate the exponential effect of their labor. Because the men of the International Council took a stand for the Bible, people outside of their own confessional traditions trusted them to defend and expound Scripture. They knew that when these men taught the sovereignty of God and the salvation of sinners, they had gotten those truths not from their own minds or from the opinions of the age, but from the Bible itself.

Calvinism thus spread through the denial of the inerrancy of Scripture by theological liberals. Don't tell me you don't serve a sovereign God, for He who sits in heaven says: "How will I spread the glories of grace? I'll raise up a generation of men who deny the Bible. Then I will raise up others who stand fast by My Word. I will win people to the teaching of that Word through the defenders of that Word."

5. Two Church Controversies

In the 1940s, a medical missionary to China was run out of the country during the Maoist Communist takeover. Along with hundreds of other Presbyterian missionaries, he came back to his native South to a church that was not the one he had left years before. It was a church rife with theological liberalism, and he was shocked.

This man, L. Nelson Bell, was the father of Ruth Graham Bell and the father-in-law of Billy Graham. Bell set about to establish a movement to recapture the Southern Presbyterian Church for the Bible, for the gospel, and for evangelism in missions. His dream was never realized; the old church did not recover.

However, in 1973, fifty thousand people left their churches to establish the Presbyterian Church in America, with a commitment to the Bible, to the Reformed faith, and to the Great Commission of Jesus Christ. That church has now grown to about a half-million people. It is the largest conservative Presbyterian church in the English-speaking world. Its Reformed University Fellowship is the largest campus ministry of a conservative Reformed group in the English-speaking world. Its Reformed missionary force is the largest in the history of the world. God has blessed that little backwater Southern gathering of Christians in spreading the Reformed faith around the world.

At about the same time, there was a resurgence in Calvinism in another Southern denomination of about 15 million people, the Southern Baptist Convention, because of the influence of R. Albert Mohler Jr., president of the Southern Baptist Theological Seminary.

In the nineteenth century, there was a shocking revival of Calvinism at the seminary because of its Abstract of Principles, which had been drafted by two professors who had studied under Charles Hodge and Samuel Miller at Princeton Theological Seminary. Hodge and Miller were thoroughgoing Calvinists. But over the years, Southern Seminary had drifted away from those confessional roots, largely due to the influence of Karl Barth.

When Mohler was a student at Southern Seminary, he was deeply influenced by the theological liberalism of Barth. However, a man named Carl F. H. Henry, a former editor of *Christianity Today* and author of *God, Revelation, and Authority*, came to visit the campus, and Mohler was assigned to show him around. When Henry asked Mohler, "What is your view on inerrancy?" Mohler admitted had never heard of the doctrine. What Henry taught him in the next hours dramatically transformed his theology, bringing him back to the confessional roots of Southern Seminary.

Years later, when Mohler was asked to be president of the seminary, he did so with the understanding that he would turn things around. When he first preached for the entire seminary, his sermon was titled, "Don't Just Do Something; Stand There." It was a call to stand up for the authority of Scripture. The bulk of the student body of fourteen hundred turned their backs on him. What's more, several deans followed Mohler back to his office, where they said: "We will not stand for this. We are calling for a vote of no confidence on you at the faculty meeting tomorrow morning."

Mohler's response was, "Fine, you're fired." And the seminary turned its back on liberalism and began finding its way back to Calvinism.[4]

When Mohler invited me to come to Southern Seminary four years after its dramatic turn away from liberalism, I wept uncontrollably at what God had given back to His people and His churches. Southern Seminary is now the largest theological seminary in the world. Every professor without exception supports the Abstract of Principles.

You don't think God is sovereign? Mohler and others at the Southern Baptist Seminary *know* He is.

6. A Book and an Anglican
Knowing God was written by Packer, an evangelical Anglican theologian. Packer was already respected by British evangelicals because of his book *Fundamentalism and the Word of God*. There had never been a finer brief defense of the authority, inspiration, and inerrancy of Scripture than that book. After writing that book, Packer wrote a series of magazine articles, which InterVarsity Press later compiled and published as *Knowing God*.

Because Packer was trusted by the larger evangelical world through *Knowing God*, which Billy Graham and other centrist evangelicals approved, a new generation of believers was introduced to a sovereign God and the fullness of His grace. Packer also taught believers about the doctrines of grace in his famous introduction to John Owen's *The Death of Death in the Death of Christ*. Ten times more people in our time have read Packer's introduction to Owen's *Death of Death* than have read the book. They could not read that introduction without learning about the doctrines of grace.

Whatever differences we may have with Packer, our dear brother, about Evangelicals and Catholics Together (ECT), we are eternally grateful to him for teaching Christians today about the doctrines of grace.

7. A Theologian Philosopher
You cannot give a top ten list of factors in the Reformed resurgence

---

4. See Collin Hansen, *Young, Restless, Reformed: A Journalist's Journey with the New Calvinists* (Wheaton, Ill.: Crossway, 2008), 72–74.

without mentioning R. C. Sproul. For almost fifty years, Sproul has faithfully taught the Reformed perspective on church history, systematic theology, philosophy, and the Bible to hundreds of thousands of people in seminaries, on the radio, in books, and in conferences all over the Western world.

I am always astounded at the diversity of people who gather at Sproul's conferences. At one of his recent conferences, I saw a mother, a father, and their seven children, ranging in age from about three to fourteen. I thought they must be from a Bible church, but they were members of a United Methodist congregation outside Chicago. The father listened daily to Sproul on the radio and wanted his children to hear him speak. When I asked whether they knew that Sproul was Reformed, the father asked, "What's that?"

8. A Force of Nature

The eighth influence on the Reformed resurgence is John Piper, of whom it was recently written, "His Desiring God Ministries is the conduit through whom so many of these others who had preceded him now find their word mediated to this rising generation."[5] That is especially true of Jonathan Edwards. Piper is intoxicated by Edwards, and that appreciation is channeled into nearly every sermon he preaches.

The powerful message of Piper's ministry is that all unction about God's truth comes from God and all fruit of our labor comes from God. But in terms of human observation, what sets John's labors apart from others is his theological precision meeting up with spiritual, life-consuming passion, and his profound hope of imparting a serious joy that leads to satisfying sacrifice. The starkness of John's statements and the uncompromising nature of his sermons, calls, and claims have captivated the world-weary generation of today. Piper may have turned sixty not long ago, but his discipleship, Bible reading, preaching, and writing have the freshness of a young convert. This man has no fear; he serves only One. That is evident in everything he says and does.

Collin Hansen tells the story of a young woman who sat under

---

5. Mark Dever, "Where'd All These Calvinists Come From? Part 9 of 10" 9Marks Ministries blog post, Aug. 2, 2007, http://blog.9marks.org/whered_all_these_calvanists_come_from/ (accessed Jan. 9, 2010).

Piper's preaching for the first time. "I was terrified," she said. "I realized I had never named the God of the Bible. Then I fell down and worshiped Him."

9. The Decline of a Movement
One final influence of the Reformed resurgence is not a person, man, seminary, denomination, or movement. It is the *decline* of a movement.

One of the key things that has led to a Reformed resurgence is the decline and death of liberalism. Liberalism today is sustained only by the life support of endowment. Try to name a liberal church, denomination, or seminary that is growing. There are none. The liberal alternative to secularism is gone.

What is left? The non-Calvinistic denominations of our day are fading in an increasingly hostile, secular environment. Mark Dever writes:

> The theological climate in which weaker, more vapid versions of Christianity pale and fade, and in which more uncut vigorous versions thrive, is upon us. The lies of secularism and the decline of Christian nominalism has caused a generation of young people to grow up looking for something that they can pin their lives to the mast on. They are not looking for compromise with the world. They are looking for full-bore, high-octane, no-holds-barred, sold out commitment, and they cannot find that from nominal Christianity anywhere. So where do you find it? Well, irony of ironies, they've looked to the Calvinists!

This yearning for deep preaching is evident everywhere in the young Reformed awakening. Have you personally been attracted to Piper, Mohler, or Sproul? These men didn't hold their fingers to the wind to find out what this generation wanted; they preached what their generation needed. Their listeners weren't used to someone telling them the truth, no matter what. They found themselves drawn to Piper, Mohler, or Sproul because these men neither feared nor flattered any flesh, only God. These leaders were consumed by passion for God. And thousands of people were attracted to that.

It was amazing to see people with bodies covered with tattoos and piercings at the 2009 Gospel Coalition conference in Chicago, grabbing every Reformed book they could buy at the book tables. Only God could inspire such thirst!

This generation needs the doctrine of the church. It desperately wants community but it doesn't want authority, and you can't have community without authority. The only way we can serve these hungry people is to tell them: "You inspire us with your zeal, and your commitment to service is contagious. Could we serve you by showing you some things that we have learned from Scripture about how to minister together in the church, which is the family of God, the assembly of the living God, and the pillar and support of the truth? Could we serve you by showing you these things?"

This generation is also confused about methodology. Even the best of them will say: "We must be strong and biblical in our theology, but we can do that any way we want. Methodology is neutral." They have bought into the great error of evangelicalism, which says methodology is unrelated to theology, that the method does not affect the message. We must serve them by saying: "God has given us a gospel message, but He also has given us the means of grace, which are: the faithful preaching of the Word, the biblical administration of the sacraments, and the exercise of church nurture and discipline. He has told us how to preach and how to pastor. And these principles, however applied in different cultures and generations, are universally applicable. What's more, they are required of all by the apostle Paul. We cannot define ministry as we go along. We must follow the Book. And we must respect those who say to us, 'Let's learn not only to *preach* by the Book but also to *minister* by the Book.'"

This generation is fatherless. If you have worked among young people in the world, you will find them aching for a godly man to pour life into them. They come from homes that are broken. They come from homes where fathers were too busy and too distracted to invest themselves in their children. They come from homes where the fathers couldn't have led them in family worship to save their lives. So they have an aching void in their lives for fathers to come alongside them and pour their lives into them. Would you be that for them? Do you see why it is important for you not just to criticize them? They expect that of fathers who have rejected them all of their lives. What they need is for you to come alongside them and love them by shepherding and nurturing them. They need gentle correction that shows them a more excellent way, praying that God will deal with them. Tell them what encourages you, then pour your life into them.

Conclusions

The key characteristics of the first eight factors of this Reformed resurgence are, first, that every single one, from Spurgeon, Lloyd-Jones, and MacArthur to Piper, from the Banner of Truth Trust to the PCA, has been *motivated to seek faithfulness, not success*. When we begin seeking numbers, prominence, and the praise of the world, our labors will surely be in vain. None of these men, institutions, and denominations sought the success that God gave them. They sought only to be faithful and left the fruit of that faithfulness to God.

Second, all of these men, institutions, and denominations had *a big view of God*. The only churches that are growing in the Western world today are churches with a big view of God. That does not surprise me, because you can't meet the skepticism of this generation with a little God and a little gospel. When men have peered into telescopes and seen a universe fourteen billion light years across, they cannot be captivated by a little God. It is the old, faithful, tried-and-true Bible teaching, the old confessional Calvinism, that is drawing this new generation to the vivifying air of a sovereign, colossal God.

Third, all of these men, institutions, and denominations had *strong confessional convictions held with broad sympathies for others*. For a hundred years, evangelicalism has said the way to stay united as a movement is to downplay our theological differences and to play up sharing the gospel. That is wrong because the gospel is theology, and if we can't agree on what the gospel is and what the Great Commission entails—as Jesus said, "teaching them . . . all that I have commanded you" (Matt. 28:20)—then scaling down theology and scaling up mission will not unify us.

Today, thousands of like-minded brethren are standing up to say: "We are not for doctrinal minimalism but for doctrinal maximizing. We are for confessional commitment, but alongside it we will have broad sympathies with those who have a high view of Scripture, a high view of God, and a high view of the doctrines of grace, and who understand the gospel as we understand it. We will work with them, not minimizing or belittling our differences, but recognizing how important those differences are in the lives of our churches and working together for the gospel.

Fourth, in all these men, institutions, and denominations, *God in His inscrutable wisdom chose to favor them outside of their narrow ecclesiastical constituency.* Spurgeon was part of a theological minority in the British Fellowship of Baptist Churches. Controversy dogged him at the end of his career as he saw his church forsake its commitment to doctrine and the gospel. Yet today you can hear Africans and Australians preaching like him. Someone in China and someone in Russia is preaching like him. In just this way, all over the world, God has favored men outside of their own narrow ecclesiastical constituencies and given them broader influence to fuel a new understanding and appreciation for Calvinism. Praise God for His blessing in all of these men, institutions, and denominations that He has used to bring a resurgence of Calvinism to America. Let us pray that that resurgence will be multiplied, deepened, and prolonged, to the glory of His grace.

CHAPTER 15

Twelve Reasons Calvin is Important Today

Joel R. Beeke

Honoring John Calvin may seem a little peculiar to people today. Calvin did not do anything as dramatic as heal a man with his passing shadow or nail his *Institutes of the Christian Religion* to the door of a cathedral. His teaching, which may be summarized as "the knowledge of God and the knowledge of ourselves," is hardly the kind of stuff that most would consider important half a millennium after it was written.

So why is Calvin important today? Why do we celebrate his legacy? What did he teach and do that merits perpetual remembrance in the church of Jesus Christ? I asked that question of three dozen Calvin scholars and friends. I received scores of pages in response. In this concluding article, I will share with you the gist of what I received.

Twenty-four of the thirty-six friends I contacted responded. Many of the respondents mentioned similar or identical reasons for Calvin's continuing importance. For convenience, I have grouped all the responses under twenty-one headings, each corresponding to a role Calvin played. Nine of these were mentioned only once by my correspondents. They are:

- Calvin the historian, who unfolded redemptive history for us
- Calvin the polemicist, who combated error and heresy on every hand
- Calvin the pilgrim, who longed for home with eschatological hope
- Calvin the traditionalist, who respected tradition so long as it was biblical
- Calvin the catechist, who stressed the need to catechize children
- Calvin the deacon, who showed sympathy to the poor
- Calvin the vocationalist, who developed a sense of the sacredness of work
- Calvin the law-promoter, who taught the law as a rule of life for believers
- Calvin the author, who promoted God's kingdom through scores of writings on an astonishing number of subjects

Though these nine roles teach us much about why Calvin is important today, I want to concentrate on the twelve that received more than one vote from my correspondents. I will briefly develop each of these, quoting heavily from this correspondence.[1] Behind each heading I have placed the number of correspondents who listed the role as one of the three primary reasons Calvin is still important to study today. The reasons follow the order of the number of responses, moving from the least to the most. I trust you will find these results as fascinating as I do.

CALVIN THE EDUCATOR

Reason #12: *Calvin models for us a proper recognition of the importance of education—especially seminary training, which is the backbone of the Christian enterprise (2).*

David Hall provides an apt summary of this point:

Calvin broke with medieval pedagogy that limited education primarily to an aristocratic elite. His academy, founded in 1559, was a pilot in broad-based education for the city....

Calvin's academy, which was adjacent to St. Pierre Cathedral, featured two levels of curricula: one for the public education of Geneva's youth (the college or *schola privata*) and the other a seminary to train ministers (*schola publica*).[2] One should hardly discount the impact that came from the public education of young people, especially in a day when education was normally reserved only for aristocratic scions or for members of Catholic societies. Begun in 1558,[3] with Calvin and Theodore Beza chairing the theological faculty, the academy building was dedicated on June 5, 1559, with 600 people in attendance in St. Pierre Cathedral. Calvin collected money for the school, and many expatriates donated to help its formation. The public

---

1. These quotations, all of which are derived from personal e-mails sent to me in the summer of 2009, are not footnoted.

2. E. William Monter, *Calvin's Geneva* (New York: John Wiley & Sons, 1967), 112. The *schola privata* began classes in the fall of 1558, and the *schola publica* commenced in November 1558.

3. Public records for January 17, 1558, refer to the establishment of the college, with three chairs (theology, philosophy, Greek). See Henry Martyn Baird, *Theodore Beza, the Counsellor of the French Reformation, 1519–1605* (New York: G. P. Putnam's Sons, 1899), 104.

school, which had seven grades, enrolled 280 students during its inaugural year, and the academy's seminary expanded to 162 students in just three years. By Calvin's death in 1564, there were 1,200 students in the college and 300 in the seminary. Both schools, as historians have observed, were tuition-free and "forerunners of modern public education."[4] Few European institutions ever saw such rapid growth.[5]

The Geneva Academy had a critical role in sending missionaries all over Europe to proclaim the gospel and to organize Reformed churches. Philip Hughes writes:

> Calvin's Geneva was something very much more than a haven and a school. It was not a theological ivory tower that lived to itself and for itself, oblivious to its responsibility in the gospel to the needs of others. Human vessels were equipped and refitted in this haven…that they might launch out into the surrounding ocean of the world's need, bravely facing every storm and peril that awaited them in order to bring the light of Christ's gospel to those who were in the ignorance and darkness from which they themselves had originally come. They were taught in this school in order that they in turn might teach others the truth that had set them free.[6]

Influenced by the academy, John Knox took the evangelical doctrine back to his native Scotland; Englishmen were equipped to lead the cause in England; Italians received what they needed to teach in Italy; and Frenchmen (who were the bulk of the refugees in Geneva) were trained to spread Calvinism to France.

Calvin's convictions about education were so influential during his lifetime that the Heidelberg Catechism (1563), a thoroughly Calvinist document, listed as God's first requirement for keeping the Sabbath holy the need to financially support the ministry and theological schools (Q. 103). Would we have listed this as the first item God requires in keeping the fourth commandment? Calvin and those whom he influenced gave seminaries priority because they realized

4. See Donald R. Kelley, *Francois Hotman: A Revolutionary's Ordeal* (Princeton: Princeton University Press, 1973), 270.

5. David W. Hall, *The Legacy of John Calvin* (Phillipsburg, N.J.: P & R Publishing, 2008), 13–14.

6. Philip Hughes, "John Calvin: Director of Missions," in *The Heritage of John Calvin,* ed. John H. Bratt (Grand Rapids: Eerdmans, 1973), 44.

that without them, there would be no solid training of ministers or missionaries. Calvin reminds us that seminaries are the backbone of the church and the entire enterprise of God's kingdom on earth. Considering that Calvin's seminary, and nearly every sound Reformed seminary established since then, abandoned its biblical and Reformed moorings and became liberal within several generations after its founding, do we not have all the more reason today to support the few sound seminaries that exist with earnest prayer and generous giving?

CALVIN THE SOCIO-THEOLOGIAN

Reason #11: *Calvin models for us the wide-ranging impact of his theology on Western European and North American civilization, whether it be the rise of the Western democracies; the development of economic life and international commerce, scholarship, and scientific discovery; or the promotion of the values of human dignity, personal freedom, social justice, and the rule of law (3).*[7]

Andre Bieler writes: "[T]he sum of medieval knowledge was theology—the study of God. The sum of the knowledge of the Renaissance was humanism—the study and knowledge of humanness. Now, the science of Calvin is a theological and social humanism which includes a study of man and society through a twofold knowledge of man by man, on the one hand, and knowledge of man through God, on the other."[8] In other words, Calvin's writings display a rare combination of the legitimate fruits of human inquiry, science, and scholarship completed by—and interpreted in the light of—the unchanging truths of the Word of God.

Calvin discussed many aspects of man's life in society and in the world as a necessary corollary to his exposition of man's relationship to God and the way of salvation through Christ. For example, he devoted an entire chapter of *The Institutes* to a wide-ranging and thorough discussion of civil government.[9]

Significantly, in the light of subsequent debates and develop-

---

7. I thank Rev. Ray Lanning for his assistance on this section.

8. Andre Bieler, *The Social Humanism of Calvin*, trans. Paul T. Fuhrmann (Richmond: John Knox Press, 1964), 12.

9. *Institutes* 4.20.

ments among Calvinists, Calvin held that "the Lord through the hand of Moses did not give that [Mosaic] law to be proclaimed among all nations and to be enforced everywhere."[10] Rather, God granted freedom to each nation to frame its own laws, according to its circumstances, so long as those laws "press toward the same goal of equity," that is, the equity found in the moral law of God, "a testimony of natural law and of that conscience which God has engraved upon the minds of men...this equity alone must be the goal and rule and limit of all laws."[11]

As John T. McNeill writes: "Calvin sets the example of a positive attitude to government and a deep appreciation of the ruler's office.... The aim of government is the public good, conceived in the broad sense of service to every human person in his welfare, his education, his opportunity to inherit the treasures of culture and religion.... [Yet,] Calvin is a realist in his political expectations. He sets the standards high; but he does not expect sinless perfection in political man."[12]

Similarly, Calvin had much to say about the freedom of the individual, the stewardship of earthly goods, the dignity of labor, and the rights of working people. As a social force, he reformed the morals of great cities, established the rule of law, and opened the way for people to raise themselves by education and by the diligent use of their knowledge and abilities. Calvinism promoted and encouraged scholarship of all kinds, including scientific research. Calvinism also promoted the right of people to limit the powers of their governors and to change forms of government, if necessary.

But Calvin discussed none of these things in isolation from God and His Word. Rather, he placed his vision of man's life in the world squarely in the context of man's twofold identity as a creature made in the image of God and as a fallen sinner redeemed and delivered from bondage to sin through Jesus Christ. The potential for great achievement by the first identity is recovered and enabled only by the second.

---

10. *Institutes* 4.20.16.

11. Ibid.

12. John T. McNeill, "Calvin's Ideas Still Politically Relevant Today," *in Calvin and Calvinism: Sources of Democracy?*, ed. Robert M. Kingdon and Robert D. Linder (Lexington, Mass.: D.C. Heath and Co., 1970), 75–6.

Admittedly, Calvinism's ideas of human freedom and dignity often ran ahead of the actual practice of Calvinists at any given point in time. Even today, some Presbyterians may not be altogether comfortable with the degree of personal freedom of faith and practice set forth in the Westminster Confession of Faith, which says, "God alone is lord of the conscience, and hath left it free from the doctrines and commandments of men which are in anything contrary to His Word; or beside it, in matters of faith or worship."[13]

Nonetheless, Calvinism has been a great force for freedom wherever it has influenced people. Calvinism also has fostered economic development, advances in knowledge, political and social change, and establishment of the rule of law.

Many people today are unaware of the debt they owe to Calvinism for the personal freedom, economic opportunities, and cultural attainments that they value so highly. The emptiness of modern culture, the pessimism of the age, and the excesses of capitalism, socialism, and nationalism that have bedeviled our past and imperil our future prove the folly of separating Calvinistic values for society from Calvinism's vision of who man is, under God, and what he can be only in Christ, according to the Word of God.

Economist and lay theologian Douglas Vickers sums it up well: "The Reformation was first and essentially a theological movement that spread its influence to the socio-cultural level in its implications, chief among them being the sanctity of individual freedom. That influence has been tarnished, notably in its economic aspect, by a failure to recognize that sin is abroad in the world and in the hearts of men."

CALVIN THE EVANGELIST

Reason #10: *Calvin models for us how to teach and practice evangelism and missions (5).*

One of the most fallacious charges against Calvin is that he did not fuel a passion for evangelism and missions.[14] Others assert that Calvin was responsible for relighting the torch of biblical evangelism

---

13. *Westminster Confession of Faith,* "Of Christian Liberty, and Liberty of Conscience," 20.2.

14. William Richey Hogg, "The Rise of Protestant Missionary Concern, 1517–

during the Reformation[15] and thus should be credited with being a theological father of the Reformed missionary movement.[16] Views of Calvin's attitude toward evangelism and missions have ranged on the positive side from hearty to moderate support,[17] and on the negative side from silent indifference to active opposition.[18]

Calvin's teaching and his practice both confirm that he was a model evangelist. Calvin taught evangelism in a general way by earnestly proclaiming the gospel and by reforming the church according to biblical requirements. More specifically, Calvin taught evangelism by focusing on the universality of Christ's kingdom and the responsibility of Christians to help extend that realm.

Calvin asserted that both God's sovereignty and our responsibility are involved in evangelism. The work of evangelism is ultimately God's work, not ours, but God uses us as His instruments. Calvin writes that the gospel "does not fall from the clouds like rain," but is "brought by the hands of men to where God has sent it."[19] God "uses our work and summons us to be his instruments in cultivating his field."[20] The power to save rests with God, but He reveals His salvation through the preaching of the gospel.[21] God's evangelism thus causes our evangelism.[22] He allows us to participate in "the honor of constituting his own Son governor over the whole world."[23]

1914," in *Theology of Christian Mission,* ed. G. Anderson (New York: McGraw-Hill, 1961), 96–7.

15. David B. Calhoun, "John Calvin: Missionary Hero or Missionary Failure?" *Presbuterion* 5, 1 (Spr 1979): 16–33—to which I am greatly indebted in the first part of this section; W. Stanford Reid, "Calvin's Geneva: A Missionary Centre," *Reformed Theological Review* 42, 3 (1983): 65–74.

16. Samuel M. Zwemer, "Calvinism and the Missionary Enterprise," *Theology Today* 7, 2 (July 1950):206–216; J. Douglas MacMillan, "Calvin, Geneva, and Christian Mission," *Reformed Theological Journal* 5 (Nov 1989):5–17.

17. Johannes van den Berg, "Calvin's Missionary Message," *The Evangelical Quarterly* 22 (1950):174–87; Walter Holsten, "Reformation und Mission," *Archiv für Reformationsgeschichte* 44, 1 (1953):1–32; Charles E. Edwards, "Calvin and Missions," *The Evangelical Quarterly* 39 (1967): 47–51; Charles Chaney, "The Missionary Dynamic in the Theology of John Calvin," *Reformed Review* 17, 3 (Mar 1964):24–38.

18. Gustav Warneck, *Outline of a History of Protestant Missions* (London: Oliphant Anderson & Ferrier, 1906), 19–20.

19. *Commentary* on Romans 10:15.

20. *Commentary* on Matthew 13:24–30.

21. *Institutes* 4.1.5.

22. *Commentary* on Romans 10:14–17.

23. *Commentary* on Psalm 2:8.

According to Calvin, this convergence of divine sovereignty and human responsibility in evangelism means that we must pray daily for the extension of Christ's kingdom.[24] We should not become discouraged by a lack of visible success in evangelism but pray on, believing that "Christ shall manifestly exercise the power given to him for our salvation and for that of the whole world."[25] We must also diligently work for the extension of Christ's kingdom, knowing that our work will not be in vain.[26]

We evangelize for many reasons, Calvin says: God commands us to do so,[27] God leads us by His own example,[28] evangelism is our duty to God,[29] we want to glorify Him[30] and please Him,[31] we are grateful to Him,[32] and evangelism is our duty to fellow sinners.[33]

Calvin taught we must make full use of the opportunities God gives to evangelize. "When an opportunity for edification presents itself, we should realize that a door has been opened for us by the hand of God in order that we may introduce Christ into that place and we should not refuse to accept the generous invitation that God thus gives us," he wrote.[34] On the other hand, when opportunities are restricted and doors of evangelism are closed to our witness, we should not persist in trying to do what cannot be done. Rather, we should pray and seek other opportunities. "The door is shut when there is no hope of success. [Then] we have to go a different way rather than wear ourselves out in vain efforts to get through it," Calvin wrote.[35]

Difficulties in witnessing, however, are not an excuse to stop try-

24. *Institutes* 3.20.42.
25. *Commentary* on Micah 7:10–14.
26. *Commentary* on Hebrews 10:24.
27. *Commentary* on Matthew 13:24–30.
28. John Calvin, *Sermons on the Epistle to the Ephesians,* trans. Arthur Golding (Edinburgh: Banner of Truth Trust, 1973), sermon on Ephesians 4:15–16.
29. *Commentary* on Isaiah 12:5.
30. Jules Bonnet, ed., *Letters of Calvin,* trans. David Constable and Marcus Robert Gilchrist (repr., New York: Simon and Schuster, 1957), 4:169.
31. Ibid., 2:453.
32. *Commentary* on Psalm 51:16.
33. John Calvin, *Sermons of Master John Calvin upon the Fifthe Book of Moses Called Deuteronomie* (repr., Edinburgh: Banner of Truth Trust, 1987), sermon on Deuteronomy 33:18–19 (Hereafter, *Sermons* on Deuteronomy 33:18–19.)
34. *Commentary* on 2 Corinthians 2:12.
35. Ibid.

ing. To those suffering severe restrictions and persecutions in France, Calvin wrote: "Let every one strive to attract and win over to Jesus Christ those whom he can."[36]

Calvin practiced what he taught. His efforts can be categorized into four concentric circles. First, Calvin evangelized in his local congregation of Geneva, beginning with preaching. Calvin reached out to unsaved people through his preaching, impressing them with the necessity of faith in Christ and what that meant. Calvin made it clear that he did not believe everyone in his flock was saved. Though charitable toward church members who maintained a commendable outward lifestyle, he referred more than thirty times in his commentaries and nine times in his *Institutes* (only counting references within 3.21 to 3.24) to the small numbers of those who received the preached Word with saving faith. "If the same sermon is preached, say, to a hundred people, twenty receive it with the ready obedience of faith, while the rest hold it valueless, or laugh, or hiss, or loathe it," Calvin said.[37]

Second, Calvin used preaching as a tool to spread the Reformation throughout the city of Geneva. On Sundays, the Genevan Ordinances required sermons in each of the three churches at daybreak and at 9 a.m. At noon, children went to catechism classes. At 3 p.m., sermons were preached again in each church. Weekday sermons were scheduled at various times in the three churches on Mondays, Wednesdays, and Fridays. By the time Calvin died, a sermon was preached in every church nearly each day of the week.

Third, Calvin sought to evangelize all of Europe. The reputation and influence of the Genevan community spread to neighboring France, then to Scotland, England, the Netherlands, parts of western Germany, and sections of Poland and Hungary. Calvin increasingly viewed Geneva as a kind of model for the Reformed movement and for Christ's reign throughout the world.

Inspired by Calvin's ecumenical vision, Geneva became a nucleus from which evangelism spread throughout the world. In 1561 alone, 142 men were sent out from the Geneva Academy on missions to different places in the world.[38] That is an amazing accomplishment

---

36. Bonnet, *Letters of Calvin*, 3:134.
37. *Institutes* 3.24.12.
38. Philip Hughes, "John Calvin: Director of Missions," 45–6.

for an effort that began with a small church struggling within a tiny city-republic.

Finally, Calvin became involved in overseas missions, most notably, a mission effort among the Indians in Brazil. With the help of a Huguenot sympathizer, Gaspard de Coligny, admiral of France, and the support of Henry II, then king of France, Nicolas Durand (also called Villegagnon; 1510–1571) led an expedition to Brazil in 1555 to establish a colony. When trouble erupted in the new colony near Rio de Janeiro, Villegagnon turned to the Huguenots in France, asking for better settlers. He also appealed to Coligny, to Calvin, and to the church in Geneva.

The Company of Pastors chose two ministers and eleven laymen to send to Brazil. As Neal Hegeman writes:

> The first Protestant congregation in the New World was started in Coligny, Brazil, in April of 1557.[39] The Coligny Expedition turned out to be short lived as the Vice Admiral Nicholas Durand de Villegagnon (1510–1571) betrayed the French Huguenots and the colonists. The fruit of the first Protestant entrance into the New World was the martyrdom of Jean du Bordel, Matthieu Vermeil, and Pierre Bourdon, who died at the hands of Villegagnon. These men wrote the "Coligny Confession,"[40] the first confessional and theological document to be written in the New World.

Later, the Portuguese destroyed the remainder of the settlement.

Calvin was clearly interested in spreading the gospel overseas, but that interest was limited by time constraints, his work at home, and by government restrictions. Nearly every door to the heathen world was closed to Calvin and fellow Reformers. The world of Islam to the south and east was guarded by Turkish armies, while the navies of Spain and Portugal prevented access to the recently discovered New World. Additionally, most of the governments in Europe were controlled by Roman Catholic princes, kings, and emperors.

The conclusion is seamless: both Calvin's writings and practice

39. G. Baez Camargo, "The Earliest Protestant Missionary Venture in Latin America," *Church History* 21 (1952):135–45.

40. Jean Crespin, "Los mártires de Rio de Janeiro," trans. G. Baez Carmargo (México City: CUP, 1955), 109–114, as recorded in appendices of Cornelius Hegeman, "El Origen y el Desarrollo de las Iglesias y las Misiones Presbiterianas y América Latina y el Caribe (1528–1916)" (Miami: MINTS), 365ff.

showed his large heart for evangelism to extend the kingdom of our Lord Jesus Christ to the ends of the earth. Establishing the heavenly reign of God upon earth was so important, Calvin said, that it "ought not only to occupy the chief place among our cares, but even absorb all our thoughts."[41]

CALVIN THE PASTOR

Reason #9: *Calvin models for us how to faithfully pastor the sheep of God as under-shepherds of the Chief Shepherd (7).*

John Calvin was first and foremost a pastor. He faithfully pastored in Geneva for more than twenty-five years and in Strasbourg for three years. As Jim Garretson writes:

> Calvin's work as a pastor to his respective flocks has been a matter of growing academic interest in recent years. Biographers and historians alike have come to realize the profound pastoral focus that characterized his labors in Geneva and Strasbourg. The more one reads his letters and listens carefully to his sermons and treatises, the more one recognizes a shepherd who carried the burdens, hopes, and fears of his people upon his heart. His transparency and humility reveal a tender-hearted man who, like his Master, went about doing good while seeking to act in the best spiritual interests of those entrusted to his care.

Erroll Hulse adds:

> As a pastor, Calvin was exemplary in personal godliness, in family life, and in the ministry of prayer. His pastoral care for people is reflected in his letter writing, there being four thousand letters extant. Calvin stuck to his pastoral calling through trials of every kind and persevered through terribly painful physical afflictions.

When Sinclair Ferguson was asked at Ligonier Ministries' pre-conference seminar on Calvin in March 2009, "What have you learned from Calvin's life or writings?" he answered:

> For me, Calvin has been the model of what a gospel minister in a local congregation should be. He preached every second week, preaching probably eight sermons, and the other week

---

41. Bonnet, *Letters of Calvin,* 2:134–5.

probably five. He counseled, but he understood that the counseling arose either out of emergency crises that he was able to help, or because under the ministry of the Word all the filth and sludge of human hearts came to the surface. I feel the church desperately needs to get back to the centrality of the ministry of the Word that characterized Calvin's preaching and pastoring. You just need to read his sermons to think, *You know, if I could take my lunchtime and listen to him for forty minutes, asthmatic as he was, struggling for breath, this would be mind-changing and life-changing.* Here is this totally unspectacular man, who never had a laugh in his church, patiently unfolding the Scriptures. It transformed lives pastorally and it gave multitudes of young men the courage to be martyrs for the gospel.

We are crying out for ministries like that—just ministers in local congregations feeding the people of God with the Word of God. And at the end of the day, this is all Calvin thought he was doing. He was a local pastor.

CALVIN THE PIETIST

Reason #8: *Calvin models for us how to bring all of life under the rubric of a biblical, comprehensive piety (8).*

Piety (*pietas*) was the primary reason Calvin wrote his *Institutes.* For Calvin, piety is best defined as the development of a right attitude to God. This attitude includes six things: true knowledge, heartfelt worship, saving faith, filial fear, prayerful submission, and reverential love. All of these have the glory of God as their goal. Calvin's notion of piety comprehensively impacted his worldview theologically, ecclesiastically, and practically.

Theologically, Calvin rooted piety in the believer's mystical union with Christ, which produces communion with Christ and participation in His benefits. He viewed the Holy Spirit and saving faith as the double bond of piety, for the Holy Spirit works piety in us through faith. Then, too, Calvin presented us with the central doctrines of salvation, justification, and sanctification through the grid of piety, for justification is imputed piety and sanctification is imparted or actual piety.

Ecclesiastically, piety is nurtured through the Word and the church. The Word gives content and shape to genuine piety. The church nurtures piety through preaching, which is our spiritual

food and medicine for spiritual health. The church also nurtures
piety through members using their gifts to strengthen each other in
the fear of God. The communion of saints encourages the growth of
one another's gifts and love, since to grow in grace, Calvin said, we
are "constrained to borrow from others."[42] Calvin called the sacraments exercises of piety, for they help promote a right attitude to
God. He defined them as testimonies "of divine grace toward us,
confirmed by an outward sign, with mutual attestation of our piety
toward God."[43] The Lord's Supper, in particular, prompts piety of
grace received and given. Psalm singing also promotes piety, Calvin
argued, for the psalms are "an anatomy of parts of the soul," and
therefore relate to all of a believer's experiential life with God.[44] Calvin viewed the book of Psalms as the canonical manual of piety.

Practically, Calvin's section in the *Institutes* (3.6–10) on the Christian life strongly promotes piety. *Prayer* is the principal and perpetual
exercise of faith and the chief element of piety, both privately and
corporately. *Repentance*, which involves both mortification (the kill-
ing of sin) and vivification (coming alive to life and righteousness in
Christ), is the way of piety. God has always intended to give repentance as a lifelong grace. *Self-denial* is the sacrificial dimension of piety
by which we learn that we belong to God rather than to ourselves,
and we are to learn to yield ourselves and everything we own to God
as a living sacrifice. While self-denial focuses on inward conformity
to Christ, *cross-bearing* centers on outward Christ-likeness. If Christ's
life was a perpetual cross, ours also must include suffering.[45] Cross-
bearing tests piety, Calvin said. Through cross-bearing, we are roused
to hope, trained in patience, instructed in obedience, and chastened
in pride. Through a *proper estimation of this life,* believers learn that
they are stewards of this world and recognize that God is the giver of
every good and perfect gift. Thus, they are called to unconditional
obedience to God's will, which is the essence of piety.

For Calvin, piety involves the entire life of the devout believer
and the entire family of the church community. Living piously means

---

42. *Commentary* on Romans 12:6.
43. *Institutes* 4.14.1.
44. *Commentary* on Psalms, vol. 1, p. xxxix.
45. Richard C. Gamble, "Calvin and Sixteenth-Century Spirituality," in *Calvin and Spirituality,* Calvin Studies Society Papers, 1995–1997, ed. David Foxgrover (Grand Rapids: The Calvin Studies Society, 2002), 34–5.

dedicating every minute to living *coram Deo* (in the presence of God) with intense consciousness, realizing that we must yearn for God every minute of our lives.

How urgently we need to recover this kind of pious living—and how richly Calvin's own life models it for us! When Calvin died, Theodore Beza wrote, "Having been a spectator of his conduct for sixteen years…I can now declare, that in him all men may see a most beautiful example of the Christian character, an example which it is as easy to slander as it is difficult to imitate."[46]

Through Calvin's influence, theology always pursued piety, for Protestant theology and spirituality focused on how to live the Christian life in solitude with God, in the family, in the fields, in worship, and in the marketplace. Few today realize the importance of this comprehensive piety. A few years ago, when I studied Calvin's view of piety for a chapter in the *Cambridge Companion to Calvin*, I asked one of the world's leading Calvin historians how I should commence my study. Her response was, "Why would you want to study that outdated subject?" Though sadly neglected, comprehensive piety, as much as anything else, is what makes Calvin so important today.

CALVIN THE COMMENTATOR

Reason #7: *Calvin models for us what good commentaries ought to be and thereby sets a high standard for all successive Protestant commentaries (9).*

Calvin's *Commentaries* are a great gift to Christ's church and laid a foundation for the dynamic theology of the Reformation. They show us that Scripture truly is the living Word. For accurate, reverent, and erudite exposition, Calvin has no equal. His method of exegesis has been followed by ministers of God's Word until today, and the church has been blessed and edified as a result.

The *Commentaries* are a sterling example of the benefit of doing exegesis under Scripture's authority. Calvin's *Commentaries* are an exemplary display of the vital principle *Scripturam ex Scriptura explicandam esse* ("Scripture is to be explained from Scripture"). We must not "rush headlong and rashly" into Scripture, Calvin said, "because

---

46. John Calvin, *Tracts and Letters* (repr., Edinburgh: Banner of Truth Trust, 2009), vol. 1, page c.

the Spirit, who spoke by the prophets, is the only true interpreter of himself."[47] We must be reverent, obedient, and teachable, he continued, for the whole world together cannot produce living faith through any interpretation of Scripture. Only the Holy Spirit can illuminate the humble soul seeking after the true knowledge of God.

As pastors and students of the Word, we would be wise to make use of the *Commentaries* in our ministries. As Paul Helm writes:

> We should study his commentaries, one of Calvin's greatest permanent legacies to the church.... Calvin writes tersely and without any personal showiness. "I love brevity," he once said. He lets the Word of God do the work. He was granted great insight into the meaning of the text of Scripture, the intentions of the writers, and the scope of each passage. He produced a shelf full of commentaries, one on almost every book of Scripture, but each is made up of short comments on the text. For this reason, they are of timeless value.

The veteran preacher Al Martin says of Calvin's *Commentaries*:

> Several years ago, someone asked me what I would do differently if I could turn back the clock some thirty to forty years and restructure my personal ministerial priorities. I said that I would purpose to read all of Calvin's commentaries in conjunction with my regular devotional reading of the Bible. Over the years, I have worked through many Puritan volumes in this way, taking just four or five pages each morning as part of my devotional exercises. I wish someone had directed me to do the same with Calvin's commentaries early in my ministry.

Finally, the Calvin scholar John Hesselink writes:

> Contemporary biblical scholars often pay tribute to the special value of Calvin's *Commentaries* because of the theological insight and spiritual depth of Calvin's handling of biblical texts. As an Old Testament scholar, L.P. Smith, points out, "No modern commentator equals Calvin for penetrating the depths of the passage and pointing the way to its application by Christians to the problems of later time." It is noteworthy that the Barthian scholar, George Hunsinger, always reads Calvin's commentaries as well as modern ones in his preparation for the Bible class he

---

47. *Commentary* on 2 Peter 1:20.

teaches each Sunday at Nassau Presbyterian Church in Princeton. He writes, "The reason is that Calvin thinks theologically about what he reads and that he does so at a level of brilliance beyond anything that recent scholars have to offer."[48] This kind of testimony is repeated again and again by biblical scholars.

CALVIN THE CHURCHMAN

Reason #6: *Calvin models for us what it means to maintain a high view of the church and her worship without idolizing her or falling into the absolutism of Rome (10).*

While breaking with the clericalism, authoritarianism, and absolutism of Rome, Calvin maintained a high view of the church: "If we do not prefer the church to all other objects of our interest we are unworthy of being counted among her members," he wrote.[49] Calvin agreed with Cyprian and Augustine, who said, "He cannot have God for his Father who refuses to have the church for his mother."[50] To this Calvin added, "For there is no other way to enter into life unless this mother conceive us in her womb, give us birth, nourish us at her breast, and lastly, unless she keep us under her care and guidance until, putting off mortal flesh, we become like the angels."[51] So the church is essential for spiritual nourishment and maturation.

Calvin teaches us today that we must avoid a church that is an absolute authority, an infallible teacher, and a center of habitual grace. But we also must avoid a church that is a center for rallies, entertainment, rehabilitation, or politics; in short, one that becomes a music hall, a social institution, or an evangelistic circus. Instead, Calvin calls us back to Scripture to consider what Christ has said about His church.

In the past, Reformed believers profoundly cherished the church. Today, that sense of appreciation is waning. Many Protestants have a depreciated view of the church as Christ's institution.[52] This lower view of the church is fostered by a misunderstanding of what the

---

48. *Theology Today* 66, 2 (July 2009):131.
49. *Institutes* 4.1.1.
50. Ibid.
51. Ibid., 4.1.4.
52. John Murray, "The Church—Its Identity, Functions, and Resources," in *Collected Writings of John Murray* (Edinburgh: Banner of Truth Trust, 1976), 1:238.

church truly is as Christ's institution. It disregards Jesus' words to Peter: "Upon this rock I will build my church" (Matt. 16:18). Calvin would say that we cannot really understand what the church is and why we should appreciate her until we truly understand the meaning of those words. In Matthew 16, Jesus teaches us three critical truths about the church: first, her *status* belongs to Christ ("my church"); second, her *substance* is founded on Christ ("upon this rock"); third, her *success* is due to the workmanship of Christ ("I will build")—all of which should increasingly move us to cherish the church.[53]

Calvin's ecclesiology impresses us with the truth that Christ is the Head of the church. The living church is the bride of Christ here on earth, which Christ will perfect and bring to glory. Calvin loved the church dearly and often expressed anxiety over her lack of progress in sanctification and grace.

Calvin modeled what it means to be a real, biblical churchman. Garretson writes:

> Calvin's work as a churchman remains an important example to today's Christian leader. His was a pastoral theology rooted in the life of the church for the sake of the church. It came to expression in a beehive of activity at the local, regional, and international levels as he tried to constructively contribute to the advancement of Reformation principles with friend and foe alike. His labors as pastor and preacher kept him focused on the spiritual welfare of the church as it is nurtured through Word and sacrament; all his efforts as pastor and churchman were infused with these convictions as he sought to apply God's intentions for His church and society at large.

Too many churches today overlook what Calvin and the Reformation had to say about worship. John Thackway warns us:

> The danger today is that we focus on Calvin's doctrine and omit its proper application to the issues of our day. Divine worship is one example. So much Calvin celebration material this year has not included this. It is a strange anomaly in some places, that Calvinistic doctrine can be preached from the pulpit and yet charismatic-style worship can ascend from the pew.

53. Cf. Joel R. Beeke, "Glorious Things of Thee are Spoken," in *Onward, Christian Soldiers: Protestants Affirm the Church* (Morgan, Pa.: Soli Deo Gloria, 1999), 23–67.

Psalm singing was a critical part of worship, Calvin believed. As Hall writes:

> One of Calvin's early initiatives was to translate music designed for use in public worship into the language of the day. Realizing that what people sing in a holy context has an enduring impact on how they act, Calvin wanted worship—in all its aspects—to be intelligible. Shortly after his settling in Geneva, he urged a talented musician, Clement Marot, to translate the psalms into mid-sixteenth-century French. Calvin wanted participants in worship, not only the clergy, to be able to understand and reiterate the truths of Scripture—this time in poetic structure. His democratizing of holy song and other elements of worship made parishioners participate in divine liturgy.[54]

CALVIN THE TRINITARIAN

Reason #5: *Calvin models for us how to hold an exalted Trinitarian view of God (11).*

Calvin was utterly God-centered in his theology and life. True Calvinists should thus be filled with a holy obsession with the triune God, as He has revealed Himself in the Scriptures, in all His majesty, sovereignty, and grace. Ferguson says:

> What seems to dominate the development of the *Institutes* is Calvin's immense Trinitarianism: the unity of the Trinity, his appreciation of the distinctives of each person within the Trinity, and his appreciation of how God Himself is the gospel. That leads him to the high-water mark of Christological thought that you get in Calvin. In some areas of his thinking it seems as though he is the first Christian writer to get this just right. Today, we have very much lost this consciousness of Trinitarianism. It is very difficult for twenty-first-century people to understand why the early fathers fussed so much about how they described the Trinity. Their answer was, "We love Him so much that it is our responsibility to describe Him as magnificently as we can." That was something that really gripped Calvin, and is one of the great things we need to learn from him today.[55]

---

54. Hall, *The Legacy of Calvin*, 32.
55. Sinclair B. Ferguson, remarks during question-and-answer session, Ligonier Ministries National Conference, Orlando, Fla., March 21, 2009.

First, then, Calvin focused on the fatherly sovereignty of God. Calvin had an exalted view of God in His predestinating grace, His providential government, and His preeminent glory. Curt Daniel writes:

> Calvin is known (and unfortunately hated by some) for his rediscovery of the great truth of the sovereignty of God. Some would specifically point to Calvin's appreciation of the majesty of God. I would add that twenty-first-century Christians would do well to emulate his reflection of the seriousness of God. Calvin preached no silly godling but rather an awe-inspiring Lord that towers over the universe. Calvin reminds us to approach the triune God in reverence and not presumption or religious triteness.

Such a view of the majestic heavenly Father has profound consequences in the life of a believer. Maurice Roberts says:

> When I read the *Institutes* as a young believer, it was Calvin's doctrine of God that shook me most. I had not until then considered what it means that God is sovereign in every way. I recall the amazement and profound shock that stunned me at the time when I first came to see that God is infinitely in control of all things and knows even my own inward thoughts. It staggered me to think that I had come to Christ only as a result of a divine decree of election. God therefore might have left me in my sins to perish had He chosen to reprobate me. It seems commonplace now to think of God as sovereign in every way, but then it was a shock and one with profound consequences for my own spiritual development. It is Calvin's view of God which, in my opinion, is most needed in the world today.

Second, Calvin focused on Jesus Christ. To Calvin we owe the Reformed development of Christ in His threefold mediatorial office as Prophet, Priest, and King, as well as much of our doctrine of divine Sonship and, perhaps most of all, our focus on believers' mystical union with Him. As David Willis-Watkins writes, "Calvin's doctrine of union with Christ is one of the most consistently influential features of his theology and ethics, if not the single most important teaching that animates the whole of his thought and his personal life."[56]

---

56. David Willis-Watkins, "The *Unio Mystica* and the Assurance of Faith

Calvin did not intend to present theology from the viewpoint of a single doctrine. Nonetheless, his sermons, commentaries, and theological works are so permeated with the union-with-Christ doctrine that it becomes one of his primary focuses for Christian faith and practice.[57] Calvin inferred this when he wrote, "That joining together of Head and members, that indwelling of Christ in our hearts—in short, that mystical union—are accorded by us the highest degree of importance, so that Christ, having been made ours, makes us sharers with him in the gifts with which he has been endowed."[58]

This union must be our starting point in understanding spiritual life.[59] This union is possible because Christ took on our human nature, filling it with His virtue. Union with Christ in His humanity is historical, ethical, and personal, but not essential. There is no crass mixture (*crassa mixtura*) of human substances between Christ and us. Nonetheless, Calvin states, "Not only does he cleave to us by an indivisible bond of fellowship, but with a wonderful communion, day by day, he grows more and more into one body with us, until he becomes completely one with us."[60] This union is one of the gospel's greatest mysteries.[61] Because of the fountain of Christ's perfection in our nature, the pious may, by faith, draw whatever they need for

According to Calvin," in *Calvin Erbe und Auftrag: Festschrift für Wilhelm Heinrich Neuser zum 65. Geburtstag,* ed. Willem van't Spijker (Kampen: Kok, 1991), 78.

57. E.g., Charles Partee, "Calvin's Central Dogma Again," *Sixteenth Century Journal* 18, 2 (1987):194. Cf. Otto Gründler, "John Calvin: Ingrafting in Christ," in *The Spirituality of Western Christendom,* ed. Rozanne Elder (Kalamazoo, Mich.: Cistercian, 1976), 172–87; Brian G. Armstrong, "The Nature and Structure of Calvin's Thought According to the *Institutes:* Another Look," in *John Calvin's Magnum Opus* (Potchefstroom, South Africa: Institute for Reformational Studies, 1986), 55–82; Guenther Haas, *The Concept of Equity in Calvin's Ethics* (Waterloo, Ontario: Wilfred Laurier University Press, 1997).

58. *Institutes* 3.11.9.

59. Howard G. Hageman, "Reformed Spirituality," in *Protestant Spiritual Traditions,* ed. Frank C. Senn (New York: Paulist Press, 1986), 61.

60. *Institutes* 3.2.24.

61. Dennis Tamburello points out that "at least seven instances occur in the *Institutes* where Calvin uses the word *arcanus* or *incomprehensibilis* to describe union with Christ" (2.12.7; 3.11.5; 4.17.1, 9, 31, 33; 4.19.35; *Union with Christ: John Calvin and the Mysticism of St. Bernard* [Louisville: Westminster/John Knox, 1994], 89, 144). Cf. William Borden Evans, "Imputation and Impartation: The Problem of Union with Christ in Nineteenth-Century American Reformed Theology" (Ph.D. dissertation, Vanderbilt University, 1996), 6–68.

their sanctification. The flesh of Christ is the source from which His people derive life and power.[62]

Finally, Calvin is the theologian of the Holy Spirit. As Helm notes:

> We should always remember that Calvin is the theologian *par excellence* of the Holy Spirit. This means two things: he discredited, in the most thorough and emphatic way, the Roman Catholic medieval doctrine of grace as divine assistance in the production of human merit (channeled through the sacramental system of that church). He replaced it with an emphasis upon the joint operation of the Word of God and the Spirit of God. The Spirit applies the Word's message of sovereign grace to dead sinners through the mediatorship of Jesus Christ; He brings regeneration, illumination, penitence and justifying faith, and the graces of sanctification. So the ministry of the church is the ministry of the Word and two sacraments, and the invocation of the Spirit to make it fruitful, in place of the supposed *ex opere operato* power [literally, by the work performed, hence, containing operative power] of seven sacraments.

Calvin is a preeminent example of a man dependent on the Spirit of God for the interpretation of Scripture. This is especially true when we consider that Calvin did not have scores of other Protestants to lean on as we do today. He was reliant on the works of the fathers and the Scholastics. The church in our time is greatly in need of examples of Spirit-led pastors and teachers. Regardless of the distracted spirit of worship, the church today continues with the same dependence on the Spirit for illumination, justification, sanctification, and the communion of saints as in Calvin's day.

For Calvin, then, a wonderful harmony exists between the three persons of the Trinity. Hesselink captures this well when he writes:

> Calvin was thoroughly Trinitarian. No one was more overwhelmed by the majesty and glory of God than he. At the same time, Jesus Christ and His salvific work are at the center of Calvin's theology. Yet, it is still quite appropriate to dub Calvin "the theologian of the Holy Spirit," as did B. B. Warfield, Werner Krusche, and others. "For Calvin, every apprehension of God depends on the activity of the Spirit.... At the edges and limits

---

62. *Commentary* on John 6:51.

of Calvin's thought the Spirit takes over" (John Dillenberger). However, for Calvin, the Spirit can never be separated from the Word; nor can Christ be separated from His Spirit. Thus, Calvin's focus on the Spirit is always circumscribed by the doctrine of the Trinity. Herein is another distinctive contribution of Calvin to the church.

CALVIN THE PREACHER

Reason #4: *Calvin models for us how to preach God's Word faithfully and powerfully in an expository, experiential, and applicatory manner to God's glory, the edification of believers, and the salvation of the lost (12).*

For Calvin, to live was to preach. William Bouwsma writes: "He preached regularly and often: on the Old Testament on weekdays at six in the morning (seven in winter), every other week; on the New Testament on Sunday mornings; and on the Psalms on Sunday afternoons. During his lifetime he preached, on this schedule, some four thousand sermons after his return to Geneva: more than 170 sermons a year."[63] Preaching was so important to Calvin that when he was "reviewing the accomplishments of his lifetime on his deathbed, he mentioned his sermons ahead of his writings."[64]

Calvin called the preaching office "the most excellent of all things," commended by God that it might be held in the highest esteem. "There is nothing more notable or glorious in the church than the ministry of the gospel," he concluded.[65] In commenting on Isaiah 55:11, he said, "The Word goeth out of the mouth of God in such a manner that it likewise goeth out of the mouth of men; for God does not speak openly from heaven but employs men as his instruments."[66]

The primary motivation behind Calvin's preaching was the conviction that the preaching of the Word of God *is* the Word of God. Preaching is the Word of God because its content is the Word of God. The preached Word does not rival the written Word but rather derives its authority from it. In T. H. L. Parker's words, preaching has no authority in itself, but rather borrows its authority from the

---

63. William Bouwsma, *John Calvin: A Sixteenth-Century Portrait* (New York: Oxford, 1988), 29.

64. Ibid.

65. *Institutes* 4.3.3.

66. *Commentary* on Isaiah 55:11.

written Word and thus becomes the Word of God inasmuch as it remains faithful to God's revelation.[67] Preaching, for Calvin, is also the very Word of God because the preacher is sent by God Himself. This high view of the ministry means that each true preacher is a specially commissioned ambassador of God (an image Calvin liked to use) and thus is the mouthpiece of God to His people.

Despite the emphasis Calvin placed on the importance of preaching, the minister of the Word is not alone in his work. Calvin believed that the Holy Spirit is the "internal minister" who uses the "external minister" in preaching the Word. The external minister "holds forth the vocal word and it is received by the ears," but the internal minister "truly communicates the thing proclaimed [which] is Christ."[68] Thus, God Himself speaks through the mouth of His servants by His Spirit. "Wherever the gospel is preached, it is as if God himself came into the midst of us," Calvin wrote.[69] Preaching is the instrument and the authority that the Spirit uses in His saving work of illuminating, converting, and sealing sinners. "There is…an inward efficacy of the Holy Spirit when he sheds forth his power upon hearers, that they may embrace a discourse [sermon] by faith."[70]

Calvin preached series of sermons based on various Bible books, striving to show clearly the meaning of a passage and how it should impact the lives of his hearers. Much like a homily in style, his sermons had no divisions or points other than what the text dictated. As Paul Fuhrmann writes, "They are properly homilies as in the ancient church: expositions of Bible passages [in] the light of grammar and history, [providing] application to the hearers' life situations."[71]

Calvin was a careful exegete, an able expositor, and a faithful applier of the Word. His goals in preaching were to glorify God, to help believers grow in the grace and knowledge of Christ Jesus, and to unite sinners with Christ so "that men be reconciled to God by the

---

67. T. H. L. Parker, *Calvin's Preaching* (Louisville: Westminster John Knox, 1992), 23.

68. John Calvin, *Tracts and Treatises,* trans. Henry Beveridge (repr., Grand Rapids: Eerdmans, 1958), 1:173.

69. *Commentary* on Synoptic Gospels, 3:129.

70. *Commentary* on Ezekiel 1:3.

71. Paul T. Fuhrmann, "Calvin, Expositor of Scripture," *Interpretation* 6, 2 (Apr 1952):191.

free remission of sins."[72] This aim of saving sinners blended seamlessly with Calvin's emphasis on scriptural doctrines. He wrote that ministers are "keepers of the truth of God; that is to say, of his precious image, of that which concerneth the majesty of the doctrine of our salvation, and the life of the world."[73]

The image of the preacher as a teacher motivated Calvin to emphasize the importance of careful sermon preparation. How he accomplished that with his frequent preaching and heavy workload remains a mystery, but he obviously studied every text he expounded with great care and read widely what others had said about it. He then preached extemporaneously, relying heavily on his remarkable memory. Calvin taught that no one will ever be a good minister of the Word except he first be a scholar.

On average, he would preach on four or five verses in the Old Testament and two or three verses in the New Testament. He would then consider a small portion of the text at a time, first explaining the text, then applying it to the lives of his congregation.

Calvin's sermons were fairly short for his day (perhaps due to his asthmatic condition), ranging from forty to sixty minutes. He reportedly spoke "deliberately, often with long pauses to allow people to think," though others pointed out that he must have spoken rapidly to complete his sermon on time.[74]

Calvin's style of preaching was plain and clear. In a sermon titled "Pure Preaching of the Word," Calvin said, "We must shun all unprofitable babbling, and stay ourselves upon plain teaching, which is forcible."[75] Rhetoric for its own sake or vain babbling must be shunned, though true eloquence, when subjected to the simplicity of the gospel, is to be coveted. When Joachim Westphal charged Calvin with "babbling" in his sermons, Calvin replied that he stuck to the main point of the text and practiced "cautious brevity."[76]

---

72. *Commentary* on John 20:23.

73. John Calvin, *The Mystery of Godliness* (repr., Grand Rapids: Eerdmans, 1950), 122.

74. Philip Vollmer, *John Calvin: Theologian, Preacher, Educator, Statesman* (Richmond: Presbyterian Committee of Publication, 1909), 124; George Johnson, "Calvinism and Preaching," *Evangelical Quarterly* 4, 3 (July 1932):249.

75. Calvin, *The Mystery of Godliness*, 55.

76. John C. Bowman, "Calvin as a Preacher," *Reformed Church Review* 56 (1909):251–2.

Calvin's sermons were not short on application; rather, the application was often longer than the exposition. He taught that preachers must be like fathers who divide bread into small pieces to feed their children. Short, pungent applications, sprinkled throughout his sermons, constantly urge, exhort, and invite sinners to act in obedience to God's Word. "We have not come to the preaching merely to hear what we do not know, but to be incited to do our duty," Calvin said to his listeners.[77]

Parker suggests that Calvin's sermons follow a certain pattern: (1) Prayer; (2) recapitulation of the previous sermon; (3a) exegesis and exposition of the first point; (3b) application of the first point and exhortation to obedience of duty; (4a) exegesis and exposition of the second point; (4b) application of the second point and exhortation to obedience of duty; (5) closing prayer, which contained a brief, implicit summary of the sermon.

John Gerstner says that although Calvin often followed this structural order, he frequently departed from it because "he was so eager to get at the application that he often introduced it in the midst of the exposition. In other words, application was the dominant element in the preaching of John Calvin to which all else was subordinated."[78]

In short, Calvin provides us with one of the greatest models of biblical preaching. Jim Garretson writes:

> Calvin's model of preaching continues to provide a helpful historical example of what disciplined, expository, experimental, applicatory preaching looks and sounds like. His published sermons evidence a God-honoring, Christ-exalting, Spirit-empowered example of biblical-theological preaching that is direct, discriminating, and profoundly personal in application. The reader of his sermons quickly feels that this is a man who knows, feels, and has experience of the things of which he is preaching. This personal dimension gave great force to his words as preacher, and people were swept up into the realities that were theirs in and through Christ Jesus.

When Steve Lawson, author of *The Expository Genius of John Calvin*,

---

77. Bonnet, *Letters of Calvin*, 3:134.
78. John H. Gerstner, "Calvin's Two-Voice Theory of Preaching," *Reformed Review* 13, 2 (1959):22.

was asked during the 2009 Ligonier Ministries National Conference what he had learned from Calvin, he said:

> To understand Calvin is to understand him as preacher. He was many things—theologian, author, statesman, reformer—but on the four hundredth anniversary [of his birth]...what was reinforced was *Calvin the preacher*. I think that is what is so desperately needed in the church.... Calvin is just a preacher of the Word, but he was committed to verse-by-verse exposition, which required even greater mental energy to make every text sit up and walk and to give life to the congregation. That impresses me as I study Calvin—his devotion to the pulpit and to the preaching of the Word of God.

CALVIN THE CHRISTIAN

Reason #3: *Calvin models for us how to live an experiential Christian life of suffering and persecution in humility and godliness (13).*

Listen to what several colleagues write about Calvin's life. Malcolm Watts notes:

> Calvin was a theologian of *the heart*. Spiritual experience really began for Calvin when "by a sudden conversion, God subdued and brought my heart to docility." Thereafter, as he grew in grace, he discovered that the Lord graciously admits us to "greater familiarity with himself." "How then is it possible for thee," he once wrote, "to know God, and to be moved by no feeling?" When under "the heavy affliction" of his wife's death, Calvin was able to write to Guillaume Farel that the grief would "certainly have overcome me had not He who raises up the prostrate, strengthens the weak, and refreshes the weary, stretched forth His hand from heaven to me."... Calvin was profoundly experimental. He would have had no sympathy whatsoever with that contemporary "Calvinism" that despises the spiritual feelings of the heart. Instead, he would surely impress on us—we who are so lacking in life within—that the vital essence of authentic Calvinism is "to glorify God and to enjoy Him forever."

Tom Ascol writes:

Calvin has left a great legacy for the church by virtue of his personal testimony of grace, humility, industry, and perseverance through desperate times. It is far easier to vilify him than it is to consider his life carefully in light of his historical context. In a hard age when church and state were in complete upheaval, he maintained a steady course as a faithful pastor. Despite his preference to "die a hundred other deaths" than to give himself to pastoral ministry in Geneva, he nevertheless took up that cross and bore it well. Despite threats, opposition, sickness, and mistreatment from those who should have been his supporters, he pressed on in his calling to shepherd the people of Geneva, strengthening the church through consistent preaching and teaching, and leading them to send out missionaries to preach the gospel in hard places.

Howard Griffith says:

Calvin is important today as an example of the spiritual life. Paul tells us to live in this good creation, remembering that "the fashion of this world passeth away" (1 Cor. 7:31). It has always been difficult for the church to do this—to live with joy in this world, avoiding asceticism—yet willingly to give up good things for the sake of Christ's kingdom. Calvin, it seems to me, is a remarkable example of that. He urged Christian freedom, yet he owned almost nothing. He gave others rest in Christ, but he worked himself to death doing it. I think he did this because he really understood the life-giving power of suffering with Christ. He embraced the cross of discipleship and found the resurrection power of the Spirit.

Donald McKim writes:

In Calvin's view, the Christian life was all about denying one's self and serving God by serving other people. Calvin wrote: "We ought to embrace the whole human race without exception in a single feeling of love; here there is no distinction between barbarian and Greek, worthy and unworthy, friend and enemy, since all should be contemplated in God, not in themselves" (*Institutes* 3.7.6). This was Calvin's expansive definition of the neighbor and love.

Calvin's impact is on our head, heart, and hands: what we believe; where our confidence is found; how we love and serve others. This covers all our bases. Calvin's theology can nurture our faith, can nourish our lives, and can call us forth into wider arenas of service today.

Martin Holdt says:

Calvin was an example of consistent godliness throughout his life. When he expressed his devotion to Christ as "my heart a sacrifice for God," he was epitomizing Romans 12:1 in his life. What loyalty to Christ! There was no letup to the very end of his life. Humility alongside godliness is in short supply in the ministry today, but the life of Calvin is an inspiration to follow him as he followed Christ.

Al Mohler remarks:

When people think of Calvin in terms of his biography, what is often missed is the suffering of the man. Calvin suffered almost every day of his adult life. He was a man who had infirmities, sickness, physical strains, and stresses and pains that would go beyond what we would even discuss in this context. He had to read and study under the most excruciating of circumstances. He had emotional and relational sufferings—suffering of the heart, suffering of being rejected, suffering of opposition, suffering in his family life, which was very tragic. There was death—losing his wife after such a short time, and the grief that comes from loneliness. When you know that, what strikes you is the joyfulness of his writings and of his piety.

Ferguson notes:

Another striking thing about Calvin was that his friends would die for him. They just loved him to death. He had an amazing number of friends, as his correspondence demonstrates. In some of his correspondence, you just get little moments when he kind of breaks through the pain barrier. He'll say, "We read this and we had a really good laugh." They obviously loved him, and he loved them deeply. That is, in many ways, the measure of the man by contrast with the caricature we get of him.

Finally, Thackway writes:

In addition to his massive intellect, Calvin's heart religion is deeply moving and challenging. His self-effacing outlook is linked to this: for if knowing and serving God is one's sole end, promoting self will be irrelevant. His insistence on a plain coffin and unmarked grave shows whom he wanted everyone to remember when he was gone.

CALVIN THE THEOLOGIAN

Reason #2: *In bequeathing* The Institutes of the Christian Religion *to us, Calvin models marvelous systematic theology by combining the best of exegetical, doctrinal, historical, and pastoral theology for the church rather than for the academy (14).*

Within a few short years of his conversion and amid the mounting persecution of Protestants, especially in France, Calvin wrote the first edition of the most substantial and foundational statement of the Reformed faith, *The Institutes of the Christian Religion* (1536), a six-chapter book. Enlarged editions followed, culminating in his final eighty-chapter definitive edition in 1559—which virtually amounts to a new book.

Calvin's *Institutes* are still important to us today for several reasons:

First, they are of great historical value. For centuries, they have served as a gift to God's church, inspiring and edifying both pastors and pilgrims. Stephen Westcott writes:

> John Wicliffe (in part), Martin Luther, William Tyndale—all these were used of God to give the Bible back to the people, but if the boy who followed the plow was to know more of Christ than the lordly prelate, Calvin knew that he needed more than just the Bible in his hand. He needed guides and teachers, pastors and preachers. They, in turn, required training, and that necessitated a concise method of extracting the core truths of Scripture, and then fitting them together into a comprehensive scheme: a logical and systematic arrangement to confound the gainsayers and a framework to ground a lifetime of Bible study upon. Calvin provided that in his *Institutes*—not as a book to rival the Bible, but a handbook to help understand the Bible, a handmaid to Bible study, a servant to lead into the depths and wonders of the Bible scheme of redemption. Calvin was the first true Reformed dogmatician, the pioneer Reformed systematic theologian. All Calvinist "systematics" since his day have merely followed in his steps and attempted to refine his work.

Second, they are of great foundational value. Calvin gets at the basics with his emphasis on two-fold knowledge, beginning his *Institutes* with the statement: "Nearly all the wisdom we possess, that is to say, true and sound wisdom, consists of two parts: the knowledge of God and of ourselves."[79] For Calvin, the knowledge given us in Scripture of God and of ourselves is the beginning and end of theology. The knowledge of God is the issue; the knowledge of ourselves is derivative. McKim writes:

> What really counts in life is two things: knowing God and knowing ourselves. These two things are related. Calvin says we cannot gain a true knowledge of ourselves unless we have first looked on the face of God. What really counts about who we are in life is who we are in relation to God. We are to know God, and by this Calvin does not just mean to believe or know that there is a God. He means we are to know who God is, the nature and character of God. As Calvin puts it: "We ought to observe that we are called to a knowledge of God: not that knowledge which, content with empty speculation, merely flits in the brain, but that which will be sound and fruitful if we duly perceive it, and if it takes root in the heart" (1.5.9). Not just "brain knowledge," but "heart knowledge" of God—that's what counts, says Calvin. This basic sense of reality is as true for us today as it was in Calvin's time. Calvin guides us in our most basic beliefs.

Third, they are of great didactic and catechetical value. Mohler writes: "Calvin was a teacher in his *Institutes* and everywhere else. He understood that the church needs to be a learning people. The church should be a school.... At the end of the day, I want to die like Calvin died, studying to the end, preaching and teaching and learning until there comes that day when we see no longer through a glass darkly."

Fourth, they are of great practical value. Mohler referred to this when asked why Calvin was still important during a question-and-answer session at the 2009 Ligonier Ministries National Conference:

> One particular aspect of Calvin's life that helps to explain why he is so relevant today is that he was the combination of the systematician and the pastoral theologian, the preacher and the teacher, the founder of institutions, and the reformer of the church. Certainly we can look back with much appreciation to Martin Luther, but Luther did not leave us a systematic theology. If you look back to the great figures of the church, no one seems to have left anything like all of what we have from Calvin....

---

79. *Institutes* 1.1.1.

Here is Calvin's responsibility, considering what was at stake. He understood the gospel of the Lord Jesus and the church was at stake. The crucial questions were: Where is the true church? What is the true gospel? How would a church be established upon the Word of God? The theological maelstrom in which all of this happened, the confrontation with Rome, meant that Calvin was doing theology with his life at stake. This wasn't an esoteric ivory tower endeavor for him. He understood that life and death hung in the balance and that the integrity of the church and of the gospel was in the balance.

Fifth, they are of great spiritual value. Calvin wrote his *Institutes* as a "sum of piety," not as an academic, speculative, dogmatic treatise. He was concerned that our theology should express itself in piety, and that piety be rooted in Scripture. He wanted all our activity to be doxology that flows out of our theology. The *Institutes* establish Scripture as a standard by which we express our faith in worship and guard our faith against error and hypocrisy. For Calvin, the purposes of theology, doxology, piety, and activity of the church are all inseparably connected. This combination promotes a genuine biblical spirituality that is acutely needed today.

Sixth, they are of great contemporary value. In a time of rampant religious pluralism, Calvin's *Institutes* serve, Hesselink notes, as "a necessary corrective for what passes for theology today. *The Institutes* are far more readable than much modern theology, and like most classics, they never grow old or stale. Wherever people long for theology that is biblical, balanced, edifying, and thoroughly Trinitarian, the *Institutes* will be read with appreciation and profit."

No one in church history has matched Calvin as a theologian for pastors and people. It is no wonder Philipp Melanchthon called him simply "the theologian." All of Calvin's theological writings are rich, readable, and real. His *Institutes* are magisterial; in some places, they are definitive and sublime. Calvin also gives us room to grow as we stand on his shoulders, for theological service to God's Word requires new life and the cultivation of this new life in the Spirit. As Phil Eveson says, "Calvin's astounding capacity to present the gospel truths rediscovered at the Protestant Reformation and the Christian way of life based upon them in a clear and winsome way is particularly important as our present generation struggles to come to terms with the clash of world views."

CALVIN THE EXEGETE

Reason #1: *Calvin models for us how to handle the text of Scripture with conscientious fidelity (16).*

Whether in his commentaries, sermons, *Institutes,* other theological treatises, letters, church meetings, or interactions with people, Calvin strove to be governed by sound exegesis of the Scriptures. While admitting his failures on his deathbed to his fellow pastors and the members of the town council and asking for their forgiveness, Calvin could say with a clear conscience, "I have not falsified a single passage of the Scriptures, nor given it a wrong interpretation to the best of my knowledge."[80]

Calvin was extremely cautious in interpreting Scripture so as not to yield to his preconceived notions and desires. Consider how careful he was to make Christological applications of many texts in the Psalms that seem to be patently messianic. As Walt Chantry says, "Because he was rigidly bound by the text of Scripture, his exposition of texts often surprises us."

Ligon Duncan writes:

> Calvin was the best exegete in the history of Christianity. This is not to say that he was always right in his interpretation, or that the church has no exegetes who have surpassed him in a variety of areas in the last half millennium, but who can rival him among the great theologians for comprehensiveness, accuracy, and succinctness of biblical interpretation? Not Augustine. Not Aquinas. Not Luther. Not Owen. Not Edwards. Not Barth. Only Warfield matches his reliability (but not his scope of exposition, nor his brevity). Who among the great preached and commented so well on so much of the Bible as Calvin? None.

One reason why Calvin was such a great exegete is that he was committed to being governed by Scripture rather than governing Scripture himself. He was a servant of the Word who bowed under its authority.

Al Martin writes:

> [Calvin was] ready to embrace in faith all that God has spoken, and also in faith to be content when God is silent. The following

---

80. John Calvin, *The Necessity of Reforming the Church* (Audubon, N.J.: Old Paths, 1994); http://worldwidefreeresources.com/upload/CH320_SG_09.pdf

words of Calvin are oft repeated in his writings. He says, "Let us, I say, permit the Christian man to open his mind and ears to every utterance of God directed to him, provided it be with such restraint that when the Lord closes His holy lips, he also shall at once close the way to inquiry. The best limits of sobriety for us will be not only to follow God's lead in learning, but, when He sets an end to teaching, to stop trying to be wise."

How much we need to learn today as Christians, and especially as preachers, that to acknowledge ignorance where God has not given us light is not shameful. Rather, as Martin concludes, "it is an expression of a humble mind that gladly embraces God's declaration that 'the secret things belong unto the LORD our God: but those things which are revealed belong to us and to our children forever, that we may do all the words of this law' (Deut. 29:29)."

Stephen Westcott enlarges this thought:

Calvin's relation to the Bible is the hinge upon which his God-given success swung open. It is not nearly enough to say that for Calvin the Bible was central and authoritative: it was almighty God speaking directly to him, and his awed reaction was like that of Samuel, "Speak, LORD, for thy servant heareth." He was hungry and thirsty for the Word, to make it the very fabric of his own being: and then to offer its riches and wonders to the whole earth, so far as it was in his power to do so. Hence his great series of commentaries, opening and enforcing Scripture, and his equally great series of expository sermons, often covered the same ground but with greater human application and pathos. In both Calvin brings all of life under the searchlight of the Bible, and the corollary of reformation in the individual, the family, and the state flow naturally from this.

Hart says: "Calvin was a remarkable expositor of God's Word. His commentaries, sermons, and lectures show a keen attention to Scripture. He obviously knew and interacted with church fathers. He also knew the value of systematic teaching, that is, of theology proper. That's why he is so well known for the *Institutes*. But for all of his humanistic and Christian learning, Calvin devoted his intellectual energies to understanding God as He has revealed Himself in His holy Word."

It is no wonder, then, that so many have called Calvin an exegete of the Word, a theologian of the Word, or a preacher of the Word.

What has been said of John Bunyan—"Prick any vein in his body, and his blood will be bibline"—could be said even more profoundly of Calvin. He reminds believers today of our great need to be thoroughly submissive to the Word of God in all that we think, say, do, and teach.

CONCLUSION

To gain a true appreciation of Calvin's life and legacy is next to impossible in a single book. Scarcely is there an area of life in modern history and Western civilization that is not permeated by Calvin's influence. Not just church, theology, missions, and worship, but education, government, economics, industry, and social work bear the imprint of Calvin's thought. Some have said that Calvin had the greatest influence of any individual in the last millennium or since the close of the New Testament canon. The nineteenth-century Scottish church historian William Cunningham writes, "Calvin was by far the greatest of the Reformers. He is the man who next to Paul has done most for mankind."[81] Spurgeon is even stronger: "Among all those who were born of women there has not risen a greater than John Calvin. No age before him ever produced his equal. And no age after him has seen his rival.... The longer I live the clearer does it appear that John Calvin's system is the nearest to perfection."[82] The English scholar Lord John Morley says: "To omit John Calvin from the forces of Western civilization is to read history with one eye shut."[83]

Calvin was the foremost leader of the sixteenth-century Reformation. During his lifetime, his teaching affected hundreds of thousands of people—as did his numerous books, which were printed by the thousands even when they were banned.[84]

Today, a fresh hunger for Calvin and Calvinism's biblical doctrine and spirituality is helping the Reformed faith spread throughout the world. Calvinism has a bright future, for it offers much to those who

---

81. William Cunningham, *The Reformers and the Theology of the Reformation* (repr., Edinburgh: Banner of Truth Trust, 1967), 292.

82. Charles Spurgeon, *Autobiography* (Pasadena, TX: Pilgrim Publications, 1992), 2:372; Iain Murray, *The Forgotten Spurgeon* (Edinburgh: Banner of Truth Trust, 1986), 79n.

83. Cited in *Christian History*, 5, 4 (1986):2–3.

84. Hall, *The Legacy of Calvin*, 33–5.

seek to believe and practice the whole counsel of God as revealed in the Scriptures. Calvinism offers a complete theology, a complete way of life, a complete kind of piety. As Tony Lane says: "Calvin offers a model of a theology that is orthodox without being Fundamentalist, a theology that combines respect for tradition with ultimate loyalty to Scripture, and a theology that combines careful exegesis and theological acuteness. Calvin belongs to the first rank of *both* theologians and exegetes."

To this, Mark Johnston adds: "Perhaps the greatest thing of all that Calvin has left the church is an appreciation that all of life is religion. In a generation for whom life has become carved up into isolated compartments—for Christians as much as for anyone else—we desperately need to be reminded that our chief end and most comprehensive enjoyment in life is always and only God Himself!"

Finally, Duncan summarizes well why Calvin is important today:

> Calvin is important today because he presented a unified, gospel-based exposition of the Christian life that is thoroughly biblical, deeply christological and vitally practical—and desperately needed even in the Reformed community. For Calvin, our theology, doxology, piety, and activity are all of a piece. They are inseparably connected. He was concerned that our theology express itself in piety, and that our piety be rooted in biblical theology. He wanted all our activity to be doxology, and to flow from our theology, and for our doxology to reinforce our theology and piety.

Let me close by answering a question you may be asking if you have not read Calvin up to this point: *Where shall I begin?* I recommend that you begin with three edited books that get to the heart of what Calvin was all about: *The Golden Booklet of the True Christian Life,* which is an extract from Calvin's *Institutes* (3.6.5–10) on how to live as a Christian in this world; *The Soul of Life: The Piety of John Calvin,* which presents forty-five bite-size pieces of Calvin with chapters on his life and piety; and *365 Days with Calvin,* which provides small doses of Calvin's commentaries and sermons, with practical applications appended to each day's portion.[85] All three of

---

85. John Calvin, *The Golden Booklet of the True Christian Life* (Grand Rapids: Baker, 1952); Joel R. Beeke, ed., *"The Soul of Life": The Piety of John Calvin* (Grand Rapids: Reformation Heritage Books, 2009); Joel R. Beeke, ed., *365 Days with Calvin*

these books are easy to read. But don't stop there. Having gotten a taste of Calvin, you will be surprised how easy it will be to transition to Calvin's *Institutes,* which may look daunting, but is anything but. Read a section or two of the *Institutes* every day and complete the book in one year. You will not be sorry. Upon completion, you will be, by the Spirit's grace, a far more informed, mature, Christ-centered, and sanctified believer than when you began.

(Grand Rapids: Reformation Heritage Books, 2008, and Leominster: Day One Publications, 2008).

Contributors

DR. JOEL R. BEEKE serves as President and Professor of Systematic Theology and Homiletics at Puritan Reformed Theological Seminary. He has served as a pastor of his current church (HNRC in Grand Rapids) since 1986. He has written, co-authored, or edited sixty books and contributed over fifteen hundred articles to Reformed books, journals, periodicals, and encyclopedias. He is frequently called upon to lecture at Reformed seminaries and to speak at conferences around the world.

DR. GERALD M. BILKES is Professor of New Testament and Biblical Theology at Puritan Reformed Theological Seminary. He has written several articles on biblical-theological themes and given addresses at several conferences. His areas of special interest include hermeneutics, the history of interpretation, and conversion in the Bible.

DR. J. LIGON DUNCAN, a native of Greenville, South Carolina, was born and reared in the home of an eighth-generation Southern Presbyterian Ruling elder. Since 1996 he has served as Senior Minister of Teaching at First Presbyterian Church of Jackson, Mississippi. He is President of the Alliance of Confessing Evangelicals and Chairman of the Council on Biblical Manhood and Womanhood. He is the author and editor of several books and speaks at numerous conferences around the world.

DR. MICHAEL A.G. HAYKIN is currently Professor of Church History and Biblical Spirituality at Southern Baptist Theological Seminary and Adjunct Professor of Historical Theology at Puritan Reformed Theological Seminary. He is the author and editor of over ten books and has made several hundred contributions to journals and periodicals. He also serves as the director of The Andrew Fuller Center for Baptist Studies.

DR. NELSON D. KLOOSTERMAN teaches Ethics and New Testament at Mid-America Reformed Seminary. He serves as associate minister of Community United Reformed Church, Schererville, Indiana. He gives weekend seminars on Christian marriage and family, Christian medical ethics, and

Christian cultural worldview. He serves as co-editor of the *Mid-America Journal of Theology*.

DR. DAVID P. MURRAY is Professor of Old Testament and Practical Theology at Puritan Reformed Theological Seminary. He was a pastor for twelve years, first at Lochcarron Free Church of Scotland and then at Stornoway Free Church of Scotland (Continuing). From 2002 to 2007, he was Lecturer in Hebrew and Old Testament at the Free Church Seminary in Inverness. Dr. Murray joined the faculty of Puritan Reformed Theological Seminary in 2007.

DR. JOSEPH A. PIPA, JR. serves as President and Professor of Historical and Systematic Theology at Greenville Presbyterian Theological Seminary. He pastored the Tchula Presbyterian Church, Tchula, Mississippi, Covenant Presbyterian Church, Houston, Texas, and the Trinity Presbyterian Church, Escondido, California. He was also a Guest Lecturer at Westminster Theological Seminary and Associate Professor of Practical Theology and Director of Advanced Studies at Westminster Theological Seminary, Escondido, California. He has written or edited numerous books and contributed to a number of journals and periodicals.

REV. CORNELIS PRONK is Visiting Professor at Puritan Reformed Theological Seminary, where he teaches Church History and Systematic Theology. Along with many articles published in various magazines and theological journals, he is the author of *Expository Sermons on the Canons of Dort*, and *No Other Foundation than Jesus Christ*, as well as the translator of several books from the Dutch language. He served as radio pastor of the Banner of Truth broadcast and is editor of *The Messenger*, the monthly magazine of the Free Reformed Churches of North America.

DR. DONALD SINNEMA has been the Professor of Theology at Trinity Christian College since 1987. His areas of expertise are Dutch immigration to North America and Post-Reformation studies. He has written a number of articles for journals and periodicals. He belongs to the Sixteenth Century Studies Conference, Calvin Studies Society, and the Association for the Advancement of Dutch American Studies.

DR. DEREK W. H. THOMAS is Instructor of Historical and Practical Theology at Puritan Reformed Theological Seminary. He is currently the Minister of Teaching at First Presbyterian Church of Jackson, Mississippi and Professor of Systematic and Practical Theology at Reformed Theological Seminary. He has written or edited dozens of books, and serves as the Editorial Director for The Alliance of Confessing Evangelicals and the editor of its e-zine, Reformation 21. He also speaks at numerous conferences around the world.

DR. CORNELIS P. VENEMA serves as President of Mid-America Reformed Seminary and teaches Systematic Theology. He serves as an elder in his church and preaches on a regular basis. Dr. Venema also speaks and teaches in a variety of church and conference settings. His special interest lies in Reformation theology, particularly the work of the Reformers John Calvin and Heinrich Bullinger. He has authored numerous books and is a co-editor and frequent contributor to *The Outlook* and the *Mid-America Journal of Theology*.

Please consider partnering with us in carrying out our mission of offering the following degrees: M.A.R. (Master of Arts, 2 years), M.Div. (Master of Divinity, 4 years), and Th.M. (Master of Theology, 2 years). Above all, please continue to pray for us that our institution may remain faithful to biblical, Reformed truth.

- -

YES, I WOULD LIKE TO DONATE!

❑ I would like to financially support PRTS by giving $_____, designated for:

    ❑ Operation Fund   ❑ Scholarship Fund   ❑ PRTS Foundation
    ❑ Puritan Resource Center

❑ I would like to enroll in the monthly donation program.
    ❑ I will send a check for _____ each month.
    ❑ Please charge my Debit/Charge card $_____ per month.

PAYMENT METHOD
    ❑ Check/cash enclosed

    ❑ Charge my Debit/Charge card: Card # _____

        Exp. Date ____ / ____ Security Code _____

❑ Please send me the PRTS catalog and DVD.

        ~~~~~~~~~~~~~~~~~~

Name   _____

Address   _____

City/State/Zip   _____

Phone _____ E-mail _____

American donors and donors from countries other than Canada,
please send your gifts and this form to:
    Puritan Reformed Theological Seminary
    2965 Leonard Street, NE, Grand Rapids, MI 49525

Canadian Donors please send your gifts and this form to:
    Burgessville Heritage Reformed Church, Attention: PRTS
    685 Main Street, P.O. Box 105, Burgessville, Ontario N0J 1C0
    Donors may also give on-line through www.CanadaHelps.org. Make donations to the
    Heritage Netherlands Reformed Congregation, PRTS operating fund.

Thank you for supporting Puritan Reformed Theological Seminary. Were it not for the prayers and financial gifts of friends like you, much of what takes place on a daily basis at the seminary would need to be reduced or eliminated.

For more information regarding the seminary, visits, or ministries affiliated with the seminary, please contact our registrar, Mr. Henk Kleyn, at 616-977-0599 ext. 120, or send an email to henk.klyen@puritanseminary.org.